No Longer
on Pedestals

02/06/2015

To Linda & Moe

I'm thankful for your friendship all these years.

Best Regards,
Carol

No Longer on Pedestals

Carol Kuhnert

Carol A. Kuhnert

iUniverse

NO LONGER ON PEDESTALS

Copyright © 2014 Carol A. Kuhnert.

All rights reserved. No part of this book may be used or reproduced by any means, graphic, electronic, or mechanical, including photocopying, recording, taping or by any information storage retrieval system without the written permission of the publisher except in the case of brief quotations embodied in critical articles and reviews.

iUniverse books may be ordered through booksellers or by contacting:

iUniverse
1663 Liberty Drive
Bloomington, IN 47403
www.iuniverse.com
1-800-Authors (1-800-288-4677)

Because of the dynamic nature of the Internet, any web addresses or links contained in this book may have changed since publication and may no longer be valid. The views expressed in this work are solely those of the author and do not necessarily reflect the views of the publisher, and the publisher hereby disclaims any responsibility for them.

Any people depicted in stock imagery provided by Thinkstock are models, and such images are being used for illustrative purposes only. Certain stock imagery © Thinkstock.

ISBN: 978-1-4917-5067-4 (sc)
ISBN: 978-1-4917-5068-1 (hc)
ISBN: 978-1-4917-5069-8 (e)

Library of Congress Control Number: 2014918996

Printed in the United States of America.

iUniverse rev. date: 12/29/2014

To the children who were raped and abused by
my brother, Father Norman H. Christian,
and to all clergy abuse victims.
May they find compassion and the courage they require to heal.

Contents

Foreword ix
Acknowledgments xiii
Introduction xv
Chapter 1: Childhood Years 1
Chapter 2: Sabbatical 21
Chapter 3: Struggle 31
Chapter 4: Betrayal? 38
Chapter 5: I Know 47
Chapter 6: Marriages 61
Chapter 7: Meeting with Monsignor 63
Chapter 8: Removed from Active Ministry 73
Chapter 9: A Friendly Response 80
Chapter 10: Panic 91
Chapter 11: Seeking Advocacy 94
Chapter 12: Subpoena and Stroke 110
Chapter 13: Child Abuse Unit 116
Chapter 14: Media Exposes Father Christian 125
Chapter 15: Enlightenment 128
Chapter 16: Criminal Investigator 132

Chapter 17: Sad but True 134

Chapter 18: Norman on Deathbed 142

Chapter 19: Family Speaks Out 163

Chapter 20: Another Victim 178

Chapter 21: Archbishop Naumann Transferred 194

Chapter 22: Persistence 197

Chapter 23: Editorial 205

Chapter 24: Grief 208

Chapter 25: More Victims Come Forward 211

Chapter 26: Not Welcome 216

Chapter 27: Monsignor Visit 218

Chapter 28: And Yet Another 225

Chapter 29: Press Conference 230

Chapter 30: And Another 233

Chapter 31: *Twist of Faith* Controversy 235

Chapter 32: Destroyed Clergy Records 240

Chapter 33: My Supportive Family 247

Chapter 34: Father Tom Doyle 252

Chapter 35: Disagreements 255

Author's Note 261

Appendix 277

Appendix 2 345

Timeline and Works Cited – Part One 351

Timeline and Works Cited – Part Two 377

Foreword

Why is it that when we hear that a priest has raped a child, we are unwilling to believe it? Is it so horrific that we cannot process it and it is easier to just believe it did not happen? If that same priest—or a teacher—spanked the child for disciplinary reasons or took away his or her recess, the parents would be outraged and demand that the offender be punished immediately. Unfortunately, when a child is sodomized or raped, no one wants to know. The child and his family are the ones who end up being blamed, persecuted, and ostracized.

Victims of sexual abuse or rape never forget that these horrific things happened to them. Even if it is repressed, the trauma manifests itself in some way. Some work through their many problems in seemingly productive ways: going to years and years of counseling, attending school and obtaining advanced degrees, finding employment that focuses on helping victims who are helpless in the system. But it never is enough. Every day is a fight within to wake up and look in the mirror, forever to feel like "damaged goods," even decades later.

Others may succumb to the struggle. These are men and women who daily relive the forty-year-old man raping them while their mothers trusted that the respected man was counseling them. The victims may become promiscuous; they may become drug addicts, unwed mothers, or unemployed, nonproductive members of society. And what happens then? Do people understand and feel sorry for them? Not on your life. They are judged yet again, more harshly this time. When will society wake up and realize that it is up to us to do something besides close our eyes to make this problem go away?

When was the last time you looked at someone like I've mentioned above and thought, "I wonder what happened in her life that made her hate herself so much? Why doesn't she ask for help or go to a shelter? Why does she abuse drugs? Why does she have an eating disorder? Why does she cut herself? Why did he try to commit suicide? What happened to him that he doesn't have any self-confidence?" It is easier to judge the sleazy, weak, lazy, dishonest, ungrateful, or even insane members of society. If we ignore them, maybe they will go away. Perhaps their pain is too much to bear and impossible to take away. We just might not want to know what deep, dark secret has caused such severe human scarring. We are unable to face something so evil.

The problem is that acknowledging this could shatter our entire existence. We grow up and live our sheltered lives, going to church, playing ball, attending Catholic school or Parish School of Religion, and involving ourselves in social circles that develop from the Catholic parish to which we belong. Even if it is our child who is the victim, we do not want to report it to the police, because the rest of the congregation will pin that scarlet letter to our daughter's or son's shirt, and everyone will blame our child for either lying or "asking for it" by wearing certain clothes or being pretty.

We Catholics choose to blindly follow and have things never change in our view of the world. Just push the images away. "They are so horrific," we might think. "I can't even begin to think about that. They just cannot be true." Unfortunately, they are—for many young, innocent boys and girls.

The Catholic Church is not a bad ideology. In fact, it could work rather well with less corruption and more equality for man and woman alike. Clean up the "good old boys" network, and you'll get rid of much of the corruption. When the mentality is "us against them," one tends to stand up for even the bad apples on the "us" team. Practice what we are supposed to be about—Christ. Jesus would not have hidden the perpetrators. Yes, He would have forgiven them, but He wouldn't have allowed them to keep hurting children. And He would have carefully held the child victims in His arms and let the children know that He loved them, that He was sorry these men hurt them, and that He would keep them safe. Unfortunately, pedophile priests are still being hidden. With just a personal apology and a show of empathy, the hierarchy could unload much of the huge burden from the child and family, but instead much additional pain and suffering is inflicted on them by the denial of justice, love, and compassion.

My aunt is the author of this book. All her life she was a no-questions-asked Catholic, a very kind, giving, and loving woman. She has always put the Christ in Catholic. Imagine her confusion when the people she trusted, who promised they would take care of a crime against children and do the right thing, not only deceived her but dismissed her when she began to question them and personally reach out to the victims with love and compassion, grieving with them for all that was done to them.

You will read how the diocese and the higher powers knew about her brother, my pedophile priest uncle, for more than twenty-five years before finally taking him out of ministry. My aunt documents her fervent struggle with the church and their concealing the criminal activities of her brother. He wasn't sorry and never apologized to anyone for raping and abusing numerous children. My uncle always felt they "wanted it" and that he compensated the ones he needed to. He felt completely supported by those above him, even to his death. When he died, he was buried with full priestly honor—a large gathering with the archbishop presiding at his funeral! There is no excuse for celebrating the life of a nonrepentant serial child rapist.

The secrecy must stop. The church must exorcise the powerful evil that exists and protect the innocence that is our future. The good people want and need a church that practices what it preaches and embraces the broken, especially those destroyed with our own hands. Shame on us for remaining silent and turning our backs on those in most need of our love.

Pete

Acknowledgments

With thanks ...
To Joe, for his patience, unconditional love, and support all these years.

To my children, for their encouragement and love.

To my grandchildren, for being a constant source of joy during turbulent times.

To my daughter and niece, for their compassion, courage, and determination and for helping me with this, even though this was extremely difficult on them.

To Jeanne, a loving big sister, through thick and thin.

To Tim, Steve, and other abuse victims I was blessed to meet: your strength inspired me to get this story told in hopes to change the hearts and minds of those in denial.

To Ken, for his assistance with documentation.

To David and Barb, two dependable sources of information and encouragement.

To Louise, Carol, Ellen, Mary, Bob, Carolyn, Joy, Charlie, and Mary Ellen. True friends willing to listen and share.

To Fran and Helen, for their validation and encouragement.

To my guardian angel, Sister Maurice.

To Archbishop Joe, for his friendship and compassion toward my family during difficult times.

To our family and friends who have continually given their love and support.

Introduction

My purpose in writing this book is to open the minds and hearts of those who find it difficult to believe clergy have been sexually abusing children for many decades and that the Catholic Church has made protecting the abusers and the church's assets its number-one priority, while leaving the victims, their families, and church members to fend for themselves in trying to heal, understand, and cope. I hope my book encourages Catholics to truly live their faith and do all they can in bringing about change in how the church deals with these issues. I also hope it will encourage those still carrying their painful secrets of abuse to inform the authorities of the unspeakable crimes committed against them by predatory clergy so many years ago, thereby putting the shame where it belongs—on their molesters and the church. Victims have endured decades of guilt that never belonged to them. They are the innocent ones.

This book is about the betrayal of one such priest, Father Norman H. Christian, and the manner in which the church's bad judgment and cover-ups further betrayed his victims, their families, and everyone who revered, trusted, and respected him.

My family learned that lesson the hard way, and the predator/Catholic priest was my own brother. Since 1988, I've learned what a flawless job the church does of covering up crimes committed by their own. The Archdiocese of Saint Louis had knowledge of my brother's pedophile behavior long before I became aware of it, yet neither my sister nor I was ever warned he could be a danger to our children. The hierarchy chose to send my brother for treatments, return him to active ministry, and move him from parish to parish, where he could continue to endear himself to unsuspecting families, all of whom were more than happy to entrust their innocent children to him. Had he not victimized his own niece and had she not found the courage to tell me about him, I would have never learned he was a pedophile. Much of the information I eventually learned came from my brother's admissions to me over the years, as I was encouraging him to follow his church-scheduled treatment programs.

The hierarchy chooses to claim it wasn't aware that such abuse was happening in the past or that, once made aware, the behavior was thought curable. For those reasons, they don't feel they should be held responsible for having used bad judgment in returning predators in the clergy to active ministry. Somewhere through the years, it had to have become apparent that the behavior wasn't curable and that some changes needed to be made.

The church must be accountable for its actions or lack thereof over the years. Showing compassion and understanding to the victims, along with an acknowledgment of wrongdoing, is the right thing to do. Removing the abuser from active ministry once they realize the accusation is true, instead of waiting for a court to force them to do so, would give the right message to everyone. Unfortunately, I have seen little change over past decades. The church's putting the protection of its reputation, assets, and clergy before anything else, with its secrecy and cover-ups, has caused more children to be abused.

It's sad that most of the older generation finds it easier to stay in denial than deal with questioning the church they have held so dear all their lives. In the Catholic Church, we are taught from infancy to trust, respect, revere, and obey clergy. It was unthinkable that any of them would do wrong, but they are human, and some do. The church must own up to that fact and accept its responsibility for the damage that's been done to so many lives.

There are many Catholics who no longer trust or respect the church because of its deceptive mishandling of child sexual abuse by clergy. Expecting everyone to look the other way, pretending nothing happened, and ignoring the victims is shameful.

Everyone needs help in coping with this. The pedestals are gone, and that's a good thing. We always should have been aware that clergy are fallible, like all human beings.

Chapter 1
Childhood Years

I was the youngest child in my family, born July 1941, and grew up in Our Lady of Sorrows parish on the south side of Saint Louis, Missouri. My parents, Henry and Verona Christian, were devout Catholics and placed great importance on Catholic education for their three children. As with any parent sending children to a private school, they sacrificed to do so. Signs of our family's Catholic faith were quite evident in our small one-bedroom home. A picture of the Last Supper hung in the kitchen. A crucifix and other religious pictures decorated the walls throughout the house. I had a habit of blessing myself with water from the small holy-water font in the hallway before going to bed every night and felt privileged when I got to refill the special holy-water bottle from the container at church. We had a special sick-call crucifix that hung on our bedroom wall, for use if a priest brought communion for someone too sick to attend Mass. It contained two small blessed candles and a bottle of holy water to use during the priest's visit.

Like many of the time, our parents preferred to keep their troubles to themselves. Dad, a tall, slender man with wavy, dark brown hair, enjoyed fishing, reading, and playing cards. He supported our family by working three different shifts as a bottler at a Saint Louis brewery. When he was working the afternoon or midnight shifts, we kids had to be quiet so he could sleep during the daytime. We were rarely allowed to bring friends into the house to play. With that being the rule at our house, Mom thought it only fair that we not be allowed to go inside our friends' homes. It was often embarrassing for me, as my friends didn't understand when I wouldn't come inside their houses to play.

Mom was slightly more than five feet tall and wore matronly, size 14 housedresses every day. She wasn't one to worry about current fashions and would only buy something dressier for a special occasion. There was little money left, if any, to put toward such luxuries after paying all the household bills. Mom wore little makeup—lipstick, powder, and a touch of rouge on her cheeks—but she permed her dark brown hair several times a year to make sure the curls she set with bobby pins every night lasted all day. She would groom her hair with the flower-patterned silver brush, comb, and mirror set that lay on top of her bedroom dresser. That set really caught my eye, but she frowned on my handling it. Mom didn't have much jewelry to put in the jewelry box that set on the dresser, but she did a lot of sewing and mending and had a very large container of miscellaneous buttons from which she could choose to replace missing ones. She often let me play with all those buttons, and my imagination would turn them into families, teacher and students, whatever. We didn't have a lot of toys back then, so those buttons brought me many hours of fun. I remember one Christmas, Santa surprised me with twin dolls; I was thrilled. The boy and girl dolls came with all kinds of clothing too. It wasn't until I was much older that Mom told me those were not new dolls. She had taken two dolls I already had and made all the new clothes for them, letting Santa bring them as twins. In all my excitement, I never noticed they were my old dolls. Once, when he was small, my brother, Norman, was surprised with an electric train set around the Christmas tree. Though we rarely got the things we craved, we learned to be happy with getting what we needed. I loved my parents and always knew what they expected of me; I never wanted to disappoint them.

Mom was a good cook, but as a kid, I was a terribly picky eater. Mom didn't cater to any of us; we ate what was served or went hungry. I picked at many suppers and sometimes just waited until breakfast. That changed as I grew older, and I enjoy just about everything now.

Being six years younger than Norman, I was only in second grade when he entered the seminary right out of eighth grade. I don't remember what he did during his early years except play the drums in the school band and the picnic parade. Mom told me, "The girls in your brother's class are disappointed he is going to enter the seminary."

By the time I was six, Norman was already twelve and keeping a frightful secret. A picture I have of him at about eight years of age shows an innocent-looking child with straight, light brown hair. Though cut short, as was the style of the day, he had a lot of it back then. Add his hazel eyes and flawless, light tan complexion, and Norman was a very handsome boy. He started balding at nineteen, but his piercing eyes and over-the-top personality mesmerized people. After spending some time with him, however, many were probably disappointed at some point to discover that Norman was all about Norman.

My sister, Jeanne, told me that Norman would often walk out of the house as Mom was reprimanding him about something. "Mom would get so angry that he'd walked out," Jeanne recalled. "He'd come back later, acting as though nothing had happened, but I don't remember there ever being any consequences for his having done it." Neither of us understands how he got away with such behavior.

Jeanne and I never blatantly disrespected our parents like that; besides the love and respect we had for Mom and Dad, we knew we'd have been disciplined in some manner, had we ever done so.

While I was still in grade school, Mom had to work part time because of financial difficulties at home. At first, she worked just a few blocks from our house. I'd let myself in the house after school, knowing she was nearby in an emergency. When I grew older, she changed companies and worked full time farther away. She remained active with church organizations and in her retirement years, she delivered Meals on Wheels.

When Jeanne, Norman, or I wanted to go anywhere, we walked, rode a bike, or took the bus. Our parents did not chauffeur us around. We had one car in our family, and it was used to take our parents back and forth to work. Sometimes our family would use it to visit relatives on weekends. Our parents enjoyed taking us to country church-picnic dinners once in a while too. Some Sundays, when the weather was nice, Dad would tell all of us, "Go get ready for a ride; it's a beautiful day to head out to the country and get some fresh air." Mom always cooked the big dinner of the day on Sunday for noon, so we'd have the rest of the day free to do whatever we decided. Occasionally, we would all go to an afternoon movie at a local theater, but we were never allowed to buy any candy, popcorn, or soda. "You are here to see the movie, not to eat," Mom would tell us. I would have loved having something to munch, but I enjoyed the movies anyway, especially the westerns, my favorite back then.

In the summer, my favorite thing to do after dinner was run five blocks to a nearby park and play with neighborhood kids on the swings and slides. The only thing I had to worry about was being home before the streetlights came on. Before leaving for the park, though, those dishes had to be washed and put away and the kitchen floor swept. Mom, Jeanne, and I would do those chores, not Norman. I think he took the trash out to the can in the alley. He'd vanish after dinner, but I don't know where he went.

Our family couldn't afford to buy a TV when they first came out, so Mom would occasionally walk with us and some neighbors to a fire station about a mile from where we lived. The firemen would let us watch their TV for as long as we wanted—and we'd be in awe. Mom was careful that we didn't overstay our welcome, and then we'd walk back home. It was exercise and entertainment rolled into one. When I think of it now, after learning of children being abused by some firemen over the years, I wonder if anyone there started grooming my brother for abuse. That enters my mind because Norman later told my sister and me that he had been sexually molested by people in the neighborhood when he was a kid, but he never gave us names.

Norman grew into a nice-looking guy. He stood about five foot ten and had a booming voice and laugh that always caught everyone's attention, anywhere he went. His heavy, dark facial hair required him to shave nearly twice a day, but he had no need for a comb or brush, as little remained on top of his head.

I never understood why, but Norman was never friendly to Joe, now my husband, when we were dating. One of the things that attracted me to Joe was that he cared so much about others, especially his own parents and family. He was the youngest of ten, and his parents had just celebrated their fiftieth wedding anniversary when Joe and I started dating. He still lived at home with them and was always looking out for and helping them in every way he could. Joe began to show that same care and helpfulness to my parents, family, and friends, and that has been his nature throughout our fifty-plus years of marriage. I asked him what he remembered about Norman back when we were dating. He said, "I don't remember his being around much. I can't recall any details, but my feelings back then were that Norman wasn't happy I was dating you. He seemed standoffish and arrogant around me." Norman's attitude toward Joe changed after we married, because Norman, recognizing how handy Joe was, called quite frequently from his various parish assignments, asking for his help with electrical problems or fixing other things for him. Joe always did as he was asked and never charged Norman for anything.

Our parents did the best they knew how in raising the three of us, and I will always be grateful to them for the values they instilled in me. I learned the importance of being truthful, respectful, compassionate, and giving. I developed self-discipline; to do what is necessary, even if it is difficult or not fun; to prioritize; to live within my means; and to maintain a high level of integrity. They taught me to do things right and get them done on time. I was fortunate that my parents were good role models; I could observe and learn. I watched many times as Mom prepared a sandwich and drink for some disheveled man who had knocked on our back door, asking for something to eat. Mom told me, "Some people are having hard times, and we need to help them when we can." Dad was a member of the Saint Vincent de Paul Society at church. Once, upon learning of a family who had no place to stay, he brought them to our home to spend the night until a permanent place was found for them. We kids were thrilled to camp out on the living room floor, letting the adults have the beds.

I am by far no saint, but because of my strict upbringing, which especially stressed the church's teachings about God and morality, I've felt compelled to confront the wrongs I have witnessed within the church since learning of my brother's shameful secret. The manner in which the church has dealt with Norman's and other clergy's sexual-abuse cases is deplorable. It certainly is not the kind of behavior that was ingrained in me by the school Sisters of Notre Dame or by my parents. What the church has done goes against everything that has ever been taught to me throughout my entire life. Something is terribly wrong.

When my siblings and I were in grade school, the day began with daily Mass, which was said in Latin. Only boys were allowed to be altar boys back then. As I reflect on it now, I think that helped me to feel inferior to the boys. Throughout elementary school, our Catholic faith was drilled into us: don't question anything; just believe what is taught and obey. At home, Mom and Dad told us that going to church for confession once a week was mandatory. We were taught in religion class that when we went to confession, in addition to having sins forgiven, we received graces from God that would help us live less sinful lives. That meant that even with no sins to confess, we were to go to confession—my parents made sure their children received those graces every week. Those were the days when everyone dressed nicely to go to church, and women always covered their heads with a hat or scarf. So every Saturday afternoon, I'd stop what I was doing, change into nice clothes, put a scarf on my head, and walk two blocks to church to get there by four o'clock, before the lines got too long. Usually, there were four priests hearing confessions. The longest lines were always at the most-liked priest's confessional. Everyone figured out quickly which priests to avoid because they were known for giving longer penances.

There seems to be quite a change in confessional lines in the church today. The lines are shorter, and people have the choice of speaking with the priest face-to-face. Learning what I have over the years about predator priests' behaviors, it disturbs me to think of how many predator priests may have gotten pleasure from their time spent in the confessional.

Over the past several decades, I have learned of numerous victims worldwide with painful stories of abuse and the horrible things that were done to them by clergy. I realize now how easily predator priests could lead into inappropriate or abusive "confessional" conversation with intimidated children, who would most likely be too afraid or embarrassed to say anything. It could happen with emotionally vulnerable adults as well. Susceptible people, children or adults, are easily manipulated by a predator. They trust him, as they were taught to do from the time they were small. The priest holds all the power and sadly, the predators use it for their own sick advantage. Pleasuring themselves as they listen to a confession that excites them is another possibility.

The website BishopAccountability.org offers examples of the "abuse crisis in the Roman Catholic Church." One such example is from a *St. Louis Post-Dispatch* article of August 8, 2002, written by Norm Parish. Titled "Area Priest in Sex Case is Laicized by Pope; Saint Louis Archdiocese Had Removed Joseph D. Ross from Saint Cronan Church," it reads, in part: "Ross, 58, had been accused of grabbing and kissing the youngster several times during confession. The eleven-year-old boy also reported that while he was attempting to confess his sins a month later, Ross grabbed his arm and attempted to pull him onto his lap."

During my childhood, I held all clergy, priests, and nuns as people with a very special calling from God. I was taught to trust them completely. They were right next to God in my eyes, and I felt very common and lowly in their presence. There was no one I respected more. Sadly, I no longer feel that way.

I was a shy kid back then. I did what was expected of me so that I wouldn't upset anyone. I avoided confrontation completely and concentrated on pleasing others; I felt that I didn't matter anyway and neither did my opinion. It was not uncommon for my mom to tell me, "You're nobody special; the answer is no." Or "What do you think, that you're someone special? Just do what you were told." After becoming an adult with children of my own, I realized our mom did what she thought was best in raising us. She had grown up with only a dad, as her own mother had died suddenly in an accident when she was just a toddler.

We kids knew our parents expected us to do as we were told, and permission to stray from the routine work schedule of the house was rarely given. Once we finished our chores, we could play. We routinely helped with the laundry, dusting, vacuuming, washing the floors, cleaning the bathroom, making beds, washing and drying dishes and putting them away, taking out trash, cutting the grass with an old-fashioned push-mower and clippers for trimming, raking leaves, and shoveling snow. We learned responsibility and got lots of exercise in the process.

I did pretty well with classes in school but had to work at it and was always glad when summer vacation arrived. During high school, I wasn't good at sports, but I did enjoy volunteering at a hospital in Saint Louis after school a couple times a week. The staff would assign various duties to me. I'd take dinner trays to patients, at times feeding those who needed the help. I earned spending money by babysitting for neighbors occasionally, and after I turned sixteen, I was able to get a job working evenings and Saturdays as a salesclerk at the Woolworth's dime store, which was not too far from our home. The pay wasn't much—around sixty cents an hour—but it was nice to have the extra money. My time was pretty well spoken for with school, homework, household chores, and my part-time job. I worked at the dime store for two years before graduating from high school and finding a full-time job as a secretary, with higher pay, insurance coverage, and paid vacation. I continued working after I married but quit after I had our first child so that I could be a stay-at-home wife and mother. I truly enjoyed this last position the most.

Jeanne and Norman were three years apart in age but were my seniors by nine years and six years, respectively. Neither was too eager to spend time playing with a kid sister. Jeanne had sparkling deep-blue eyes and long, silky dark brown hair that fell into soft curls below her shoulders. She had a beautiful voice, and I used to enjoy listening to her and some friends singing in our home, accompanied by Mom on the piano. There were times when I begged Jeanne to sing me to sleep. Listening to her sing relaxed me, and I really loved the times she did. One time, when Jeanne and I were in our small backyard, she gave me a ride on the back of her bike. She made a sharp turn around a tree, and I instinctively gripped my feet to the wheel to keep from falling off. My foot got caught in the spokes. We both went down with the bike, and I ended up with a badly sprained ankle. While it was painful, and I was immobilized for many weeks, there was a bright side to it for me. Our parents made Jeanne and Norman play board games with me, something, as with older siblings, they never wanted to do. I enjoyed their playing with me, even though they were feeling forced to do so.

Jeanne married when I was twelve, and I was a junior bridesmaid in her wedding. She was an accomplished seamstress, and when I was in high school, she graciously made me beautiful formal gowns for both my junior and senior proms. Jeanne and I had little in common until I married and began having children. She and Al wanted children but were not blessed with any in the first years of their marriage. When their children started arriving around the same time as mine and Joe's, it brought Jeanne and me closer. We celebrated birthdays and holidays together, babysat for each other, and did things together with the kids; it was nice.

During my childhood, I usually spent free time playing outside with school and neighborhood friends or cousins who lived nearby. Jeanne said her childhood years were spent playing with a friend who lived two blocks away, but she doesn't know who Norman played with or where. She is as much in the dark about our brother's childhood activities as I am.

By the time I was in third grade, Norman was already going to the seminary. Up until then, I watched him play the drums in our grade school band. He seemed grown up in that band uniform, marching in the parade on picnic days. Our annual school picnic was as exciting to me as Christmas. There were rides and game booths with prizes, and the thought of it had me so excited that I could hardly fall asleep the night before. After the parade, Norman would change from his band uniform to his regular clothes for the day. I never saw him in the schoolyard, going on any rides, but Mom made sure he checked in with her throughout the day. I did not feel I ever mattered to my brother, as he never made an effort to spend time with me.

The house we grew up in on Henry Avenue was very small. Mom always referred to it as a cigar box and had hopes of one day moving into a larger house, but my parents never could afford to do it. All the rooms were small; there was only one actual bedroom, one bathroom, a kitchen, dining room, and front room with an extra small room next to it. The house had a basement and a wooden porch on the back, with a single-car garage by the alley. Our parents had made the dining room into their bedroom when we were young, putting bunk beds and a roll-away bed in the one bedroom for us kids. Eventually, they had the back porch redone and made into a closed-in sunroom. I then got to sleep out there on a roll-away bed, but it was cold in the winter because the room wasn't heated. I can remember sharing a roll-away bed with Norman when I was really young. At some point, the bunk beds were moved into that extra small front room, and Jeanne and I shared that room for a while. The house had no air-conditioning, so in the very hot Saint Louis summers, we'd all set up beds and cots in our basement, where it was cooler. We ate our meals down there, too, and always left the basement screen door unlocked for Dad, as he'd come home from work late at night. No one worried about intruders coming in back then.

The house only had one closet in the bedroom and one in the bathroom. It amazes me now that my mom's, Jeanne's, and my clothes and shoes all fit in that one small closet. They eventually bought a metal cabinet for hanging clothes and placed it in that small front room; Dad's and Norman's things were put in there. I guess the truth is, none of us had many clothes back then.

Mom grocery shopped a couple times a week, as there were no freezers or large refrigerators then to keep foods fresh. I'd pull my little red wagon, sometimes getting a ride in it, as we walked the many long blocks to the store. Occasionally, we had a case of twenty-four empty glass Pepsi bottles to return to the store. We'd put the heavy case into the wagon, and we'd take turns pulling it. For returning the bottles for recycling, Mom would receive two cents per bottle. She received a whopping forty-eight cents for the returned case. I used to look around our neighborhood and pick up bottles that people had just tossed away, earning me enough money to buy a Popsicle or candy for a treat. When we walked home from the grocery store, pulling the wagon full of bags packed with groceries, we had to be really careful, especially going up and down the curbs at street corners. Mom would cry out, "Slow down! Watch out for the eggs! Watch not to crush the bread, and don't bruise the peaches. That bag has glass jars in it; be careful." We didn't buy soda very often; our main drinks were milk, iced tea, and sometimes Kool-Aid, which Mom liked to call "bug juice"—not her favorite. We were allowed soda only once in a while, and I never outgrew the habit of asking my parents, "Is it okay if I have a soda?"

Monday meant helping Mom put the family's dirty clothes through her wringer washing machine. She filled it with extremely hot water from a hose she connected to a faucet in the basement and added the laundry soap. Three square rinse tubs stood around the washing machine. The washer and tubs all had wheels to move them around and hoses to empty them. Mom added bleach to the first tub, so we had to be careful not to put any colored clothes into it, as they would get ruined. Mom carefully lifted the clean clothes from the hot, soapy water with a long wooden spoon and fed them, one by one, through the wringers, letting them fall into a rinse tub. Jeanne and I were very careful not to get our fingers caught in the wringers as we moved the clothes from one rinse tub to the next. We sometimes popped buttons off dresses and shirts by putting them through the wringer the wrong way. Mom didn't empty the water from the washing machine until after the last batch, using the same soap water for all the clothes. She started with the whites and worked through to the dark clothes last. Mom strung a clothesline in the yard and when each batch was ready, she, Jeanne, and I took it outside and hung each piece with clothespins to dry in the hot sun. Meanwhile, the next batch was washing in the machine. Jeanne or I would prop up the full lines of clothes with long, thin wooden poles to keep things from dragging on the ground. The clothes smelled so fresh from drying outside, but sometimes, birds flying over would make it necessary to wash them again. If it rained on Monday, we just hung the clothes in the basement to dry. Mom turned on an electric fan to help create a breeze for drying. Dried clothes were taken down, folded, and put away. Mom dampened whatever clothes needed to be ironed, rolled them up, and placed them in a basket.

Tuesday was ironing day and was always done in the basement. I learned to iron on Dad's handkerchiefs and moved up from there. I always enjoyed ironing. Since Mom worked outside the house, we kids knew we were to help with the routine housecleaning every Saturday. No one got to sleep in. We were up by seven and ready to get the jobs done. The times I dreaded most were the arrival of spring and fall, when we had to help wash all the windows in the house, inside and out, wash the metal venetian blinds, and also wash and change all the curtains to the current season. That was a huge undertaking that took us an entire exhausting day as we moved ladders around along with pails of hot water, rags, cleaners, and squeegees, working together to make our house sparkle and smell fresh for the new season. She was bound to hear, "Ouch, my finger's bleeding, Mom," from whoever was washing the metal blinds. Wiping too fast over those slats was dangerous for our fingers, but we wanted to get finished with that dreaded job as quickly as possible.

I also needed to clean my pet canary's cage a couple times a week. I dearly loved little Pete and made sure he had food and fresh water every day. I loved watching him splash in his little plastic bathtub when I attached it to the opening of his cage. He would sing on my command, even when perched on my finger. Pete became very tame, flying to me when I left his cage door open to let him fly around the room. I had more of a relationship with my pet than I had with my brother while growing up. He had been a gift from my parents after recovering from pneumonia when I was five. My parents promised me a pet if I'd get well. Every animal I asked for was vetoed, but they suggested a canary and took me to pick one from a place filled with them in small individual cages. I loved my bright yellow songbird right from the start. He sang to the top of his tiny lungs almost to the day he died, when I was eighteen—by then I was a high school graduate and working full time. As I checked on my little friend before going to work one morning, I found him sitting on the bottom of his cage, pitifully looking up at me. I hurried off to catch my bus to work with an uneasy feeling that my thirteen-year-old pet might be dying. Dad, who hadn't left for work yet, called me that afternoon at work. "Carol, I just wanted to let you know that Pete died." It was a sad day, as I had grown up with my little friend. I missed him for quite a while, but he left me with many happy memories.

After we kids all were grown and had left home, Mom and Dad used the bedroom for themselves and bought a dining room set for the other room, for times they'd have our families over, especially when we'd all be together, as for Thanksgiving. It'd be crowded but manageable. The little house on Henry Avenue may have been small, but it held an abundance of our parents' love for us.

It was my brother, Norman, however, the only son, who was the golden child in our family. I was told he always expressed a desire to become a priest. It was no surprise when he went from eighth grade right into Kenrick Seminary. My parents were so proud, as was Grandpa Christian. The Christian family was quite large, and Grandpa had many grandchildren. Every Christmas, the entire family would gather together and enjoy singing songs around a piano at an aunt and uncle's large house. Eventually, the time would come when Grandpa would call each grandchild to him to receive an envelope that contained a small monetary Christmas gift from him. Every year, he'd purposely forget to call one child's name, and then he'd watch to see the child's reaction. He enjoyed his little tease every year. Grandpa always tucked a larger amount of money into Norman's envelope than in the others because he was going to become a priest. The extra money was supposed to be kept a secret, but I once heard my parents talking to Norman about how nice it was of Grandpa to do that. So it had started that far back—Norman's being treated special, better than the other grandchildren, just because he was going to become a priest.

Looking back, maybe that was the beginning of impressing on me that my brother was someone special. I wasn't jealous of him, but I never felt comfortable around him. I didn't feel I could relate to him, because I put him on a level way above me. Part of me was proud of him, but a bigger part of me knew little about him. I can't remember a time he ever showed interest in something I was doing during my childhood. I never knew his likes and dislikes, his friends, or any of the usual things one might know about a sibling. All I knew was that my brother planned to enter the seminary after eighth grade. Memories of Norman are few. I remember him looking for garden snakes under the rocks in our mom's flower garden and then playing with them. He and my sister would take long bike rides together. Mom once told me, "I expected Norman to grow up to be a road builder because of the way he played so much in the gravel underneath our back porch. When he was young, he'd make all kinds of roads for his toy cars and trucks with his little bulldozer."

During his seminary years, I would accompany Mom every week to pick up his dirty laundry from the seminary and drop off his clean clothes. We did this from the time he entered the seminary, all through high school, college, and the time he was at the seminary until his ordination. Our family attended the many musicals in which Norman performed at the seminary, too.

Father Norman Christian was ordained a priest March 18, 1961, and I became engaged to be married in December of the same year. My parents assumed that since my brother was now a priest, he would perform our marriage. I really didn't have a preference, so I agreed. It was silly of me to think his pattern of behavior toward me would change, and he'd actually spend some time with me and my intended. I was brought back to reality quickly when Norman told Joe and me to just go to our parish priest for our marriage preparations. (Before a couple could marry in the church, they were required to meet with the priest several times to discuss spiritual, emotional, financial, and child-raising instructions. They also discussed everyday happenings of married life.) He said that he'd only be performing our wedding ceremony because he didn't have the time to do the rest of the stuff with us. That was disappointing but not surprising—I had learned not to expect much from him when I was growing up. I believed God was calling my brother to the priesthood, and when I saw how proud my parents were of him for entering the seminary, I recognized that Norman was very special. I foolishly felt he was better than I was, that he had more important things to do than to bother with a kid sister.

After Joe and I married, when we invited Norman to spend time with us, he'd show up if he had nothing better to do, but he made no secret of it if he had another offer of something he'd rather do. He never gave me any reason to feel that I or my family was anything special to him.

Norman did what Norman wanted to do, regardless of others' feelings. Once, he was very excited about receiving a black lab puppy. He quickly bonded with the dog, named him Delta, and took him everywhere, even where he knew the dog wouldn't be welcome. I don't know if it ever occurred to him to ask people if they minded having his large dog in their homes. Our mom was one who wasn't happy around dogs because of a bad experience with one early in her marriage. She definitely didn't like dogs inside her house, and we kids all knew it. That didn't stop Norman. He would bring Delta into her small house when it was full of people, such as for Thanksgiving dinner, and the dog would run through the house and sniff the food on the table. It was as though Norman was daring Mom to say something, and of course, she never did. None of us asked him to put the dog outside. After all, this was a priest's dog, and back then, everyone catered to priests. My sister and I couldn't understand, however, why Norman would deliberately bring the dog when he knew it upset our mother. It wasn't until we spoke with him regarding his pedophile behavior that he made it clear to us how much he hated our mother. It seemed he had intended to aggravate her.

Our parents loved us and did the best job they knew how. They weren't the kind of parents who gave hugs or compliments, and they weren't easy to talk to, but they certainly taught us right from wrong. As I've mentioned, Norman was their pride and joy, and they went out of their way to do whatever they could for him. Somehow, though, Norman developed a deep hatred for our mother and was disgusted with our father for not exerting stronger authority in the household—something else he admitted to Jeanne and me later in his life. We three children knew to ask Mom if we wanted permission for anything. Dad was a kind, quiet, religious man who loved to read and enjoyed being active with his church organizations. He never wanted to have the final say on things at home. If we went to Dad for something first, he'd automatically tell us to ask Mom. For some reason, that really bothered Norman.

As a young priest, Norman had joined a Big Brothers group. The thought of his being brotherly to anyone surprised me, because he had so little to do with me. Then I figured it was probably because I was a girl, and he just never knew how to relate to me, especially since I was years younger. He was probably more comfortable with boys. It never occurred to me he would have plans to molest those children. Those poor "little brothers" of his were easy prey for such an evil monster in clerical garb. I remember that Norman brought one little boy with him to one of our family get-togethers. I can only hope that boy didn't become one of Norman's victims.

I am not aware of anyone from the Big Brothers organization making accusations of abuse against him, but now, knowing Norman's history of sexually abusing vulnerable young boys, I question his motives for joining the organization. Most likely they were excited about having a priest as a big brother—what a wonderful role model some young boy would have. If you couldn't trust a priest, who could you trust? It is that fact that makes Father Norman Christian's crimes—and all the others like him—even worse than the common pedophile.

We had a small family gathering in September 1969, consisting of Mom and Dad, Jeanne and her husband, their four children, Joe and me, our three children at the time—Jeff, Lynn, and Sue—and Norman. My brother, surprisingly, had invited us to his assigned parish, Sacred Heart Catholic Church in Festus, Missouri, to celebrate our parents' fortieth wedding anniversary. Our parents were quite happy about it. After celebrating a special Mass for them in the church, he told us we were all invited to the rectory dining room to enjoy a delicious dinner that the parish cook had specially prepared for us.

The dining room was just big enough for all of us to sit around the large mahogany table. The enticing aroma of roast beef with gravy, mashed potatoes, rolls, green beans, carrots, and applesauce drew us all to the beautifully set table. I cautioned my children to be careful with the lovely napkins, dinnerware, and crystal glasses.

Wine was served to the adults and grape juice to the children for toasting our parents, before we began enjoying the scrumptious food and beverages of iced tea, milk, water, or coffee. While eating, we reminisced about Mom and Dad's life together, as well as talking about what was going on with all of us. Cake and ice cream were served after the meal for those who could manage to eat another bite.

After finishing dinner, everyone went into the spacious living room and settled into the large, comfortable couch and chairs. As we adults continued talking, the kids were occupied on the floor with toys and coloring books that I had brought along from home. Norman started filling us in on how things were going for him at the parish, giving us the impression he was happy there. Later, he decided to give us a tour of the rectory and church. I watched closely that the kids didn't touch anything while we followed Norman throughout the premises. Everything there was old, but it was well cared for, beautifully polished or painted, and well maintained. Earlier, after the Mass, I had asked someone to take a snapshot of our family group with my camera. I treasured that picture because our dad became very ill not too long after that celebration. He was in and out of the hospital for several years before passing away in August 1974, just three months after the birth of my last child.

None of us was aware of the pedophile in our midst as we smiled happily for the camera that day. We had no clue the priest we loved, trusted, respected, and called our brother and Uncle Norman was a danger to children.

Years later, after learning my brother was a child molester, looking at that picture made me feel sick. I realize now that he was molesting the children of that parish at the time.

I had enjoyed cake decorating for many years. Sometimes I'd get a phone call from Norman, telling me that a kid he knew was having a birthday. He'd ask if I'd make a cake for him, and then he'd give me the child's name, any special details he wanted on the cake, and when he needed it. He'd come by to pick up the cake, give me a quick thanks, and be on his way. I never thought anything about making the cakes back then, but now I feel he may have used me to help groom some of his victims.

In 1979, some of his parishioners threw him a surprise birthday party, and I offered to bring the cake. Since he enjoyed riding motorcycles at the time, I wrote across the top, "Happy Birthday to one of Heaven's Angels gang members." If only I had known the truth about him then. The years that followed brought about more parties and decorated cakes for my brother.

As the parish priest, Father Christian was well liked in every parish to which he was assigned. He made special efforts to connect with the kids in each parish, and the parents trusted him with their children—they had no reason not to. Among other events, he enjoyed showing movies on weekends for them. Norman asked my husband to install motorized movie screens at the various parishes, as he was moved around over the years. He told us the kids loved coming to the movies when he showed them; he always had a crowd.

One of Norman's victims later told me, "Father Christian used to save me a seat right next to him when he was showing those movies. It always made me feel special that Father liked me that much. I was just a shy kid who enjoyed the special attention." He didn't realize that Norman was grooming him for sexual abuse; neither did his parents.

Joe and I both regret that we allowed Norman to use us—with the decorated cakes and motorized movie screens—to help lure innocent children to him. The fact that we didn't know at the time that he was a pedophile doesn't take away the sickening feeling we have over this.

Chapter 2
Sabbatical

Norman had been a priest for twenty-four years by 1985, when he phoned a female cousin of ours to whom he was close and asked, "How about we have dinner together sometime soon? I've got some important news to tell you."

When my cousin related this story to me, she still seemed agitated by it. She said that she and her husband had invited Norman to a very nice country-club restaurant, where they planned to pick up the check. "I was embarrassed when Norman showed up at the restaurant to meet us," she said. "He was dressed like a bum—disheveled and unshaven. We had to ask if they had a coat and tie he could borrow, because they weren't going to let him come in as he was dressed." She shook her head in disbelief. "We both thought Norman's news was going to be that he had gotten a promotion in the church, but we were way off. We were enjoying our wonderful dinners when suddenly, Norman dropped a bombshell—he had 'gotten into a predicament with some kids' a while back and now was in trouble for it."

She told me that Norman just shrugged his shoulders and said matter-of-factly, "It happened, but now the church is taking care of everything, and I have to do what they say. So I wanted to let you know I'm being sent to a Catholic-run treatment facility for the next six months, because I sexually abused seven or eight boys in Festus. It happened back in the early seventies."

Then my cousin told me, "He strongly emphasized that it was important we keep this to ourselves and not tell anyone, because the church would suffer terribly if word got out. We couldn't understand how he could nonchalantly tell us of his history of sexually abusing young boys. He completely stunned us, not only by what he said but by how he said it. He didn't seem at all embarrassed by talking about it and appeared excited about going to wherever it was the church was sending him for therapy. When Norman said that the church was taking care of everything, we assumed that meant the victims' needs, too."

My cousin and her husband both also assumed Norman would never do any such thing again, so they kept his shocking secret, saying nothing to anyone about what he had told them, not even to my sister or me. They did what Catholics were taught to do: trust the church to do no wrong.

I felt terribly let down and irritated when my cousin finally told me, many years later, that she and her husband had learned Norman's secret back in '85. She hadn't tried to warn me or Jeanne so we could protect our kids from him; maybe she thought Norman had confided in us. I don't know, but the longer I thought about it, the more I began to recognize how alike my cousin and I were when it came to our Catholic faith. We were both very faith-filled, trusting Catholics, raised from birth to believe in God and to obey, revere, trust, and believe that the church will do no wrong. Shortly after talking to my cousin, I began questioning my own actions for not going to the police the minute my daughter told me what Norman was doing. As horrid as her facts were about my brother, at that point there was no doubt in my mind that the church would take care of it all. My cousin had acted in the same Catholic Church–controlled mode as I had. That blind trust in the church/clergy had been ingrained in us from the time we were small children, in Catholic schools, at church, and in our homes, where our parents reinforced what we learned at school. That's why I'd always put clergy on pedestals, thinking they were far above me—God had specially called them to lead others. That blind trust, however, gives clergy abusers power over their innocent victims.

I can't help but wonder what motivated Norman to tell our cousin and her husband he was going into treatment for having abused the boys. He certainly couldn't have been proud of it. How strange that he told them and how difficult it must have been for them to have kept his horrid secret, while trusting the church was doing the right thing. Obviously, Norman felt closer to our cousin than to his siblings, as at that time, he had told my husband and me that he was going away on a sabbatical.

It was nearing Christmas 1985 when Norman called and said he'd be leaving Saint Louis for six months to attend a sabbatical. "I can't let you know where I'm being sent," he said, "and there won't be any way to contact me once I'm there."

I really didn't know what occurred on a sabbatical. I just assumed it helped priests learn more about their vocations, making them better priests. I knew Norman enjoyed the fine things in life and greatly enjoyed the many invitations he received, from affluent parish members and others who found him captivating, to luxurious country clubs and lavish trips, some out of the country. I had come to realize that not all priests were humble and prayerful. I had met some over the years who showed signs of narcissism and realized now that Norman fit that description. I guess I longed to see a Christlike, compassionate attitude in him during difficult times, but I was disappointed, time after time, with Norman.

I wasn't happy to hear about his "sabbatical," because Joe's and my youngest child, eleven-year-old Joan, had been diagnosed with a brain tumor. It had all happened so fast, I hadn't had the chance to contact Norman with the news. The surgery to remove it was scheduled for December 27, and it would have been nice to have had him close for a little extra support. I told Norman about his niece's diagnosis, but I don't remember much of what he said, other than he'd pray for her. I just figured, *What else is new?*—he'd never been there for us. Somewhere over the years, I had accepted that Norman wanted to keep his personal life private. At this point, I was too concerned about my daughter's life to dwell on what my brother was doing. I thanked Norman for letting us know he'd be gone and wished him well before saying good-bye.

Our good friend at the time, Father Joe Naumann, a young priest assigned at our parish, was at our side in the hospital to offer his support and prayers as soon as he learned of Joan's diagnosis and scheduled surgery. We were very blessed with support from family, friends, and almost everyone who knew Joan or our family. It was quite a contrast to the lack of support we'd receive many years later with Norman's arrest and later his death.

Joan had been a normal eleven-year-old girl. She was a petite redhead who loved to play soccer and baseball, ride her bike, swim, and enjoy life with her friends. The brain surgery left her with severe side effects—double vision, and she couldn't walk, write, or do any of the things she loved doing before the surgery. Excruciating headaches, nausea, and dizziness also were with her constantly. The surgery affected the entire right side of her body. She was not going to have an easy time of it or break any speed limits on her road to recovery. It took her many years of determination and a lot of hard work, but we were all extremely happy for her that she eventually recovered and got on with her life.

Around the middle of January, mixed in with the many get-well cards for Joan, came a letter for Joe and me from Norman. He was writing from the Servants of the Paraclete, Jemez Springs, New Mexico. I was happy he had changed his mind about keeping his location a secret and now wanted us to have his address and phone number.

My brother's letter, dated January 12, 1986, read as follows:

> Dear Carol & Joe,
>
> Once I thought I would like to remain totally anonymous and tell no one where I am for this sabbatical period. But I have changed my mind where family is concerned. Especially please let me know of Joan's progress. I was very glad to get the message that she got home already, but I understand that it will be some time before we can declare her out of the woods.
>
> I am 1,140 miles away in Jemez Canyon, where this community lives who will be leading my special program. I wish I could say that this experience will be rest 'n' recreation, but it will be rather difficult. I have found that I am not totally unlike your other daughter, Sue. I will be sorting out my life and its related emotional problems, together with an overhaul of my spiritual life and its values. I probably

never will tell anyone what my "addiction" is, so I hope you and the family will have the kindness not to ask too many questions. When you live alone, it is possible that no one would ever be aware of any problem because there are no close-in family persons to pick up on it. So I have had myself studied, and this sabbatical is "what the doctor ordered." Be sure to keep me in your prayers, too.

Finally, it will be OK to write to me here (phone in emergency); tell Jeanne the address too. I am looking forward to June and my return to regular life. I will be happy to write to Sue, if you find it might be helpful.

With much love,
Norm

I had been extremely busy taking care of my family, trying to keep up with the usual household chores and caring for an extremely sick child, and I was quite exhausted. My mind was full of worries about Joan's recovery from brain surgery. Now, in the midst of all that, I felt guilty for having been upset with Norman about his secretive manner in dealing with whatever was bothering him. It totally surprised me when I read his admission of dealing with an addiction of some kind. He told me something of his situation by writing "I have found that I am not totally unlike your other daughter, Sue." Norman knew she had been in treatment for months, working with the doctor and staff of a program to help sort out her own young life's emotional problems. I understood him to mean he would be doing what she was doing in her doctor-ordered program. I didn't realize he felt connected with my daughter in some inappropriate way, being drawn by her vulnerability. The fact that Norman actually told me he had a problem and was reaching out to me for support made me feel good. I wanted to let him know that I did care about him and would help him in whatever way I could.

Within days, I had written to Norman (entire 01-19-86 letter in appendix), thanking him for letting us know where he was and telling him I was disappointed with myself for not having recognized that he might be having serious problems. "I'm glad you're taking action on whatever it is that's troubling you," I said, although I couldn't help but wonder what that might be. I updated him on Joan's recovery and mentioned how things were going for Sue. I tried to be encouraging, saying, "God sends troubles to families in order to bring them closer together, to strengthen them, and to make them realize how much they really love one another." That's what I had come to believe. Maybe by reaching out to each other for support, I thought, we'd become closer.

Thank God, our son and our eldest daughter were both holding their own. Other than the familiar signs of worry about their sisters, they were okay. I don't remember having any spare time to devote to them back then. Looking back on it now, I feel bad for not making the time to talk with each of them to acknowledge their fears or anger for what was happening in our family. In their early twenties, they took on a lot of extra responsibility and dealt with all of the emotional difficulties our family was facing. While they may not have understood why things happened as they did, they accepted the situation, and both kept a good attitude. They were always willing to pitch in and do whatever was asked of them.

Our son was away at college, so he was spared much of the daily stress going on within our home. Still, it must have been difficult for him, being away and trying to study while worrying about his family. Joe and I were very proud when he graduated. We admire the man he is today.

Our eldest daughter lived at home during her college years. I don't know how she managed to continue to do so well with her studies while working a part-time job and helping with the family situations in our stress-filled home, but she graduated college with honors. Her dad and I were very proud of her then and continue to be to this day.

Our children are all married now, with families of their own, and they still love and care about each other and us.

Norman responded to my letter quickly, on January 23. He described the program somewhat and made vague references to his situation. I couldn't imagine what "secret life" he could have had that would go back almost forty years, to his childhood. I figured whatever it was must have started around age eleven.

The idea that Norman might have been a child molester never

crossed my mind, not once! A priest accused of being a pedophile? No way! I simply could not imagine it—not about any priest. Priests are men of God. They are, however, also human and have their faults, as I have learned. Some priests do lie, betray trusts, and harm children.

What jumps out in my brother's letter is that the Archdiocesan Development Appeal helped pay for his treatment in New Mexico. This was at a cost of approximately twenty thousand dollars, according to Norman. The church has changed the name of that fund drive several times over the years, insisting not a penny of what's collected goes to pay for anything connected to the clergy sexual-abuse scandal, as it has continued to worsen each year.

While Norman's letter described the program's daily classes, it didn't mention the type of addiction with which he was dealing. It did, however, give me some idea of how his days were spent.

The following are excerpts from my brother's January 23, 1986, letter from Foundation House, Jemez Springs, New Mexico (entire letter in appendix.)

> Dear Carol,
> What a joy to get a letter from home! What you had to say meant more to me than I might have expected. It was very supportive indeed, and I needed it a lot today. I am attending a total wellness module offered by the Paracletes. There are 23 other priests (from monsignors to monastics, from the 60s to the 20s, who suffer from everything that human life will allow … things as simple as stress through a variety of relational problems, with many of us dealing with sexuality in our lives. Last October I had myself evaluated by professionals and, as I already knew, I would be prime material for their module. Perhaps someday I will sit down one-on-one with you and tell you my whole story. But for right now, I am where I need to be, with the right professional persons to guide us through 5 months of exercises designed to take us apart and put us back together. …
> I guess I should thank you for supporting the Archdiocesan Development Appeal, because that is

part of the resource that is helping pay this huge bill ... Archbishop May is fantastic! When I visited him he was so very supportive, too. ... Carol, for the first time in my life, I am trusting my secret life to these many others without fear of getting hurt in return. I have practiced hiding my secret life that goes back almost 40 years even to my childhood; and I guess with so much practice I became quite good at it (hiding my secrets). I am at the same time totally convinced of my vocation to the priesthood. I am a quality priest (better than many), effective in my ministry, and happy in doing it. ...

My faith has always been better than good, even in moment of depression years past, when I seriously thought of leaving the ranks of the clergy. ...

You are right about tragic difficulties being a catalyst for bringing families closer together. I have never felt as close to you as I do right now, having received and enjoyed your beautiful letter. Thank you for taking the trouble to reach out still further (even to New Mexico) with your love.

Let us love one another,
Norman
P.S. Share what you think you should of this letter's content. Know that I am still pretty fearful and sensitive about my problem.

I received a lengthy letter from Norman (page two of 2-23-86 letter in appendix), in which he responded to some concerns I had about Sue and Joan. Sue was having difficulties making a decision about college choices, and Joan's recovery was still rough. He gave me some of his thoughts about Sue's ideas and some suggestions, including that although she had been offered a full scholarship, he felt that Sue was not emotionally fit to go away to college. He said that he'd "be just as troubled" if he were in my shoes. He wanted to reassure me that I was doing well and said that I shouldn't get down on myself for how things were happening. He told me to give Joan a hug from him and know that she was on his mind and in his prayers. It did feel good to know he was praying for her recovery. He suggested I might have a talk with God, unloading on Him, letting Him know enough was enough. It seemed strange to hear that coming from a priest—to get mad at God. I was always told that what doesn't kill you makes you stronger. Today, I know that's true!

At the time, Norman's letter made me feel good that he was taking an interest in trying to help me and my family through our difficulties. I knew he couldn't give me any answers, but just knowing that for once he cared meant a lot. I was happy we had finally made a connection and that he told me what was going on in his life. He shared some things he was doing in the program in New Mexico, and I had hopes this was the start of a new relationship between us.

What follows is the second page of his letter. I saw a hint of my brother's narcissistic personality when he stated, "the program is fascinating, most of all because it is dealing with *me*."

Page two excerpts of Norman's February 23, 1986, letter:

> Things here are involved to the extreme. According to the first report (5 pages) sent to the archbishop, in the opinion of the staff here I am off to a very good start, and they believe the module will be of much value for me. It really is embarrassing to see my problem described in clinical terminology. I look at it and say, "Is that what I am? That's terrible," and run to the other guys and find out that they are having the same feelings. This is certainly the most important thing I have ever done with my life, and the program is fascinating, most of all because it is dealing with *me*. ...
>
> Last weekend we had an extra day off from programs, so five of us drove to El Paso, Texas (a 7-hour drive) and went across into Juarez, Mexico. We stayed in a motel and caught Sunday Mass at a neighborhood church. It was the 10 a.m. children's Sunday mass. ...
>
> Driving back we enjoyed the White Sands National Monument, and ... desert mountain scenery all along the Rio Grande river valley. After a perfect dinner in

Albuquerque topped off the outing, we were ready for a return to very intense programs once again. ...

I'm so busy that it doesn't seem like Lent. But I guess that my dying and rising is going on daily in the module. ...

I love you,
Norm

Three months later, judging from the last letter I received from Norman while on sabbatical, he seemed to be having difficulty in the program with the task of identifying his feelings as he prepared to return home to Saint Adalbert's as pastor.

Excerpts from the May 6, 1986, letter (entire letter in appendix):

Dear Carol,

First, thanks for writing as often as you do. It means a lot to me to feel included in the family, because before I came here, I was actually excluding myself from the family. ... Again, let me note that it was not your behavior in any way that created my problem; it was my own interpretation of my life and role. ...

One of the current tasks I am dealing with in the program is identifying my feelings (like, any kind of feelings). I don't know how to stay with them once I have discovered them present. My practice was to always suppress my feelings. But that always led to stress in my daily life and all kinds of other problems as a result. ...

I have enjoyed my 5 months in this program very much. I am also glad I have had the chance to tour the neighborhood while I am here. I've seen sights in Arizona, Utah, and Colorado, in addition to New Mexico and El Paso, Texas, ...

If you write me, be sure I will receive any mail before June 6, my last day at Foundation House.

Blessings on you all!
Norm

Chapter 3
Struggle

Our eleven-year-old found 1986 to be an extremely difficult year as she recovered from her brain surgery. Joan required intense physical therapy throughout the year. Besides having to relearn walking, she couldn't so much as hold a crayon in her right hand. Writing was so difficult that she eventually switched to writing left handed. Joan wore an eye patch, alternating which eye was covered each day, hoping to correct the double vision that resulted from the brain surgery. My sister perked her up by finding pretty materials and sewing a bunch of different eye patches for her to wear, instead of the plain old black ones. She even made some to match Joan's school uniform. Those cute patches made wearing them more tolerable.

We'd drive to the hospital several times a week for physical therapy, come rain, sleet, snow, or ice. Joan would put in a lot of hard work while there, and I counted my blessings she was a child of small stature, as I was handling her in transport.

A tutor would come to our home, Monday through Friday, to help with her schoolwork, but she could only do her schoolwork verbally. Quite often, she was feeling very sick with severe headache and nausea, and not much got accomplished. She attended summer school in order to keep up with her classmates, as she very much wanted to move up to seventh grade with her friends the next year.

I assumed that Norman must not have had any words of encouragement for her. He didn't visit, call, or send cards to lift her spirits, nor did he ever talk to us about her. He did, however, continue to call Sue throughout the year. It would be years later that we'd learn he had not been "counseling" her in the good sense. In fact, it was quite the opposite; he was filling her head with untruths, tearing down the self-worth she had worked on the past year, and taking her to inappropriate places (such as sexually explicit gay and lesbian movies, get-togethers in bad parts of town where she was propositioned and manhandled, and doing things that, had we known, would have been stopped by refusing him further contact with her).

Sue was still struggling with her own problems and now was worried about her little sister as well. Her dad and I tried to make sure she kept all her doctor appointments and attended all the self-help groups available to her. I made good use of those groups along with her. The last thing she needed was to be subjected to all of what my brother forced upon her—and all the while, Joe and I were grateful to him for making time to help our daughter work through whatever was troubling her. How trusting we were. He was my brother and a priest. We felt relieved and grateful to have him helping us through the difficulties our family was dealing with that year.

As that exhausting year was nearing its end, Joe and I discovered something else our middle daughter, Sue, was facing. I came across a poem she had written, and it led me to believe she might be pregnant. She wasn't home when I showed it to Joe. We sat in the living room, watching TV, anxiously awaiting her return.

It was late that evening before she came home. I showed her the poem I had found and asked, "Do you have something to tell us?" Tearfully, she blurted, "I'm pregnant." She started sobbing and her words gushed out. "I'm so sorry to disappoint you; I'm so sorry!"

I was very upset, wondering how she could have been so irresponsible, but before I could say anything more, Sue told us, "I've been going to a clinic, and the doctor says the baby is fine." The baby was due the following June. Joe and I were angry that she was pregnant but pleased that she had sought medical care for herself and the baby on her own. I told her, "We love you and will help every way we can, but understand that your life is going to change tremendously."

The exact details of her pregnancy are personal and not relevant to this book. What does matter is that suddenly, our troubled, unmarried, and now pregnant daughter had to take a long, hard look at herself and make some decisions. Soon, she'd be responsible for a baby. We were very concerned, because although we did not understand why, she struggled with loving herself. How was she going to love a baby?

Troubled by my daughter's unexpected news, I gave Norman a call the following morning, hoping to solicit some advice from him. He stopped by our house the next day and sat quietly in our dining room, listening to me vent as I paced back and forth, my arms flailing in sheer frustration.

"Norman, we raised her better than that. We taught her right from wrong. With all the Catholic schooling, religious education, and moral upbringing, where did we fail her?" It was embarrassing, telling my brother—a priest—that my teenage unmarried daughter was pregnant, but I was so frustrated, I couldn't stop ranting and raving.

Suddenly, it dawned on me that I was the only one in the room upset about my daughter's conduct. My brother, the priest, showed no signs of being troubled by what she had done. Actually, Norman's comments struck me as really bizarre, as he suggested what happened really wasn't her fault. "She can't help it if God made her so pretty. She has such sexy eyes, Carol! Boys are bound to be attracted to her. They can't control themselves. It happens!"

Norman's remarks made no sense to me. I didn't find those words or anything else he said helpful or comforting. His attitude left me feeling he didn't understand my frustration. I regretted having discussed it with him.

As things turned out, my daughter's pregnancy seemed to be the turning point in her life, as she seemed to start building up self-worth, at first for her son, and then she turned her life around. She found a job and took college classes while raising her son, with the help of her brother, sisters, dad, and me. Her son was six years old when Sue eventually married, and they moved into their own home. Not only did she finish her bachelor's degree, but she also later went on to earn an MBA. That first grandchild brought more joy into our lives than I could have ever thought. I can't imagine life without him.

At first, learning of Sue's pregnancy hit our whole family somewhat like when we learned of Joan's brain tumor the previous year. It caught us off guard, and we wondered why these things happened to our family. Still, we accepted the facts and supported one another as best we could. Our faith in God, our love for each other, and the help and support of family and friends brought us closer and helped pull us through the difficult times. While I wouldn't care to relive those turbulent times, I do appreciate what we gained from experiencing them.

We turned the page to January 1987, and it seemed to be a toss-up as to which would be more difficult for Joan: trying to keep up with her schoolwork while enduring constant headaches, nausea, and dizziness; or fighting exhaustion from the daily physical therapy regime so that she might be able to walk and write again. She had returned to school, but she still wasn't capable of writing. Classmates would carry her books for her and make copies of their notes from which she could study, and teachers allowed her to take quizzes orally. The length of the school day itself was very tiring for her, and then she'd still have homework to do. She was determined to stay with her class, though, and refused to give up.

Sue was as concerned about her little sister as everyone, but she was still struggling through her own troubles. I wanted her to concentrate on taking care of herself by keeping her doctor appointments and making use of the support groups that were available. Her dad and I insisted she follow the doctor's program, and I attended as many of the support group meetings as possible. By listening and interacting with others in similar circumstances, I was learning better communication skills and finally came to realize I couldn't control my daughter—or anyone. I could only control how I reacted to what she or anyone else did or said.

As time went on, Sue was often out with Norman. Joe and I took comfort in thinking he was giving her guidance. Maybe he'd be able to convince her of the beautiful person she was, both inside and out. She certainly wasn't willing to believe us when we told her so. It never entered our minds that his "counseling" was damaging her further.

By the middle of January 1987, the doctors decided Joan had waited long enough for the double vision to correct itself. Since it hadn't happened, it was time for surgery to fix the vision problems that had plagued her for over a year. I let Norman know Joan would be having the surgery and asked him to pray that all would go well. He assured me he would and added, "Let me know how the surgery goes."

Joan remembered the condition she was in when she awoke from her brain surgery, and she was extremely frightened about undergoing surgery again a mere year later. We were very grateful for the skilled, caring doctors and nursing staff at Cardinal Glennon Children's Hospital in Saint Louis, Missouri, who helped Joan manage her fears through the entire eye surgery procedure.

The surgery was successful, and at last, happily, Joan could put the eye patches away. Though her vision problems have reoccurred and are ongoing, they haven't stopped her from enjoying life. She learned very early in life the importance of one's attitude. Do the best you can with what you've got, and trust that God will take care of the rest.

Our household seemed happier after Joan's vision improved, and with spring arriving, she was looking forward to enjoying fishing and swimming again. Norman seemed happy when I called to tell him Joan's eye surgery was successful, but he made no efforts to visit or even talk with her on the phone. But many family and friends encouraged Joan in her recovery. She may not have noticed her uncle's absence. Norman had been assigned as pastor of Saint William's Parish in Woodson Terrace, Missouri, on June 18, and I assumed he was most likely busy settling in there.

At the end of June, Joe and I became grandparents—we had no idea how much we were going to enjoy our new role in life! I called Norman, asking if he could baptize our new grandson. After scheduling a date when he was free, he performed the baptism at our parish church after a private Mass. Sue had arranged for a vocalist and guitarist, making the occasion even more special. Many friends and family members celebrated the event with us.

Life really seemed to be improving for Joan, but then one day in the middle of October, as she was coming home from school, she was crossing the street, only one block from home, and was hit by a pickup truck. After an ambulance ride to the emergency room and many tests, we were told Joan had no broken bones or internal injuries. She did have many bruises, scrapes, and a very sore body. She ended up wearing a leg brace for quite a while but took it all in stride as her body healed again. I informed Norman of her accident, but Joan heard nothing from him, not even a card wishing her a speedy recovery. All his attention seemed to be directed toward her older sister, who remained busy working through her own difficulties.

When bad things happened, I realized the importance of looking for the good that was around and making the most of it. At the end of November, the kids and I completely surprised their dad with a fiftieth birthday party. We found his favorite disc jockey to play '50s hits in a small hall we rented for all the family and friends who gathered to celebrate Joe's birthday. Several nuns and clergy joined the crowd assembled that evening. Joe received a bumper sticker from Norman that read "I'd rather be 29." He had written on his card for Joe, "I really hope this is turning out to be the happiest birthday of your long career of birthdays." Those attending were invited to write a favorite memory they had of Joe and bring it to put into a "memories book." I had suggested Joe would need it to jog his memory in the years to come, as he would be entering his second half-century. He was always a big teaser all his life, so this was an invitation for everyone to take a shot at him for once. Many turned in a special memory, including Father Naumann, who had several amusing ones. They were collected on a designated table, where everyone could read them. Much later, when assembling all the memories in an album, I noticed Norman hadn't joined in the fun of submitting one.

That surprise party was in November 1987, and the photos-and-memories book continues to become a more special treasure as each year passes. Reading everyone's memories, looking at the snapshots from the party, and remembering the old times makes that book absolutely priceless. It's a wonderful reminder of all the people who have been with us through our difficult times, and fun times, and how blessed we've been.

I recalled the many times I answered our door to family, friends, and neighbors who stopped by, saying things such as, "Here's your dinner for tonight, Carol. You must be exhausted from running back and forth to the hospital," or "I've made you some food because you're probably so busy taking care of Joan, you don't have time to cook," or "I'll stay with Joan while you go to the store or take a break." That was expecting a lot of someone, because Joan was so frail for a considerable time after the brain surgery and was queasy more often than not. Remembering what so many had done for us during her long recovery and seeing Joan happy and physically doing well emphasized just how blessed we were. Whenever browsing through the pictures in Joe's party album, I'm reminded of all the special people in our lives.

Joe's party was a really fun time, and I expected that life would be returning to normal. Instead, I was in for a dreadful shock.

Chapter 4
Betrayal?

With a baby in the house again, our family's routines had changed, but we all made it work. I was feeling somewhat relieved with Joan's recovery as she slowly improved, and I found that I liked helping to raise our grandson—he brought great joy into our home. Our lives were brightened by the playfulness we shared with him. He had all of us wound around his little finger. Joe and I had baby-proofed the house again, knowing the little guy would be crawling before long. His mom had gotten a job and also was taking some college courses. That meant she had schoolwork to do in the evenings, in addition to attending self-help group therapy sessions twice a week through her doctor's program. Busy as she was, Sue always made sure she spent time with her son. She loved him immensely and found it increasingly difficult to be away from him all day. I could see my daughter was becoming more moody and disagreeable as months went by, and I worried if she had taken on too much. I'd try to talk with her, but she'd get angry and leave the room. I became frightened, sensing something was really wrong.

Norman had been making frequent phone calls to our house. I'd answer the phone to hear, "Hi, Carol. Norm. Just wondering if Sue is around," or "Hi, Carol, is Sue free tonight? I want to see if she'd like to do something." Often, Sue wasn't home, but when she was, she angrily would say, "Tell him I'm not home, or I'm working on my homework." I'd do what she asked, but Norman would call again another day. His niece remained adamant in refusing his calls.

I did not understand why she wouldn't talk with her uncle, and I became very angry with her. For once, my brother was being a part of my life and was trying to be supportive by making time to counsel my troubled child—or so I thought. Joe and I were frustrated that she no longer wanted anything to do with him. I angrily asked her, "Why are you turning your back on your uncle? He's just trying to help you." She'd walk away without answering, which made me all the angrier. I'm not sure why but at that time, I didn't want to tell Norman she wanted him to leave her alone. Maybe I feared he would go away, and I desperately wanted him to help her. So I made excuses for her when he called. "Sue said to tell you she's sorry, but she's got to get all her college work done," or "Sue's bathing the baby. She'll get back to you later." Of course, she never did return his calls. As she continued to refuse calls from her uncle, Joe and I became more frustrated. The tension in our home was becoming unbearable. Many weeks went by with Sue barely speaking to me; I was walking on eggshells, weighing my words in speaking to her, for fear she'd take whatever I said the wrong way. I wanted so badly for her to tell me what was wrong.

Finally, one evening, Sue quietly approached me, nervously murmuring, "Mom, I have to tell you something. Please come to my room." Her son was in the other room with his grandpa, so we'd be able to talk. The shakiness and tone of her voice, along with the fearful look in her eyes, worried me. Following her up the stairs, I couldn't imagine what she was going to tell me.

Sue sat beside me on her bed, biting her lip. She seemed frightened and had a hard time beginning to speak. Her body was trembling, and tears flowed down her cheeks as she started saying something about Uncle Norman. I know now that her greatest fear then was that I wouldn't believe what she was about to tell me. Finally, she quickly blurted out between sobs, "Mom, Uncle Norman hurts children. He has raped little boys!"

I cried, "Oh, my God!" My heart raced as she continued. I reached for her trembling hands as she said, "Mom, he has been telling me all about this since he got back from his thing in New Mexico. He has shared so many horrible details that I just can't handle it anymore.

Now that I am a mom, it's too real to me. I can't deny it or be silent anymore. I don't feel safe for my son! Uncle Norman goes to parks and picks kids up. He has raped kids from the parishes, but in his mind, they all want it. It's like he's doing them a favor. He's helping them."

By now, we were both in tears, sharing a box of tissues as she continued. "He's been taking me to creepy places—to parties with his 'friends' and to gay and X-rated movies. He scares me! When we go places, it is always in a bad neighborhood. I am afraid, but he just laughs. He took me to East Saint Louis under a viaduct to watch the fireworks for the Fourth of July celebration. He has taken me to parties where people proposition me or touch me. Even when I was pregnant, old and young men would leer at and hit on me and touch me. I didn't want to go to those places, but he insisted! He tells me my eyes are beautiful and seductive, and they tempt boys to do things to me. One time, we were in some wooded area, and he took me by the hands to do a 'confession.' Do you know what he asked God? He said, 'God, please forgive Sue for her eyes. She doesn't know what she does.' Mom, he cannot be right. I don't want him around my son, and I don't want to have anything to do with him anymore!"

I held my frightened daughter and promised that her dad and I would deal with Norman; she was finished with him. I believed every word she told me. Being there beside her, feeling her pain as she gave appalling details about my brother, there was no way I could not believe her. It had taken her three years to find the courage to tell me the shocking truth about her uncle. My evil brother had introduced my daughter to physically unsafe and emotionally detrimental places, as well as his nasty, perverted associates and people, places, and ideas, all of which her dad and I would never have allowed. I was stunned, hearing what she had to say. All I could do was hold her, and say, "I'm sorry ... I'm sorry ... I'm sorry. I'm so sorry he hurt you. Everything will be okay."

I was furious with my brother, and my head was spinning and full of questions: *Who is he? What is he? How dare he do this to my daughter? How dare he do this to anyone's child? What on earth was he thinking to have done this to his own niece, especially when he knew she was extremely vulnerable?* Of course, I know now that anyone in that state is easy prey for any pedophile. Thank God Sue gathered the courage and wisdom to tell me what Norman was doing. It was a huge risk for her to tell me such horrible things about my own brother—a priest.

Believe it or not, I was tremendously relieved when she confided in me. We finally knew what was bothering her. Now that we understood what had been troubling her, Joe and I were better able to help her. Norman held a certain power over her and had threatened her in the same way he had threatened all the boys he had molested—by teaching her to think that no one would believe her or that in some way, everything was her fault.

"Mom, he said that I am so bad the way God made me," Sue said, "that even he was attracted to me. And he prefers boys. And if I ever said anything, everyone would know I was just like him—damaged. We all are broken, he said. But he said that he and I are exactly alike. That is why he picked me. I would respect his secret. I would not betray him. But Mom, I can't. He can do what he wants to me, but he might hurt my son. And I will *not* let him do that. I had to tell you. He is a bad man. I am not like him!"

"You're right," I told her, "he is a bad man, and he is wrong—I do believe you. Everything will be okay now."

After making sure my daughter was all right and assuring her she wouldn't be involved with Uncle Norman anymore—that her dad and I would take care of this matter ourselves—I went to my husband and told him what Norman had done. It was one of those moments when you feel like pinching yourself, hoping it's all just a nightmare. We knew we had to talk with our three other children to learn if they had been victims of their uncle as well, but first, I made a call to my sister.

There was a strange silence at the other end of the line as I relayed the news about our brother. Possibly she was having a hard time believing it. Jeanne felt bad for Sue but was worried if any of her children had been victimized too. She reminded me of one occasion when Norman had invited her boys on a weekend camping trip. Jeanne said they had turned down his invitation because of a work conflict. Though they were a bit disappointed back then, she said it appeared to have been a blessing in disguise as she thought of it now.

Jeanne and I decided to check with all of our children to be sure none of them had been their uncle's victims. They might have been harmed as well and too afraid to tell us. There was no easy way to discuss this with them. Not wanting to put it off, I went to my eldest daughter's room the next evening, interrupting her studying, and simply said, "Lynn, I have something really shocking to discuss with you."

Alarmed, she immediately set her book aside and asked, "What's wrong?"

Bluntly, I told her, "I've learned that Uncle Norman is a child molester. He sexually abuses little boys."

Lynn looked stunned and stared at me in disbelief. Tears welled in her eyes as she shouted, "Who told you such a thing? That can't be true!"

"Sue just told me what's been troubling her for so long," I answered. "Among other things, Uncle Norman has been telling her graphic details of the pleasure he gets from molesting the boys. He's done inappropriate things with her, too."

Lynn was speechless.

"Lynn, has Uncle Norman ever approached you in an indecent manner? Has he ever said or done anything to make you feel uncomfortable?"

She gasped and then answered, "Mom, he's hardly ever around, and the times he was here, I don't even remember him saying much of anything to me. He's always pretty much ignored us girls. This is awful! Is Sue okay?"

I wasn't sure how to answer her. "I think she'll be better, now that she's told us what's been happening. She knows I'm talking to you, Joan, and Jeff about Norman. For all I know, he could have hurt all four of you and threatened you not to tell. Your dad and I had no idea he was molesting kids or that he had victimized Sue."

"Mom, Uncle Norman has never spent any time with me for anything," Lynn reassured me.

"I'm sorry to have upset you," I said, "but I needed to know you were okay. There just isn't a good time or easy way to lay this kind of news on you." I gave her a hug and then said, "Please come to Dad or me, should you ever be frightened or threatened by anyone."

As I was leaving her room, Lynn commented, "I don't think I'm going to be able to get my mind back on studying tonight."

I nodded in understanding, but she had eased my worries about her.

Talking with Joan about it the next day wasn't any easier. It wasn't that she was particularly fond of her uncle. As far as I knew, he hadn't formed a relationship with her. It was more like she had an uncle who was a priest and that seemed special.

Joan had returned from school and was emptying her book bag on the kitchen table when I approached her. I sat beside her and said, "Joan, before you get started on your homework, I need to talk to you about something. You haven't done anything wrong. I have to ask you something very important." Watching her puzzled expression, I tried to choose my words carefully. "I just learned something horrible about Uncle Norman, and I need to make sure that you're okay."

She didn't seem to know what I was talking about, and I dreaded going any further, but this was too important to ignore. I continued, "Uncle Norman has been hurting kids by touching their private areas and then threatening them not to tell anyone. Joan, did Uncle Norman ever do or say anything to you that made you feel ashamed or uncomfortable? Did he ever tell you not to tell anybody about something he did or said?"

She sat looking at me sadly and then slowly responded in a soft, shaky voice, "No, Mom, he's never done anything to me. I hardly ever see him. Why would he do that?"

I wasn't able to answer that question, but I did say, "I'm glad you're okay, but I want you to remember that if anyone ever makes you feel scared by what they say or do, tell Dad or me right away so we can protect you."

She nodded her head but remained quiet. It seemed my youngest daughter didn't want to discuss it any longer. I hugged her gently and suggested she get started with her homework, adding that we could talk again later if she had any questions. I wondered how she was going to get Uncle Norman out of her mind and start concentrating on homework. How does anyone get rid of such thoughts, especially when those thoughts are about a family member's depraved behavior? I loathed my brother for making it necessary to expose my child to such evil concepts.

I still needed to check with our son, a college graduate, who was living and working a distance from us. Calling him that evening was no easier. He gave me a happy, "Hi, Mom, how are you?" when he answered the phone. After we talked a while, I finally said, "Jeff, the main reason I'm calling is to talk to you about Uncle Norman. I have very disturbing news about him."

"What's happened?" he quickly asked.

I responded, "There's no easy way to say this; I've learned that Uncle Norman has been molesting kids, mainly little boys. Sue just told me what he's been doing. He had victimized her as well. Now that I'm aware, I'm checking with you and your sisters to make sure you're all okay."

Jeff seemed shocked. "Uncle Norman molests kids? Unbelievable! Is Sue all right?"

"She'll be better, now that she told."

Jeff understandably paused as the reality of his uncle hit him. He said, "I wasn't around him that much growing up, Mom. I can remember Uncle Norman coming to our house when you invited him for parties, and he used to come out to fish during the summers when we were out at the river, but Mom, I'm okay. Uncle Norman never did anything to me."

Again, I was relieved. "I'm sorry I had to give you such horrible news," I said, "but I needed to know if your uncle had ever done anything inappropriate to you. Sue is managing the best she can right now, but Uncle Norman has caused her many more problems." We talked for a few more minutes and then, before hanging up, I said, "I'll keep you updated on how Sue is doing and what's happening with Uncle Norman."

I felt bad when I hung up the phone; I was sure that Jeff was feeling down after hearing the ugly truth about his uncle. I was thankful Jeff had never joined Norman on any camping trips or other excursions for which Norman had invited his nephews and other relatives over the years.

We always had noticed that Norman favored our sons over our daughters when they were young. It was very obvious when he'd bring gifts. He'd give the boys brand-new ball gloves, trains, or any other gifts that boys loved, but he gave our girls cheap trinkets or secondhand crocheted accessories that would have appealed more to elderly ladies. The girls were old enough to notice the disparity, and they sometimes made comments to me that their uncle didn't like them. Jeanne and I never figured out a tactful way of telling him he was hurting the girls' feelings. We were dumb enough to excuse him for not knowing better because he was a priest—and we probably had a fear of confrontation at the time, as well as being inexperienced in mothering. Now, I regret that I never said anything to Norman about it. We overlooked it and continued inviting him at Easter, Thanksgiving, and Christmas and for birthday celebrations. If he did something to hurt the girls' feelings, I'd talk with them after he had left and try to make excuses for him. As they got older, it became sort of joke—what kind of oddity would they receive from him that year? This helped soften the rejection.

As if things were not already upsetting enough in our household, I received a phone call on March 2, 1988, from the police. Dorothy, an older cousin of mine on my mother's side of the family, who lived alone, had listed me as a contact in case of an emergency. I was informed that she had suffered a stroke and was in the hospital. The officer told me to pick up her purse and keys at the police station.

I called Jeanne to give her the information, and she said she'd go with me to visit Dorothy at the hospital. There, we found that Dorothy's stroke had been severe, and among other things, she could no longer speak. Her husband had been deceased for many years, and they never had children. Jeanne and I had invited her to our homes for the holidays and other get-togethers, but other than that, we knew very little about how she lived her life. Suddenly, her care was in our hands. She couldn't walk, talk, or write. Jeanne agreed to take the power of attorney for our cousin, and Dorothy agreed—her lawyer drew up the paperwork.

Life now included taking care of our new grandson while Sue was either at school or at work; checking that she was still doing all she needed to do to stay on the right track; taking care of Joan, who was recovering from brain surgery—and now, caring for Dorothy. There weren't enough hours in many of my days. I still hadn't figured out a plan of action for the situation with Norman yet.

My sister and I took care of Dorothy until her death in June 1992. In all that time, our brother, the priest, never paid one visit to his cousin, not even during the six weeks that she was in the hospital after having the stroke. A year or so before her death, she also had to have a breast removed due to cancer. Father Norman didn't pay her a visit then either, even though we had kept him informed of her condition. I wondered if Dorothy ever questioned in her own mind where he was—it was very difficult for her to communicate with us. I asked her once if Norman had stopped by to see her, and she just frowned and shook her head. Norman never asked us about Dorothy. It would have been so kind if he had shown her a bit of concern. A brief visit now and then would have lifted her spirits in those last years of her life, but he apparently couldn't be bothered.

Chapter 5
I Know

As time passed, Norman repeatedly called to talk with Sue, and I kept making excuses for her. I wanted to scream that I knew his secret, but I wasn't prepared to face him. Confrontation was something I usually tried to avoid, but after several weeks, I told Joe, "I can't take this anymore. I have to tell Norman I know."

On June 10, 1989, I sat at my kitchen table after supper, painfully writing to Norman that Sue had told me his ugly secret and how difficult it was for her to have done so. Following are excerpts from my letter:

> Dear Norm,
>
> For reasons of her own, Sue decided to tell me about the secret you told her some three years ago. She said you didn't want to tell me because I wouldn't understand, and it'd make me sick. It made me sick all right, but I needed to know. How could you have treated Sue as you did? She's so young and struggling with her own problems. I suppose at the time you felt she could handle it, since she was also undergoing therapy, but I really feel that was a bad choice. By keeping your secret all these years, her emotions have been festering inside and building like a volcano ready to erupt. ... Perhaps now I can

understand why you and I were never close. Maybe I always felt you were better than me because of your vocation. I never could understand why I felt so uncomfortable around you.

I wanted him to know we had checked with his nieces and nephews to ensure that he had not harmed them. I wrote:

I now feared that perhaps you had approached them in their earlier years growing up. I did talk with Jeanne and we both felt it was necessary to check with our families about the possibility. ... Right now I'm just confused and am going only on what Sue told me. I'd like to hear things firsthand from you; so would Jeanne. Call me when you are ready. As for Sue, I'm pretty proud of her.

It had taken many hours to compose my letter, and later, as I tried to sleep, I tossed and turned, unable to get Norman out of my mind.

I was up at the crack of dawn, before Joe left for work. After rereading what I had written the night before, I handed it to him, asking for his opinion. When he finished reading, he said, "I think he might do something to himself after reading this."

I took a deep calming breath and replied, "Norman will react however he reacts. My concern is for his victims." Putting my letter in the envelope and sealing it, I told Joe, "I'm mailing this to him this morning."

Joe left for work and within an hour, I was walking to a nearby mailbox. What an enormous sense of relief when that envelope dropped into the box. I wouldn't have to pretend with him anymore. Norman would know his sisters had learned he was a child molester.

As it turned out, Norman was not upset when he read my letter. He called me right away saying, "I was glad to get your letter. I'll be happy to meet with you and Jeanne, the sooner the better."

The three of us met at Jeanne's house a few days later. It was early afternoon, and we had the house to ourselves. Jeanne and I sat on her living room sofa across from a large picture window that faced the street. Norman positioned himself in the comfortable rocking chair across from us. He seemed pleased that Jeanne had made coffee and accepted a cup right away. We all seemed anxious as we sat down. Norman spoke first.

Glaring right at me, he yelled, "I'm really angry with Sue! She had no business telling you about me. I shared all those things with her in confidence, and I'm going to have a very hard time forgiving her for that betrayal!"

I'll never forget the harsh tone of his voice and the enraged look on his face as he spoke. My first thoughts were, *Is he nuts? What's wrong with him?* His arrogance stunned me, but I wasn't intimidated. Norman's booming voice must have carried throughout the entire two-story house and I wondered if the neighbors heard him. Jeanne seemed a bit rattled as he exploded. We both were puzzled by his ludicrous opening remarks.

I quickly responded, "I'm proud of her for having the courage to tell me what you've been doing, Norman. She did the right thing! I'm angry about what you did to her, knowing she was so vulnerable and still under a doctor's care herself!" By now, my own voice was getting louder. "You're my brother and a priest! Joe and I trusted you. We thought you were helping Sue with her troubles and were grateful! Then we learned you'd hurt her and made things worse. How could you have done that to her? If you had children of your own, you'd understand our fears and concerns."

Norman looked down his nose at me as he said, "How do you know I don't have children?"

I was shocked by his response, but it immediately brought to mind something else he had shared with my daughter—an affair he had with a woman he was counseling at the parish. I don't know if the church knew of the sexual relationship that Norman had with the vulnerable divorced woman he'd counseled at that parish—that was one of the things "Uncle Norman" had described to Sue. Norman had smugly told her, "She's in love with me and will do anything I ask. She wanted more from me. I wasn't sure that I could do it, but I did, and it was better than I thought it would be." Sue told me Norman had meant intercourse. He described the sex in more detail and said that he surprised himself by how good he was with her. Sue assumed it was his first time with an adult woman. I forced myself to stop thinking about this as Jeanne and I sat quietly, waiting for him to continue.

Composing himself, Norman sat with his eyes downcast. He spoke more calmly as he told us, "My problems started early in my childhood."

Jeanne and I listened intently to his every word. It became another one of those times that didn't seem real. *Is this actually happening?* I thought. *Am I going to wake up and discover this has all been a horrible nightmare? How could any of what he is saying be true? How could I not have had any idea in my entire lifetime that my brother was a child molester?* My mind was racing as it took in all that Norman spewed out. I tried to make sense of what he said, but there was none to be made.

Occasionally, Norman glanced at us as he spoke of being molested as a child himself. He said he was sexually abused by various people, even during his years in the seminary. Jeanne and I asked questions about that time, but his responses were vague; sometimes, he refused to answer at all. As was typical of him, he showed no concern for anyone but himself. He seemed to care nothing about how his sexual abuse of children affected anyone else—not his victims, their families, or even anyone who knew and cared about him.

Looking back now, I believe Norman intentionally distracted us that day by telling us he was gay, a label we now know is completely inaccurate. He honestly wanted us to believe that his sexual orientation caused him to become a pedophile. Raping and molesting children are not homosexual or heterosexual traits; these are the traits of a criminal pedophile.

He went on to explain about his childhood experiences. "I was molested in our neighborhood, in grade school at Our Lady of Sorrows, as an altar boy at church, and as a seminarian during my years at Kenrick Seminary." Nonchalantly, he added, "I eventually just started molesting kids myself." He quietly continued, telling of an "affair" he had in the early sixties with a teenage boy. "I was very upset when he left for seminary college. I missed him terribly." Briefly, he mentioned having sought advice from the pastor about his predicament, but he didn't say what the pastor instructed him to do.

In retrospect, I can spot Norman's skilled manipulation at work that day. He had Jeanne and me focusing on his own molestation as a child. He seemed pleased when our anger turned to sympathy for him. Our faces and sympathetic tones must have spoken volumes as we both said, almost simultaneously, "Norm, we're sorry that happened to you. Who molested you?"

He responded by slowly shaking his head and evasively looking away, refusing to answer.

"Who did you tell?" we both asked, assuming he must have told someone about being molested.

Norman squirmed nervously in the rocker, causing it to squeak. Frowning, he slowly answered, "I never told anyone."

Jeanne's expression mirrored my own—we both felt sad that he hadn't sought help from anyone. Jeanne remarked, "If only you had told Mom or Dad or even me. Somebody needed to know."

I asked him, "Norman, knowing the pain that being molested caused you, how could you do that to other kids?"

His answer was quite disturbing: "After all those years of being molested, it just became a way of life. Doing it seemed normal to me."

My sympathy quickly turned to disgust and anger at his lack of remorse for sexually abusing children. Still, I knew I had to conceal that, or he would disappear from my radar—and I wanted to keep my eye on him.

When I first told our parish priest what Sue had divulged, he assured me that the church would take care of everything. He didn't say how they would do that; I just blindly trusted them and expected I wouldn't have to worry.

Jeanne, Norman, and I had been talking for nearly two hours. Jeanne refilled our coffee and placed a tray of homemade cookies on a table for us to enjoy. We munched on a few, and then Norman resumed speaking about himself. I was sure that anything Norman had to say now could not be as shocking as what had already come out of his mouth, but I was wrong. His next pronouncement left both Jeanne and me completely stunned.

Norman grasped the arms of the rocker and angrily shouted, "Mom is the reason I am like I am! I hated her! She was a horrible gossip, and it makes me so mad that Dad never stood up to her, always letting her be the boss over us and everything!"

Neither Jeanne nor I could respond. We just let him vent further; it would have been futile to reason with him when he was so enraged.

While it hurt me to hear him say such horrible, untrue things about our mother, it helped make sense of some of his behavior that we had witnessed over the years in regards to our mother.

After another hour or so had passed, we decided to call it a day. Norman seemed relieved and grateful that he didn't have to keep his secret from us anymore. Before leaving, though, he vehemently warned us, "Make sure you are extremely careful. Don't say a word about any of this to anyone, as it could be very damaging to my reputation. If you allow it to become public knowledge, you will cause terrible harm to the church." He didn't seem to take any responsibility for the fact that his raping children could cause damage to the church. He tried to make it our fault, for causing public awareness of his crimes.

Again, Jeanne and I foolishly trusted that the church was handling everything properly, including helping any victims. We told Norman we'd let the church handle it, and he thanked us, said good-bye, and walked out to his car.

One thing Jeanne and I knew for sure as we watched him drive away: we had never really known our brother. And as ugly as the truth was, we both felt relieved that he had finally opened up to us.

Minutes later, I thanked Jeanne for letting us meet at her house. We hugged good-bye, and I headed out to my car. So many thoughts were racing through my mind as I drove home; everything that had been said kept replaying over and over. I was exhausted and anxious to get home. I knew Joe would want to hear how things went, but I was looking forward to a relaxing soak in the tub first. Having spent those stressful hours in discussion with my brother, I was tied up in knots.

I found myself torn between anger for his betrayal of our family and what he had done to my daughter and other kids and feeling sorry for him for having been sexually abused as a child, unable to tell anyone. I let out several therapeutic screams on the drive home. It helped ease my frustration, and no one could hear me.

Six and a half years earlier, on January 11, 1983, our mother had passed away following triple-bypass heart surgery. She had been in a coma for weeks following her surgery. Very early one morning, I received a call from someone at the hospital, informing me that Mom had died and saying a family member needed to view her body before it could be removed from the room. I called my sister with the news, and she said she'd be by as soon as possible to go with me to the hospital. I called Norman to let him know of Mom's death; I thought he'd want to meet Jeanne and me at the hospital. Instead, he said, "There's no reason for me to go. The two of you can take care of that."

I heard many people over the years praise what a wonderful counselor Father Christian was, yet at this time, he couldn't even comfort his own sisters. Even if he hated his mother, he should have been there for Jeanne and me. This was just one more example that eventually proved to me that Norman thought only about Norman.

He did step into his role as priest to celebrate our mom's funeral at Our Lady of Sorrows parish, where she had raised her family, attended church, and been an active member for most of her life. Because her son was a priest, a large number of clergy attended her funeral. Norman surprised everyone by not delivering the eulogy. He had asked another priest to do it. At the time, everyone assumed that Norman was hurting too much emotionally from the loss of his mother to speak himself.

That afternoon at Jeanne's house in June 1989, his true reason for not delivering the eulogy became clear—he hated Mom and couldn't bring himself to speak kindly of her. He hated his own mother, who had done everything possible for him, who had loved him dearly, and who had been so proud of him she could have burst. In his own sick and twisted mind, he saw his mom as a gossip and a controlling wife and mother. That's very sad and quite untrue. I'm thankful our mom never was aware of her son's feelings toward her and that she died not knowing he was a pedophile. Both of these things would have broken her heart.

Our mother was not the vicious gossip Norman pictured her to be. She cared about people and helped family and friends in any way she could. She may have talked about people occasionally, just as others did, and she was no saint, but she wasn't the mean-spirited person the much-loved and -adored son imagined her to be. Norman was just as disappointed with our dad, because he thought Dad was weak. Norman absolutely despised seeing our mother as the person with the final say on anything in our home. I wondered if all his years in the seminary, especially having started right out of eighth grade, had encouraged his outlandish thinking.

The Catholic Church does teach that women should be subservient to their husbands. Throughout our lives, Catholic teachings promoted women as the lesser sex. Women are not allowed to become priests. They are only to serve and revere clergy. Nuns are generally not treated as well as the priests—for example, priests often receive cash as Christmas presents; nuns get cookies, rosaries, or just prayers. Clergy get wined and dined, while the nuns receive little attention, even though they do much of the work. Possibly, seminarians develop an attitude that women are to be subservient to men, while priests are to live a somewhat privileged life.

Norman often boasted about the cooks he had as he was moved around from parish to parish. He would say, "I've really got a great cook here. She caters to me, and boy, is the food delicious," or "My waistline is starting to expand, thanks to the cook I've got. She really knows her way around the kitchen." There was a time when he was without a cook or a housekeeper, and he complained to me about it, calling it a "pain in the butt" to have to plan his own meals, grocery shop, and then cook for himself. Norman was not alone in this; the majority of priests I have met throughout my life have exhibited the privileged-life expectation. It was rare and much appreciated to meet a humble priest who didn't fit that mold.

It must have gotten on Norman's last nerve to watch Dad allow Mom to have the top authority of the household. I doubt if Norman ever understood the workings of a true, loving relationship that can be built into a marriage.

Our dad was a quiet, kind, gentle man, who would do anything within his abilities to help anyone. He was active in various organizations at our parish. The Saint Vincent de Paul Society was his favorite, and he gave from his own pockets many times to help people in need. He enjoyed fishing, reading books, and playing pinochle and was extremely proud and happy that he had a son studying for the priesthood. He wasn't much of a hands-on dad, but things changed when he became a grandpa. When I had children of my own, I saw a different side of Dad. He would sometimes take care of his grandchildren, and both he and the kids seemed to enjoy it. The children all became "Grandpa's kids," running to him before their grandma. They all took to his gentle, caring way. Grandma was more like another "mom," scolding them when they acted up. Grandpa tended to overlook some things, as grandparents sometimes do, and his softer approach made for a close relationship between them. He was a kind and prayerful man whose love of God and family was obvious.

I thank God that both my parents died before suffering the pain of knowing their son, the priest, lured children to him and sexually abused them.

Norman's mind was twisted, not only in his perception of his parents but also in his remaining a priest while molesting children. I wondered how he could look at himself in the mirror. I decided to write my brother in regard to what had transpired when we met at Jeanne's (entire 06-16-89 letter in appendix). I'm embarrassed to admit how ignorant I was at the time, when he told me of his molesting "some boys." I can see how incredibly naïve I was, so blinded to what Norman actually was to so many children all his life. I didn't understand that he had been molesting kids throughout his entire priesthood. I was still trying to make sense of the entire nightmare our family was living.

I wrote, "I could see at Jeanne's how you are really hurting and struggling, and I want to remind you that you are a good person and not to give up." What was I thinking? Now, decades later, I cringe and feel nauseated when reading the ridiculous things I wrote. I am no longer as naïve, having learned more about Norman's depraved crimes and that the church continued to cover them up. It's a crime in itself that the archdiocese allows molesters to remain priests. Think of all the children they put at risk by keeping these sex abusers in the ministry.

Another ridiculous thing I wrote was, "What makes you any less a good person now that some family members know your secret? You're still you, the same person; just another of God's imperfect human beings, like the rest of the family." It makes my skin crawl to read that now. It's true that we are all imperfect people, but sexual predators are more than just imperfect; they are unrepentant, and they are evil. I ignorantly added, "I don't feel you chose to be gay. God just made you that way." Again, I was naive enough to overlook what had really been going on in his life. He was *not* gay; he was a pedophile—a criminal! He molested and raped little boys, facts that would be made abundantly clear to me in years to come.

I had no idea what kind of help the church was giving him, but I trusted it would do the right thing, morally and legally, and I intended to be supportive as Norman accepted his own responsibility for what he had done. It sickens me now to realize that I was so brainwashed by my Catholic upbringing that I didn't go directly to the police to report him. Instead, I was a good Catholic; I trusted the church and kept his secret. Decades later, I realized that was a huge mistake. I deeply regret keeping that secret. I know now that if there is to be any hope of justice, clergy-abuse victims must go directly to the police to report their abusers and the crimes committed against them.

In that same letter, I also wrote, "I certainly want you at the family gatherings, and I feel safe in saying Joe and the kids do, too." I learned in time that I was very wrong in speaking for my family. I was even dumb enough to protect Norman's feelings, by making excuses to him for why Sue wasn't accepting his calls. Why on earth didn't it occur to me that his presence at family gatherings would be difficult on my daughter? I had just assumed she understood why I was keeping in contact with him. Now, I find it hard to read that letter without feeling ashamed and disappointed in myself.

As time passed, Norman must have thought things through and became less angry with Sue for her "betrayal." I received a letter from him in the middle of June, actually written to Sue but mailed to me with an attached note: "Carol, if you judge this is okay for Sue to handle, pass it on to her. If not, please discard it." It was written on Saint William's Church stationery, where he was assigned at the time (06-18-1989, Norman Christian letter).

Joe and I read the letter, but neither of us could make sense of it. We wondered if Sue would understand what he wrote. In hindsight, I should have discarded it, but I blundered again by asking her if she wanted to see it. Very hesitantly, she took it from me and began reading:

> Dear Sue,
> All that has taken place these last few weeks I accept as God's own way of taking my healing (spiritual and emotional) a step further. He has allowed me to experience humility's truth within the test of

my own family. It appears that I have re-entered the family I left when I became a teenager. If I am being judged by anyone, I sure do not recognize or feel it. That is quite a tribute to your family and my two sisters.

My only regret is that I thought you knew me, but I now realize that you do not know me after all. You were distracted by my sin and in your fear, you missed discovering the exciting (even contagious) holiness God is developing in my personal as well as priestly life. But now your mom will have an equal chance with you to discover it, touch it, draw strength from it, and rejoice in it. I am grateful to God for that gift. I am letting go of my embarrassment surprisingly fast. Our shared Catholic faith is working a kind of miracle. Praise God!

Sue, I set you free from any obligations you may feel toward me. I will always be there for you if you ever feel inclined to lean on me in any way. And I hope you take the chance someday to really know me. I gave my life to you before, and now I am willing and prepared to die for you, Sue. For my part I will never give you cause to fear for your son's well-being. You are a very good mother, with normal and right motherly instincts. Keep up the good work.

I am at peace with my Lord, and I am enjoying my life immensely. May yours be blessed similarly early on. (I had to wait until I turned 50!)

Peace,
Norm

After reading it, Sue handed the letter back to me, saying in disgust, "You can throw this away. I hate him! Gave me life? He took my life! He didn't set me free. I set myself free. And I'll never allow that pervert around my son, so help me God. I will not relax until the day he dies. And the only tears I will cry will be of joy and relief."

It wasn't long after Jeanne and I met with Norman that I received a note from him. He said he knew I was "confused" by his disclosure but was not judging him to be a bad person. Then he said that two issues remained for him. First, "I must ask you to help Sue understand that I am okay with her 'betrayal' of confidence; she needed to and took charge of her life in doing so. It was a mature act on her part, and she deserves praise for that courage."

It was about my daughter's betraying him—not that he (the priest, her uncle, my brother) had betrayed us by what he did to her and who knows how many children and families with his various forms of sexual abuse. He was thinking only of Norman.

Of his second "issue," he wrote: "I will feel extremely uneasy at family gatherings (worse now than ever). Can you do anything to help me get beyond that problem? I don't want to come to any family gatherings. If I do, it will be extremely difficult. I can visit and share with you because of our one-on-one sharing, but I have not done that with the others, and I don't want to. I will see everyone looking at me with suspicion and wonder at any future gathering. So, pray for me and for help to overcome this new stress at family gatherings." He closed by thanking me for suffering with him.

At the time, I only knew what Norman told me, and I wanted to be supportive to him so he would continue to keep me informed of his progress. I wrote and encouraged him to follow the program he was participating in through the church by doing exactly as he was told. I had suggested he ask Archbishop May to get a support group for "religious" started in Saint Louis. I didn't realize there already was one available to him, as Norman shared next to nothing about the program that was meant to help him. He told me his days were quite structured in hopes of keeping him, as he put it, "SA [sexual abuse] sober," and he asked me to pray for him. The hierarchy continues to keep such programs secret from the church membership.

In September 1989, he sent us a thank-you note for a birthday gift we had sent. As mentioned previously, I had a motive for staying close to him, which wasn't an easy thing to do after learning the truth, but the archdiocese offered me nothing, except repeatedly telling me, "It's not yours to worry about. We are taking care of everything." I wanted to be aware of what Norman was doing and where, so I felt I had to stay connected to him. It bothered me that he was being kept in ministry, but I continued to trust that those in charge knew what they were doing.

In thanking us for his gift, Norman added: "In terms of *life*, I measure myself at a bit over two years old. What an upheaval (the 9 months of intensive therapy, 'gestation'), like being born all over. And two years into recovery is like learning to walk through life with healthy support from family and friends!"

A month later, I received another note indicating he was struggling but not giving up. "I worked with my therapist today because I seemed to be shaming myself, isolating rather than connecting. Old patterns are hard to change. I was with Aunt Helen, and I did not reach out (shame and fear). But now I have a new day, so I will begin again and try to do things different so the end result might have a chance to be different."

At this point, Norman had been a priest for twenty-seven years, and Joe and I and our four children were coming to grips with the reality that he was a child molester. I repeatedly was assured by Monsignor Naumann that the church was handling it. Norman continued to warn me not to say anything about him to anyone! "It could bring about more lawsuits against the church, and it could be your fault for having told someone about me!" He was terribly afraid; he didn't want the church subjected to more lawsuits because of him. I was disgusted when he told me, "One person could tell another, and it'd be like someone winning the lottery. Someone could say I had molested him just to get a lot of money from the church."

Norman's top priority was to protect the church's money. He worried about what might happen to him too, but he showed no concern whatsoever for any of his victims. He had the audacity to tell me, "I never forced anybody. They [the victims] all wanted it as much as I did!"

I had made the decision to be supportive the first time I confronted Norman about his sexual addiction so I would know if he stopped doing what was necessary to help him stay "sober." I'd call him every so often, just to see how things were going.

He'd usually tell me what he had going on at the time, and it was pretty easy to tell if things had been going well for him or if he was disgusted about having to do things he disliked, such as, "I dread those parish meetings. What a waste of my time!" I'd know his days were booked if he told me, "It's hard fitting in everything I need to do to stay healthy and sober. I can hardly find time for my daily handball, therapy sessions, and doctor appointments, along with my already busy church schedule."

Jeanne and I continued to feel uncomfortable about Norman's being left in ministry. We repeatedly wondered why he wasn't removed. We often voiced this concern to each other when we were together or talking on the phone.

One time, in pure frustration, she told me, "I've tried asking questions in the confessional with various priests, but nobody offers any answers."

I told Jeanne that I had called Father Joe Naumann, our friend from the parish, but I wasn't getting any answers either. After hearing what was troubling me, Father would usually reply, "I wasn't aware of that. I'll pass along what you've told me to Norman's therapist," or "I'll mention that to the archbishop." I'd be told again that the church was "taking care of things." Father Naumann usually ended our conversations with, "I am keeping you and your family in my prayers."

Jeanne and I both felt the church wanted us to forget all we had learned about Norman, but we couldn't. It troubled us that the church continued to cover up his crimes and keep him in ministry, with no warnings to unsuspecting parents.

As time passed, we became even more bothered by the hierarchy's poor handling of the numerous, newly surfaced clergy abuse cases that were reported in the media. Joe and I often discussed what was going on with Norman and others like him. Our whole family was disgusted as we watched the same scene play out over and over—the hierarchy protected the church's image, wealth, and predator clergy, while leaving the victims to fend for themselves.

Chapter 6
Marriages

In December 1988, our son became engaged to be married. After deciding to have their wedding at our parish church, the pastor refused to allow it because our son had not lived in the parish since going away to college. Joe and I were shocked, as we and our three daughters were still very active members of the parish—not only did we volunteer, but we also were lifelong weekly monetary contributors as well.

Most likely, the pastor had based his decision on the lack of donation envelopes from our son since he moved. We were extremely hurt. Joe immediately resigned from all organizations and advised that he would no longer be available to do pro bono electrical and other miscellaneous repair work for the church. The pastor quickly changed his mind, allowing the wedding to be at the parish, but I knew he had left a terrible image of Catholicism with my non-Catholic future daughter-in-law. I doubted she would ever choose to join the Catholic faith after seeing its clergy put money before caring about its devoted members.

Jeff had already asked Norman to marry them before he learned of his uncle's criminal behavior. He assumed Norman had made amends and was getting treatment, as he hadn't been removed from ministry. Jeff decided not to replace his uncle as the celebrant. Relatives and friends were happy to see Father Christian that day, but it was an uncomfortable situation.

It was emotionally difficult to continue my relationship with

Norman, but it was the only way I could think of to stay aware of what he was doing. I was conflicted; I didn't trust the hierarchy, but my strong Catholic upbringing still told me to let them handle it. Yet ongoing disclosures of the church's cover-ups kept gnawing away at me. Uncle Norman had baptized all his nieces and nephews and had always performed family funerals. Everyone just expected my brother to celebrate at church-related family events. He was still serving in active ministry at a parish, and none of the rest of the family knew of his secret. I doubted myself every day for not saying anything, but Monsignor Naumann, whom I trusted, greatly respected, and considered a close friend, had assured me it wasn't mine to worry about—the church was taking care of everything. There was little thought given to me or how I was coping. I wondered if the hierarchy gave any thought to how Catholics in general were dealing with it.

After decades of seeing and hearing the grief of many clergy-abuse victims across the country and worldwide, I learned what they wanted most was to be heard and believed and to see their molesters removed from ministry. They hoped for an acknowledgment of wrong-doing, with a sincere apology from the church.

Court-ordered payments to help toward victims' medical bills and court-ordered letters of apology didn't give a very sincere message of being sorry for anything. It would have meant so much more if the church had given these to the victims without being ordered to do so and that those in power were truly sorry that this had happened.

Lynn and Sue both became engaged and were to be married within six months of each other. Neither wanted Norman to perform the wedding ceremony. Lynn did wonder what relatives would think when they saw another priest celebrate their marriages, as Norman had always taken that role for family weddings. Joe and I told our daughters they each needed to ask the priest they wanted and not worry about what anyone thought. They did just that, and we made it through a very busy year, preparing for both weddings—it was a refreshingly good type of "busy"!

Norman was present in the church at both weddings, sitting in the pews, blending in with everyone else. I wondered if he felt at all embarrassed, sitting there instead of being the celebrant of the wedding ceremony. I was grateful that no one asked why he hadn't performed the marriages.

Chapter 7
Meeting with Monsignor

My sister and I became more uncomfortable with our brother's situation as each year passed. We saw no sign that the church was "taking care of everything." In 1995, I suggested we make an appointment to talk with Monsignor Naumann. His being a good family friend started back when he was a young, caring, pro-life priest assigned at our parish. I felt comfortable talking with him about Norman.

I made an appointment for Jeanne and me to meet with him at his archdiocesan office. We sat across from him at his desk and talked for at least an hour that day about our concerns. We both expressed our disappointment and anger with the church's way of dealing with all the sexual-abuse reports in general. I told Monsignor, "It's wrong of the church to continue protecting clergy molesters, not removing them from ministry unless the victim is brave enough to face them and the church's pricey attorneys in court. When victims are too afraid and back down, the church just lets these predators remain in their positions, leaving children at risk. As soon as the hierarchy learns of molestation, the perpetrator needs to be removed from his position, not kept covered up until some court orders the removal."

As I wiped my tears and took some deep breaths to calm myself,

Monsignor remarked, "The church sends troubled priests for help, even when victims don't make formal charges."

"That's good to know," I responded, "but common sense would dictate not to return such clergy to active ministry, even after therapy."

Jeanne asked, "Monsignor, what kind of therapy has the church given Norman in the past?"

"I don't have access to any of that information," Monsignor replied.

"Can you tell us what the therapy is like that he is getting now?" I asked.

He replied, "I don't have any information about that either. You need to ask Norman about his therapy program."

"Jeanne and I aren't asking for any personal information," I argued. "We are looking for a general description of the program—what it consists of and what it requires of Norman. I was very pleased with my daughter's therapy program and just wonder if the church's program is similar."

Again, Monsignor told us, "You really need to direct your questions to Norman."

Jeanne and I told him of some concerns we had at that time about Norman. Monsignor said he wasn't aware of some of those things but that he'd pass that information along to his therapist. He also told me the therapist might call me about it, but that never happened.

Monsignor got our hopes up by suggesting, "Maybe the two of you could participate along with Norman in some of his therapy sessions. Of course, he and the therapist would need to give their permission."

I actually thought Norman and the therapist would be happy that we were willing to join them. We thought it might help us learn ways to be supportive of him as well as help us in coping with it all. However, when Jeanne later wrote Norman to suggest it, he immediately wrote back: "The professionals in any program like mine are not permitted to disclose what is learned during treatment. You would be refused such a meeting even if I personally asked them to meet with us."

Norman's immediate refusal caught me off guard. From what I learned with my daughter's therapy, a family's involvement in the program is a good thing. Family members are encouraged to participate as often as possible—it's helpful to the patient's recovery. Jeanne and I came away from that meeting feeling no better than when we had arrived. We had received the same old responses—the church is taking care of things; it's not yours to worry about; trust us. Our trust in the church was already hanging by a thread. We were waiting and watching, desperately hoping and praying we would see changes in the way that clergy sexual-abuse victims were treated, as well as the manner in which clergy molesters were protected by the church, but it didn't happen.

Monsignor offered to talk with us again, but why would we want to do that? There was no reaching out on this visit with offers of help for us in dealing with what our brother had done and possibly still was doing. With no feeling of comfort or satisfaction from having talked with Monsignor, we didn't see much promise for future visits.

As long as we were willing to believe and trust the hierarchy, all was well. Should we question why or try to hold them accountable, we could count on being ignored.

Then God balanced the turmoil in our lives by sending three bundles of joy in 1995, arriving within months of each other.

Our second grandson, born with beautiful, long eyelashes, made his arrival during the heat of July. Our first adorable granddaughter, with curly red hair, arrived two months later in September. Grandson number three, a clone of his dad, arrived in November. I was running out of lap space but couldn't have been happier. The babies were all beautiful and healthy. Our family was happily enjoying all the new additions; life was good.

Then came a surprise visit from my brother on a Thursday around noon. I was about to eat lunch when he arrived, and I asked if he'd like to join me. I made a couple of sandwiches and poured some iced tea for us, and we sat at the kitchen table. I could see he was extremely upset as he handed me a typed copy of a letter he'd received from Jeanne. I wasn't aware that she had written to him. Then he handed me a copy of the response he had typed and personally delivered to her (12-23-95, Norman Christian letter, entire letter in appendix).

Norman assumed correctly that I had not read Jeanne's letter before she sent it to him. His reference to it as the *"National Inquirer"* indicated his complete lack of understanding and concern for Jeanne.

Norman must have been fuming when he wrote his response to Jeanne's letter. In it, he quoted points from her letter and then wrote his irate response. In her letter, Jeanne mentioned our visit to Monsignor Naumann, in which we talked about the guilt we both felt by keeping Norman's secret. She wondered if we had been wrong in not insisting that he be removed from active ministry. She said that that thought had bothered us more and more as each year passed and rightly so.

In his letter to Jeanne, Norman responded that he was "deeply hurt—outraged might better describe it—that you went behind my back to talk to Monsignor Naumann about me."

He was furious that she tried to "cover your own ass because you have a brother-pervert-priest, which I do not believe myself to be. I have no difficulty talking with you about any aspect of my sexual compulsion/addiction and the program I am assigned to, a program that I welcome as a grace. Why did you bypass me? I should have been the first one you approached."

When we did ask Norman any questions, however, he shared very little and never gave us the impression that he wanted to help us understand or deal with any of it. I knew this was not the time to point that out to him, as he seemed irrational. I didn't want to dispute any of what he was saying for fear of his getting more infuriated. I had never seen him this angry, and it scared me.

Reading his response to Jeanne, his booming voice continued, "Actually, the history details of my compulsive sex addiction are none of your business. Aren't some things private for obvious reasons?" This comment served to convince me all the more of just how bad things were in his thought process. It was all about Norman and the effect on Norman and the church. There was no empathy for the victims or how his actions affected anyone else. He didn't understand that Jeanne and I cared about the children he had abused.

"And the danger of public disclosure is increased every time you approach some trustworthy person," he continued reading. "Had you done this in a confessional situation, you would have been safe. ... Anyone else is free to pass on the news."

I wondered if Norman had been lying to Monsignor Naumann. Maybe he was worried about what we might have told him.

A brief pause for a drink from his large glass of iced tea refreshed him, but his agitation hadn't lessened as he read on from his response to Jeanne. "The Archdiocese of Saint Louis could be sued many times over for civil damages. If this one allegation becomes public, it could awaken others to a possibility of 'winning the lottery' (some giant settlement in or out of court) for professional malpractice by one of its priests."

I felt sickened. He'd destroyed children's lives, yet there was not an ounce of concern for any of the people he'd hurt. His concern was that if a victim pressed charges and sued the archdiocese, it would be as if they'd won the lottery. It was frightening to realize this was the mentality of the church leadership.

Norman continued reading his letter to Jeanne, responding to her point that we'd felt guilt for not saying anything. "I don't think you are concerned about being sued out of house and home because you have sibling ties to me. I suppose you are feeling 'guilty' for not calling the child-abuse hotline to report child abuse and have me removed from ministry. ... If your conscience is bothering you, you too might benefit from the help of a counselor; but then they are obligated by law to report child abuse, however it comes before them. You never told me about your guilty feelings. Monsignor Naumann said not to worry, but that was not what you wanted to hear. I suppose if the archbishop himself had told you the same not to worry, you would have stuck with your prejudice toward me."

Norman wrote that Jeanne needed to be "in control of all details before the affair is handled correctly." He was right on one thing—we wouldn't have accepted the archbishop's telling us not to worry. Actions speak louder than words, and we hadn't been seeing appropriate actions taken.

Norman read more of his letter to me, in which he told Jeanne that he felt she wanted to keep a safe emotional distance from him because she was embarrassed. He felt no compassion or empathy from her, he said, and then he gave her his "permission" to "stop loving" him.

He continued to read:

> A sexaholic, like an alcoholic, is incurable. There are a lot of incurables: paranoids, [unscrupulous]

people, all the forms of phobia victims, compulsive shoplifters, compulsive liars, compulsive gamblers, compulsive bingo players, etc. Do they get cured? No; but can they be brought to function in a healthy way? Yes! If they learn what it takes to control their behavior and commit to using the means available to escape the dangerous flashpoint (trigger) that sets them off, they can live a life of sobriety relative to their addiction. That is what the 12-step group is for. "Keep coming back; it works if you work it" is said by the group as each meeting is closed. Sobriety in any dependence implies using the means at hand (other AA members, a sponsor, etc.) to be at the ready to help me be safe at moments when in the past I acted out the compulsion.

You speak as though you know about this, but I believe that your understanding is quite shallow. So I fear that you will intervene in my situation, giving your uninformed opinions to some official, thus getting me thrown out. I would then no longer be a problem for you. You will be back in the driver's seat, shaking your head that I turned out to be such a failure.

I kept thinking of Jeanne as Norman angrily read on. She had meant well in writing to him, but Norman misunderstood everything she wrote. It was shocking to learn that Norman thought we wanted to cause him harm. Jeanne and I had been kept in the dark. I expected my brother to man up, accept responsibility for what he had done, and accept the consequences. Norman never told us how the church was handling things, and it appeared to us that the church was protecting him, while we were given no help in coping with the personal issues it caused each of us. I was so incredibly disappointed to realize the church and my brother were only worried about how things affected them. I don't believe he gave any thought to how his behavior affected his sisters' lives. Jeanne was only looking for some answers that would help us feel more comfortable in answering any questions from relatives, friends, and parishioners who might inquire about his sudden departure from active ministry. He was revered and loved by many, and the church certainly didn't explain any of it.

Norman then addressed the issue of our relatives—did they know about him? Norman sarcastically referred to Jeanne as "being a chip off the old mom," and said that she probably wanted to tell our relatives about him. "If they do not know anything," he wrote, "they surely will after you disclose it." Norman hadn't even touched his sandwich, and I nearly choked while trying to swallow a bite of mine when he said, "My private sins are no more the business of any relatives than they are any business of yours. You don't have to confess my sins to anyone. Why do you want to make this your business? If you choose to make yourself uncomfortable about something over which you had no control, I guess that is your choice. Mom was a classic gossip. She always needed to be first to know and then became first to tell. She could burn up the telephone for hours, passing on the latest story to relatives."

Norman's hatred of my mother caused him to exaggerate in the extreme what he saw as her behavior—I never saw our mom in that way. He accused Jeanne of being "just like Mom," yet I've never known Jeanne to gossip either. Norman did not understand that Jeanne was only asking who in the family knew about him for her own peace of mind. She and I both were trying to be prepared for relatives and friends asking us about him. He didn't think about that, and he offered us no help in dealing with potential questions.

Norman was obviously too agitated to eat anything; his focus was entirely on reading that letter to me. I nibbled at my sandwich, amazed that he still didn't understand the damage that was done to those who had been sexually abused, especially by clergy, and who were keeping the shameful secret as they went on with their lives. He didn't seem to care, either. He only cared about how everything affected him and his life. I was astonished by the words that came from my brother's mouth.

"Mom never knew who I was," he read, still extremely agitated, "and your approach to me tells me that you know very little about who I am. You know one small part. You know my age and my sexual compulsion. The latter appears to prevent you from wanting to know who the rest of me is. If you could just get rid of me, that would take care of your self-esteem in the face of our relatives."

I was sad that Norman felt that way, as it had been his own choice to not share himself with us. It especially saddened me to know he'd never felt close to or loved by our mom even as a child. I don't know how that could have been, when I, as his younger sister, often witnessed the love and pride my parents both had for him and showered upon him.

Norman seemed particularly upset that Jeanne mentioned we'd told all of our children about him. He shouted loudly when reading his response to her: "If you have told them, you seriously violated my privacy, and I hold you accountable for it."

It took all I had to remain calm, but Norman continued reading—loudly. "How would you feel if I decided you are a compulsive gossip, and then went to every relative to tell them what I knew? You don't know that I am a pervert any more than I can show that you gossip. People will find such things out without help from either of us."

I refilled our glasses of tea, but he didn't seem to notice. He just went on with his tirade, sharing his response to our sister's mentioning Father Joe's suggestion that we have a meeting with Norman and his therapist so we could vent our concerns and get some answers. Norman seemed quite arrogant as he read, "The professionals in any program like mine are not permitted to disclose what is learned during treatment. You would be refused such a meeting even if I personally asked them to meet with us."

If it was true that such a meeting, even with Norman asking for it, would be refused, something was terribly wrong. We did not want to learn the ugly details of what Norman had done. Our hope was to gain understanding of the treatment he was receiving. Maybe we'd learn ways to help him, as well as find strength, support, and guidance for ourselves. We didn't feel right keeping his secret, but our Catholic faith held our belief that the church was handling everything properly. I still seriously question the therapy he received all those years through the church.

Norman read further, boldly stating—and apparently seeing nothing wrong with it—"They [the professionals] are careful to put in writing/notes only broad characteristics, in case a subpoena requires them to submit something to a court procedure. Details are kept off the record."

I had to bite my lip to stop myself from gasping out loud. I found it absolutely disgusting and shameful that the church would do such a thing.

Norman was nearing the end of his long letter when I glanced at the clock on the wall and saw that several hours had passed. Somewhat calmer, he read: "Jeanne, I am your family, yes; but you are not responsible for my behavior (not my crimes, not my sins, not the way I dress, not how I deal with my diabetes, not how I drink or smoke, etc.). It appears that it is your own choice to be upset by things that should upset me (and they do). I am embarrassed, ashamed, self-convicting to the point of obsession about it. I certainly will not assume responsibility for you making my problem your problem."

Norman did not know how wrong he was. It *was* our business! I believe it is everyone's business and responsibility, and it's clear to me now that if one has knowledge of anyone sexually abusing children, that person must report it to the authorities. I don't know how we could have been so naive to have not called the police right away. If Norman had been in any other career, we would have. This is a horrendous crime and the religious should not get a free pass. The hierarchy has failed repeatedly to do the right thing.

He continued reading. "The more people you disclose my sins to, the greater the risk of me becoming a public spectacle in the media."

Norman calls them "sins," but they are crimes. He was blaming us again, but it would be the choices he made, not us, that would make him a public spectacle.

"I am not going to help you deal with my problem," Norman read, staying true to form by thinking only of himself. "I believe you have manufactured a problem for yourself by wanting to be in control in advance, like Mom always needed to be in control of all possible outcomes. I am trusting myself to a program for recovery, and I hope you allow me to have the chance to complete it before you have me out of possible future ministry in the church. That remains my God-given vocation, just as yours is to remain married to grow in holiness and grace. If God has other plans, I wish you would let

Him take care of that in His own way. I am less trusting of you in the light of your going behind my back."

Norman clearly considered our meeting with Monsignor Naumann as going behind his back. It hurt that he hadn't given one thought to how any of it affected Jeanne or me and obviously didn't care about us.

He wrote that it would be more difficult for him now to share what was going on in his life, but his sharing anything personal with us during his lifetime had been extremely rare. He finished the letter by berating Jeanne. "Curious that you never asked for details about this program of recovery, isn't it? All I hear is something like, 'What are you doing to us, horrible person?'"

If that's all Norman got out of Jeanne's letter, I can only conclude that's how he was feeling about himself at the time.

After he had finished reading, he said, "Carol, I wanted to show Jeanne's letter and my letter to you, because I didn't think you knew Jeanne had written it, and I wanted you to see my response." He thanked me for listening and said he needed to leave. With his sandwich in one hand, he waved with the other as he headed out the door to his car.

Norman was way off about Jeanne's intention with her letter. It seemed even more that he didn't belong in ministry. I felt drained by his visit, and when Joe came home from work, I gave him the details while preparing our dinner.

I called Jeanne the next morning to tell her about Norman's visit and found he had terribly frightened her. She told me her doorbell had kept ringing, and she rushed to answer it. "I found Norman standing at the door, enraged, waving papers in his hand and shouting he needed to talk to me. I had no idea what was wrong. I invited him inside. He came in, yelling something at me about my questions and kept waving the papers around in the air. He wasn't making any sense."

Jeanne sounded very upset by what Norman had done. She was shocked by the things he had said to her and the way he said them. "I had only done what Monsignor Naumann had suggested we do—ask our questions of Norman directly. Somehow, he completely misinterpreted my letter. He really chewed me out, up one side and down the other, telling me how terrible I am."

Sadly, Norman succeeded in intimidating Jeanne into silence.

Chapter 8
Removed from Active Ministry

The archdiocese had sent Norman to a treatment center in Robertsville, Missouri, in 1995, because of a victim's complaint against him. In October 1996, Norman told me that he had come "a long way from the dead" in his twelve months of therapy and was looking forward to returning to his parish assignment at Saint William's. Yes, they were sending him back to active ministry.

Unfortunately, while he was at the center, the section of apartments in which he was living burned to the ground. He escaped the fire without injury but lost everything he owned. Once word of what had happened spread throughout family and friends, Norman was overwhelmed by the huge show of support in the form of clothing, monetary gifts, and whatever else people had to share. My brother happily accepted it all, but I don't think he gave a minute's thought to the sacrifices made to reach out to him by many of those on tight budgets. His attitude indicated that he felt he deserved it.

Father Christian returned to his duties at St. William's Church after leaving the treatment center, apparently thinking his life was back to normal, but the day came when he appeared at our home, visibly shaken. As I invited him inside, he began shouting angrily, "I can't believe this has happened!" He had received a letter from Archbishop Rigali, informing him to find a job; he was no longer considered safe for ministry in the archdiocese. Handing me the letter he'd received, he ordered, "Read this!" (September 25, 1996, Archbishop Justin Rigali letter; from Norman's Archdiocesan personnel file, entire letter in appendix 2.)

We sat in my living room as he continued to fume. "I've been sober for a year, and every report made during my treatment at Robertsville stated I was doing very well throughout my entire stay! I don't know why they're doing this to me!" Such devastating news had caught him greatly by surprise, and he was extremely upset. I, on the other hand, felt relief—though I didn't express that to him. The church was finally doing the right thing in removing a known pedophile from active ministry—something that they should have done when learning about the first child he abused.

I brought Norman some iced tea and listened to him vent his frustrations. Norman was petrified about what was going to happen to him. Having made only two payments so far to the current victim he was paying off, he didn't know what he'd do if he lost the salary he received from the archdiocese. I wondered where my brother was going to go and how he was going to support himself. I thought about his going to prison if the church stopped protecting him.

Norman did nearly all the talking on that visit, and he didn't stay long. As he stood up and walked to the door, he said, "I just wanted you to know what's happening to me."

The church, however, continued to look after him and made arrangements for him to live in still another treatment center, located in Dittmer, Missouri. There wouldn't be enough room for all of his furniture and belongings, but he told me that our cousin agreed to store all of it in her basement and asked if Joe and I would help him move it there.

I drove my van to Saint William's rectory early one morning. Norman and I worked for hours, loading my van and his car full to the brim with boxes. I felt very uncomfortable that day, being in the presence of the woman who worked in the parish office and the other priest assigned to the parish. I said very little and just kept carrying things out to the van. Then along came an older parishioner, who caught me loading things into my van. She asked if I knew why Father Christian was leaving, but I just looked at her sadly and shook my head.

"He is such a wonderful priest," she said. "I just love him. I am going to miss him terribly!" I didn't know how to respond to her; I was still honoring Norman's and the archdiocese's requests to say nothing. I finally said, "Father Christian is inside the rectory if you'd like to talk with him." I felt so sorry for her, as I have for parishioners everywhere over the years, being kept in the dark as to why the priest they've so trusted and revered has suddenly been taken away without an explanation. The hierarchy expects these people to keep donating their money to the church, but they don't respect the parishioners enough to be honest with them about a situation as grave as this.

Norman and I drove our cars to our cousin's home and unloaded everything into her basement. I returned home just in time to make our dinner. After Joe returned home from work and we had eaten, we rode out with his pickup truck to load Norman's larger items and took them to our cousin's for him. It took many hours to get the large, heavy things loaded, transported, and unloaded into her basement before heading back home, nearly another hour's drive. We were worn out by the time our heads hit the pillows that night.

Norman called weeks later to tell me about a meeting he had with the hierarchy, in hopes of finding another position in the church—some kind of ministry away from children. The rules stated he needed to be SA sober for ten years; he'd completed only one year. Still hopeful, he told me, "Maybe they'll consider me for a position at a retirement center." Norman needed a job to earn money, not only for his own support but also to make court-ordered payments to one of his victims. (He'd told me that when the victim's settlement had been drawn up, he'd told Norman, "Making a check out to me every quarter will make you think about the terrible things you did to me!")

It was a huge blow to Norman to be removed from ministry. He had been sober for a year and felt the church should trust him. It pained him deeply not to function as a priest. I don't know if he ever accepted that his own choices had led him to his removal from the ministry.

He continued to receive his salary, health insurance coverage, and all the rest of his priest benefits from the archdiocese. He no longer lived at a parish rectory, so he'd be paying his own living expenses, along with making the remaining payments to that victim.

By February 1997, Norman said that his therapist considered him to be safe from acting out. He was feeling pretty good about himself until he received a letter from the victim he was still paying off, sent to him in care of my home address. When I called to let him know he had mail sent to my address, and I mentioned the return address, he wasted no time in coming by for it. He quickly took it from me, put it in his pocket, and left. The abrupt way he did it left me wondering about its contents. Days later, he called, sounding much calmer, and explained he was really scared when he heard the return address on the envelope. He recognized it as coming from his victim. Norman told me, "I was angry that piece of mail had been sent to your address and scared, too, about what might be enclosed. I thought it'd be safer for me to open it at my therapist's office."

I knew then just how frightened he had been, but it had contained Xerox copies of research about pedophilia and a corrected notation regarding his last check payment. Nothing more was ever sent to my address, but I'm glad the person sent at least that one—that was how I found out about this victim and Norman's settlement. The archdiocese paid half of the settlement—$25,000—but the victim demanded that Father Christian pay the additional $25,000 himself. Norman was able to raise $16,000 somehow but was paying the remaining debt in quarterly payments, making payments to this victim from May 15, 1996, through February 15, 2001.

Father Christian finally found a job selling tickets for a major theater in Saint Louis. He loved working there, telling everyone it was a stress-free job. He could choose his own hours, thereby working around his doctor appointments, therapy sessions, and support groups. He enjoyed talking with people from all over the United States as they called to purchase tickets and discuss the various upcoming shows.

It wasn't too long, however, before he decided that the daily forty-five-minute trip back and forth from Dittmer, where he was now living, to Saint Louis was too costly, both in gasoline and time. He pleaded with the hierarchy to let him move from Dittmer to apartments on Grand Avenue, which was within walking distance of his workplace.

The archdiocese gave him the okay for the move. Again, my brother asked Joe and me to help him move all of his furniture and belongings. When we arrived with Joe's pickup truck to load Norman's things, only Norman was waiting for us—no one else was there to help with the move. The three of us lugged everything out to the truck ourselves. Upon arriving at my brother's new location, we were able to locate a freight elevator and unloaded everything from his car and our truck. We located his very small room, located on a high floor that was designated strictly for clergy—and it was dreary. It felt creepy to me, moving him into that place. It might have been all right as a residence, but our first impression was not inviting.

When March 1998 rolled around, Norman was angry about having to miss out on attending the thirty-seventh reunion of his ordination class—he had to attend his semiannual therapy aftercare workshop instead. He was disappointed and angry, but this was a consequence of his behavior, and he dealt with it.

Norman was never happy living at that small apartment and eventually managed to convince the hierarchy that he could be trusted living on his own in a regular apartment in the neighborhood. This time, he asked friends to help in getting his things moved. We gave him some furniture for this larger apartment, and he asked Joe for help in connecting the new apartment-sized washer/dryer he'd purchased and getting his computer set up and working. This apartment was on the ground level, right across the street from the YMCA and near a city park. A nearby street was full of various ethnic restaurants, which he told us about and loved to frequent. Norman was beginning to feel happy again.

It was March 1999, a little over three years since his being removed from active ministry, and his days were all planned out for him. He told me he didn't like going to his aftercare workshops but reports were forwarded to the archbishop, and he was still getting his diocese salary, so he went. Another workshop was six months away, and he looked forward to finishing assigned therapy.

The following is excerpted from a March 17, 1999, letter:

> Dear Carol and Joe,
> It is now three and a half years since I was removed from active ministry into an "eternal life" of therapy. A lot of experience and renewal has helped me change my attitudes about myself, and I will be

working on that the rest of my life. ... The happy side is that I like myself for the first time in all of my years of life. Making friends in recovery has turned out different from what I would have thought when I first began the transparent honesty of the program three years ago. It appears that my work in ministry is pointed toward the problem people like myself, who attend the 12-step meeting with me each weekday.

Working at [the theater] is apparently the right thing for me. My day is always scheduled with the kind of work that is easy (though sometimes boring). ... It is nice to live life without the phone ringing, without people pulling me into church business meetings, with freedom to say the day is over when I clock out of work.

I have my fourth aftercare workshop next week (Monday to Wednesday). ... After I complete a fifth aftercare workshop six months down the road, I think I will be finished with the expected time in the assigned therapy. So things will continue as they have for the next year of my life.

Norman decided to buy himself a new computer, thinking he'd keep himself busy, and it would help to pick up his spirits. It made no sense to Joe and me that a pedophile not only lived right by a YMCA and a city park but had an unmonitored computer. When my sister and I first talked with our brother about his sexual addiction, he told us that he enjoyed going to different parks to pick up kids for sex. His living right by the park at this time had to be a huge temptation for him, even if he had accepted that his behavior in the past was criminal. If he still felt there was nothing wrong in his past behavior, the location of this new apartment must have seemed like heaven to him. And now, he had a computer. He would often talk excitedly about being on his computer. I've always wondered what might have been found on it, if his friends hadn't shut it down at his request as he lay dying.

He had told me that he enjoyed going into adult video and book stores over the years. He once said his desire to visit them was so strong that he found himself heading into one right after having celebrated Easter Sunday Masses. Norman also made it clear that he didn't find anything wrong with computer porn. Years ago, he became quite upset when Joe made a joke about needing to be careful with the computer. Norman shouted, "That's not funny! A good friend of mine just got caught in a police sting for having child porn on his computer, and it's a shame because he's such a nice guy. Now he is going to have to go to prison for years."

Hearing him refer to his friend as being "such a nice guy" seemed odd to me. I said, "Nice guys don't have child porn—or any porn—on their computers, and if your friend got caught doing that, he belongs in prison." He dropped the subject then, but I was suspicious of his computer activities from then on.

CHAPTER 9
A Friendly Response

We had received the annual Christmas letter from Father Joe Naumann back on December 15, 1996, with a penned note on the bottom.

> Carol,
>
> You and your sister are in my prayers this Christmas. I have talked with Monsignor Gaydos about your experience and perception of our process. I think that you misunderstand if you think the church is not concerned about the needs of the victim. It is difficult to balance the needs of the victim, of the accused, of the perpetrator, and the good of the entire church.
>
> If you ever want to talk more about this issue, please call.
>
> Father Joe Naumann
> St. John the Baptist Parish

After watching the church's balancing act all these years, I was not impressed. The poor victims seemed to be the ones getting dropped on their heads, so to speak, or made to disappear.

On a positive note, our family grew again this year. God blessed us with two more bundles of joy. Another adorable granddaughter arrived at the end of April 1997, and our fourth lovable grandson arrived during a very hot August.

Our ten-year-old grandson and the three two-year-olds loved the newest additions to our family. Our get-togethers were all the more fun, watching all the cousins playing together, oblivious to anything corrupt in the world. Those times helped the adults put aside, for a while, the ugly reality we were forced to deal with on account of "Uncle Pedophile" and the church's cover-ups.

The year 1998 rolled around, and our youngest daughter, Joan, was now happily engaged to be married. They chose October at our parish church for the wedding, and they too asked someone other than Norman to celebrate their wedding Mass. However, Joan did halfheartedly invite her uncle to celebrate the Mass along with the priest who would be marrying them. She later said that she only asked him because she thought all the relatives would expect him to be there, as he had always been for weddings, baptisms, and funerals. In the excitement of wedding plans, she didn't remember that her uncle hadn't been included in her sisters' weddings, years earlier. She did ask the priest she wanted to actually perform their marriage.

This wedding was a happy occasion for many reasons. When Joan was diagnosed with the brain tumor at age eleven, I wondered if she'd ever have a wedding day. My prayers then were for her to live. When she did, I prayed God would help her be strong enough to make her way along the difficult road to recovery. Our family watched her suffer through so much during her young life and wondered why it had to be. I had no answers for her when she'd ask me why those awful things were happening to her. Now, she had some sense of normalcy in her life.

As we entered 1999, Joe and I happily anticipated the arrival of yet another grandchild. On a hot summer day in July, another cute and healthy grandson arrived. The entire family was delighted. As with the others, this child's birth helped put thoughts of Norman aside for a while.

It wasn't long before we welcomed not only another new year but a new century—the year 2000 arrived, and we also anticipated the arrival of our eighth grandchild. Springtime gave us more to smile about when another cute and healthy grandson arrived in May.

Nearly a year had passed when Norman stopped by our home the middle of March 2001, handing me an envelope containing a copy of his durable power of attorney for health care. He wanted someone in our family to have a record of his wishes. I wouldn't have to take any action, he said; it was simply for my information. He was happy to have finally followed through on getting the paperwork finished and notarized. That document was placed with all the other papers I had pertaining to him.

I had been troubled for years, watching and waiting to see what the church was doing in regard to my brother and what was being done to help his victims. I neither saw nor heard anything that told me the archdiocese was providing help to anyone Norman had harmed. All I saw was the church protecting Father Christian and others like him from being prosecuted. They continued to keep all of it hidden from the public.

While reading the *St. Louis Post-Dispatch* on March 17, 2002, an article by Jeremy Kohler on page A9 jumped out at me, along with a large picture of Reverend Joseph R. Lessard, age seventy-five.

The long article about the retired priest told how Father Lessard had acknowledged sexually abusing about twelve boys in three parishes but claimed to have never been sued or charged with a crime. He had gotten treatment at a center in New Mexico in 1979 for his pedophilia and was later assigned as a chaplain at Saint Joseph Hospital in Saint Charles, Missouri.

The article gave a lot of disturbing information regarding Lessard, but what lit my fire was the part that mentioned he'd told Archbishop John J. Carberry, in 1976, that he was going to get help for his asthma, arthritis, and sexual situation. It infuriated me that this priest ranked child molestation as a "sexual situation" and listed it after asthma and arthritis, as though it was no big deal. He hadn't denied abusing the boys. It seemed that in his mind, it was insignificant. In the article, Lessard stated, "I'd like to think that they'd forgotten about it and don't care anymore." At this point, he was concerned about himself and uncomfortable that his actions had become public—all his priestly benefits could be lost. Archbishop Justin Rigali stated in 2002 that "parish assignments given later, like [Father] Lessard received, would not be repeated these days because present policy unambiguously excludes any priest with a substantiated allegation of sexual abuse with a minor from an assignment to a parish or any ministry with children."

That sounded good, but Norman had allegations against him more than once. They were substantiated enough that the church quietly paid off one victim (that I know of), sent Father Norman Christian to treatment centers, and still reassigned him to parishes afterward.

Up to this time, when I questioned the church about my brother, I was never offered an explanation. I was told to be faithful and trust that they were doing the right thing. It took me decades to realize that was a huge mistake.

After reading how the church had dealt with Lessard, I became even less trusting and decided to let them know that I was holding them accountable for how they were handling the sexual-abuse problem within the church. I wrote a letter to Archbishop Justin Rigali. The following are excerpts from that March 17, 2002 letter (entire letter in appendix).

> The Catholic Church's reaction to the evils of clergy abuse of minors has been heavy on my mind for better than fourteen years. It was about then that I learned my own brother, a priest, was an abuser and had himself been abused in his youth by priests. ... Now today, I read Joe Lessard's disgusting interview. I can't bring myself to call him Reverend. I could hardly believe reading his comment to Carberry. "I was going to get help for the asthma, arthritis, and this sexual situation." It ranked third in his comment. Talk is cheap; the Catholic Church needs to do something other than cover up its ugly mess. Anyone else guilty of similar crimes would end up with prison time, along with therapy. I do not think clergy deserve any special treatment. If anything, the position of trust they have makes their crimes even worse.

I sent a copy of this letter with a personal note to my friend

Bishop Naumann (entire note in appendix). I was of the belief that Bishop Naumann would be able to bring about change in the way the church was handling the clergy sexual-abuse crisis. I still felt comfortable communicating with him. When our family first met him, he drove an old beat-up car, placing more value in people than material possessions. Now, I had hopes that God was directing his move up the ranks in the church for a reason. I prayed he and Archbishop Rigali would discuss the letters I sent them and give some serious thought to my concerns. I believed the church had been saying one thing and doing another when it came to these pedophiles.

I overcame my fear of confrontation, as I just knew my conscience was never going to let me sleep if I didn't confront them about leaving innocent children and unsuspecting families in harm's way.

Several days later, the phone rang as I was washing the dishes from lunch. Drying my hands, I answered it, surprised to hear Bishop Naumann's voice. After chatting for a bit, he said, "Archbishop Rigali and I received your letters, and the archbishop asked me to reply to you for him as well." No surprise there. "I'd like to discuss the concerns you've expressed in your letter."

I began telling him about my brother's incredibly selfish attitude. He responded, "Norman seems to have a narcissistic personality." I agreed, and he went on to assure me that Norman was being supervised, that someone met with him every month.

I stated my concerns about Norman's ridiculous remarks, such as telling Jeanne and me that he never forced himself on anyone. My frustration must have been obvious to Bishop Naumann when I told him, "I never heard Norman express any remorse for what he did to the children he abused. Norman thinks his behavior doesn't affect anyone but the church and him, and that troubles me."

Bishop Naumann assured me, "I will pass all of your concerns along to Norman's therapist, and if Norman needs to be told where the information came from, you'll be called first." (I never received a call.)

I then reminded Bishop Naumann of another priest who had been accused of sexual abuse and who was still in active ministry. "Why hasn't he been removed from ministry? One mother personally warned me to keep my children away from him after telling me what the priest did her child. Thanks to the Saint Louis Archdiocese's lawyers successfully arguing that the statute of limitations had expired, the lawsuits against him were dismissed. The church still allows him to continue directing that youth choir and orchestra group, endangering more children!"

Bishop Naumann gave me the same explanation he had given years ago. "There must be formal charges made by the victim before the statute of limitations expires. If an accuser doesn't follow through by pressing charges, the church feels it wouldn't be fair to dirty the priest's name by making the accusation public." Again, he assured me such priests would be sent for treatment.

What I understood of this was that it was all right to keep an accused predator in his position of trust and respect, where he could harm more unsuspecting kids. Just don't dirty his name by letting anyone know that someone made an accusation against him. The church will send him for treatment but then will return him to ministry, putting children at risk again.

My frustration grew with the bishop's approving the church's protecting priests in that manner. After taking a couple deep breaths to calm myself, I asked Bishop Naumann about the prosecuting attorney's request to the archdiocese for priests' personnel files. He quickly responded, "There are no cases in the files at this time that could be prosecuted, because they are all past the statute of limitations"—not that they were innocent, just past the deadline for filing. The immorality of the church leaders astounded me.

He went on to tell me there were no cases of obstruction of justice, and the patient reports didn't show any of the clergy to be dangerous to anyone. That one gave me pause. I responded quickly, telling him that Norman had once explained to my sister and me that the archdiocese had given orders to therapists to be careful of what they put in writing. I found it difficult throughout our conversation to curb my emotions. Norman's matter-of-fact statements about patient reports had stunned me, but the bishop's lack of concern for the dishonest tactic was extremely disappointing and saddened me as well. The man I was speaking with was not the man I once respected and called friend.

Bishop Naumann said nothing, as though he hadn't heard what I had just said. Instead, he told me there was a committee being formed to review clergy sex-abuse cases. He added, "A substantiated complaint is needed to get someone removed from ministry, and any such report would also be given to the Division of Family Services. Only the victim can prosecute."

I had been jotting down notes as we talked, so I could refer back to what we discussed. I asked him about the conditions for men presently in the seminary. He claimed there was a psychologist on staff who screened everyone. He also stated there were no abusers on the faculty. I told him, "I hope you are right, but it doesn't seem the church has been doing a very good job of policing itself."

Bishop Naumann seemed sincere in telling me, "I wasn't aware of what Norman did to your daughter. I'm sorry." Then he asked, "Please, pray for me and all priests."

"I have been and will continue, but all priests must stop their silence and report any abuse they discover to the authorities." I moved on, telling him how frustrated I was in not knowing what to say to people when they asked about my brother since his sudden removal from ministry, with no reason given as to why. People loved and respected him as a priest and were concerned. I explained, "I asked Norman what he wanted me to tell people who asked about him. He rudely told me it was none of their damn business. That certainly wasn't appropriate, but Norman didn't think or care about anyone but himself. I finally started telling people the job became too stressful for him and that he was being treated for emotional problems."

It surprised me that Bishop Naumann was fine with that explanation—it was a huge stretch from the truth. I had hoped he would have a better suggestion. Bishop Naumann was still listening patiently, even though we had been talking nearly an hour. I brought up the time Norman became so angry by Jeanne's suggestion of the two of us joining him in a therapy session. I wondered if he remembered being the one to give us that idea. I explained, "Norman didn't seem to understand or care that Jeanne and I had no one to confide in or answer our questions. Our faith in the church was weakening."

Bishop Naumann didn't comment on that but instead said, "Don't believe 100 percent of what you read in the newspaper." He assured me that what he'd told my sister and me years ago was true: the church was taking care of things. He even told me, "The two priests from your neighborhood, whose names have been all over the news media for molesting kids, were just oversights."

I disagreed, replying, "Pedophiles don't stop with just one victim." Bishop Naumann didn't argue that point.

Before he brought our conversation to an end, I wanted to mention my concerns about Norman's home computer. "Norman became quite agitated when he told Joe and me about a good friend of his getting caught in a recent police sting on computer porn," I said. "Norman thought it was unfair and claimed his friend was a nice guy and that he shouldn't have gone to prison. I have no proof, but my gut instinct made me wonder if he was involved in it too."

When Bishop Naumann didn't comment, I asked him to pass the information on to Norman's therapist.

While Bishop Naumann had been patient and polite, I still doubted that my concerns would be taken seriously by the hierarchy. At this point, I was really counting on him, trusting that his promotion to bishop was God's hand at work. Bishop Naumann would be the one to bring about change in how the church dealt with clergy-abuse victims and the priests who abused them. Holding on to that hope, I thanked him for calling, and we said good-bye. I filed away my notes, wondering if I would ever hear anything from Archbishop Rigali.

Sunday's March 3, 2002, issue of the *Post-Dispatch* ran a special report on problem priests. Patricia Rice and Norm Parish wrote an article about a prominent priest who was removed from Our Lady of Sorrows Church in Saint Louis, Missouri, in response to thirteen-year-old allegations of sexual abuse against a minor. He was the second priest to be removed from his parish within five days. Both actions, the article noted, were the result of an archdiocesan review of past allegations of sexual abuse, prompted in part by scandals in the Boston archdiocese. The mother of another Saint Louis priest was quoted in that article, saying, "I just wonder if it is true. Even if it is, so long ago and just once, it's become a witch hunt."

It saddened me that this mother could feel that way. A child being raped, even once, especially by a priest, is a horrendous thing. This was no witch hunt; this was justice. Priests do not deserve leniency because of who they are; they deserve even harsher penalties because of the positions of power and trust they have betrayed.

Not long after the removal of the pastor from Our Lady of Sorrows Church, another priest assigned there also was arrested for sexually abusing a minor. For weeks, he had expressed his horror and disappointment to the parishioners about the pastor's arrest and removal. Suddenly, one evening, this priest too was removed from the premises with no warning. The parishioners were left in shock to deal with losing both their pastor and an associate in less than a month, both having been charged with sexually abusing a minor.

Two years later the *St. Louis Post-Dispatch* newspaper, dated April 21, 2004, carried a report by William C. Lhotka, "Priest-abuse settlement may be record." Reverend Wolken had abused the son of a family friend while babysitting for them. Lhotka's article is reprinted here:

> The Archdiocese of Saint Louis agreed to pay $1,675,000 to a Saint Louis family whose son was sexually abused over a three year period by a Catholic priest. The settlement could be largest involving the church in the area."
>
> Robert F. Ritter, the attorney for the family, confirmed that he and attorneys for the church reached the settlement on Tuesday in a civil lawsuit that has been pending for about two years in Saint Louis Circuit Court.
>
> The Reverend Gary P. Wolken, 38, was arrested in 2002, and authorities said, admitted he had molested the child between August 1997 and July 2000 when he was a baby sitter for the boy, the son of a family friend.
>
> Wolken pleaded guilty in December 2002 to two counts of statutory sodomy and six counts of child molestation. The child was in kindergarten when the abuse began.
>
> In February last year, Saint Louis County Circuit

Judge John F. Kintz sentenced Wolken to 15 years in prison. At the sentencing, a family counselor read statements from the father, mother, sister and the victim.

The boy's father wrote what happened "has challenged our faith and belief not only of the church but of society as well." The victim, then 10, said he was being teased at school, was having trouble adjusting to life, was getting counseling and had lost Wolken as a friend.

Before the sentencing, David Clohessy, of the Survivors Network of those Abused by Priests, had picketed outside the Clayton courthouse with other members urging a stiff sentence.

On Tuesday, Clohessy called the settlement one of the largest ever in the Midwest. "No amount of money will restore this child's innocence," he said. "He faces a long, hard recovery as does his family. We certainly hope that this will provide for him and his family some degree of closure. We suspect, of course, that there were others that Wolken molested and we would ask them to come forward."

Prosecutor Rob Livergood disclosed after the sentencing last year that another person had indeed come forward. That person said Wolken had molested him more than 20 years ago when he was five years old and Wolken was about 15, Livergood said.

(Reprinted with permission of the *Saint Louis Post-Dispatch*, copyright 2004.)

With little time for anyone to catch one's breath, newscasters announced the arrest of the director of Vocations for the Archdiocese of Saint Louis for sexually abusing a boy in 1995. This priest was the brother-in-law of one of our neighbors. Three priests recently named as pedophiles were right in my own neighborhood. We had been led to believe there were none left in active ministry. It left people wondering how many more such priests were serving in unsuspecting parishes, endangering vulnerable children and adults.

When our eldest daughter was attending high school in the '80s, her advisor, Reverend James Funke, was later discovered to have been a child molester and eventually went to prison. Back then, a pedophile priest was publically unheard of—it was shocking news. Lately, though, these reports come frequently, worldwide. Most Catholics are disgusted and disappointed for having their trust and respect for their church betrayed by the very ones they turned to for moral guidance. Yet the church remains silent and secretive about what they are doing to correct the clergy sexual-abuse crisis.

Another article by William C. Lhotka in the *St. Louis Post-Dispatch* (March 25, 2004) told how a priest, having been sent to jail, was waging a canon-law war to remain a priest from his jail cell. He sent letters out, asking people to call his attorney if they were aware of his accuser and his personal and family history. His lawyer was an expert in canon law and was serving as this priest's defense lawyer in his bid to remain a priest. The victim had been dragged through two trials already, and his mother said that her son's molester had more rights than her son did. Where was the child's justice?

Chapter 10
Panic

It was past ten thirty on a Thursday night, April 5, 2002, when I was awakened by our phone ringing. I jumped out of bed and ran to the kitchen to answer before it woke Joe. I had barely said hello when I heard Norman's hysterical voice. "Carol, something terrible happened!" Thoughts raced through my mind as to what was causing my brother's panic. The urgency in his voice frightened me. He got right to the crux of his call, speaking loudly and angrily. "I got this awful letter in today's mail from Bishop Dolan. He's telling me I can no longer be a priest. They might even laicize me!" Norman seemed shocked. "I can't believe this has happened! As far as I know, I've been doing everything the church has required me to do since the accusation was made against me." Norman wondered if he had received this letter because of something another pedophile priest had done against orders over Easter weekend. "I might not be able to continue with therapy—without benefits, I couldn't afford it." He was also quite concerned about everything about him becoming public knowledge; besides the embarrassment, it could also bring about many more lawsuits for the church. As for being laicized—having his powers, rights, and authority removed, essentially becoming a layman—he wasn't willing to even consider that.

I had no answers for him. I could only listen as he expressed his anger. I couldn't even say I felt sorry for him. I doubt he could own up to the fact that he had brought all of this on himself by making the choices he had. While listening to his fears of what might happen to him now, thoughts of all the kids he had abused invaded my mind. I was thinking he should have been removed long before, but I continued listening to his concerns, telling him, "Norm, you're in my prayers." I had always prayed for him to do the right thing. I doubt that either of us got much sleep that night.

With initial guidance from a canon lawyer, Norman lost no time in asking Archbishop Rigali to revoke the letter decree because it didn't follow canon law procedure. What follows is Norman's April 2002 letter from Auxiliary Bishop Timothy M. Dolan, VG.

> Dear Norm,
> It is now imperative for us to state again your standing with the Archdiocese of St. Louis;
> You do not have the faculties of the archdiocese, and thus are unable to exercise the priestly ministry in any way whatsoever; the celebration of Mass (even concelebration), or any of the sacraments, preaching, or any priestly ministry.
> As of April 1, 2002, you will no longer receive a salary from the archdiocese, or as of June 1, 2002, be covered by Priests' Mutual Benefit Society.
> To regularize your situation even further, it is our recommendation that you request laicization from the archbishop. With prayerful best wishes, I am,
> Sincerely in Christ
> Most Reverend Timothy M. Dolan, VG
> Auxiliary Bishop of St. Louis

Not much later, I received a very surprising phone call from my cousin's husband early one Monday evening. These were the relatives who had met with Norman at the country club, where Norman had confided about abusing boys in Festus years ago. My cousin and her husband had been exceptionally generous to Norman throughout his years as a priest, but now, my cousin's husband, Bob, was calling to tell me the proverbial straw had broken the camel's back.

Norman apparently had said something that made Bob realize he could no longer support Norman financially or emotionally. Now,

Bob wanted to be sure I fully understood that my family and I were still welcome in their home, but he also wanted me to know firsthand what he had just done and why, because he valued my family's relationship with them. He was terribly upset but managed to say he had just finished telling Norman he never wanted to see or hear from him again. I had never heard this man say anything like that to anyone, ever. To know he suddenly said it to Norman startled me. I don't know—and didn't ask—what Norman had done to precipitate such a reaction in a man who previously would do anything for him.

I suppose reality may have finally hit him. I was very worried about Bob right then; he sounded so upset that I feared he might have a heart attack or stroke at any moment as we were talking. He vented for over an hour on the phone about his disgust, not only with Norman but with many other clergy he had come to know very well over his lifetime. He was extremely aggravated with the entire church and its cover-ups. All his life, he too had trusted clergy, who told him they were handling problems of which he had become aware. He kept the faith and trusted what they had told him. The deception and betrayals he had managed to ignore all his life by refusing to believe clergy would do anything wrong must have finally hit him dead on.

I wondered how Norman reacted to what Bob said to him, as he always enjoyed being with their family. I never mentioned the phone call to Norman, and he never mentioned to me the one he received either. Actually, he never mentioned the names of anyone from our cousin's family again. It was as though he'd deleted them from his life. From then on, whenever I would mention having heard from one of them, Norman completely ignored my comment.

I guess it never occurred to Norman to apologize for whatever he said to the man who had done so much for him throughout his priesthood. It was as though that family wasn't of use to him now, so he wouldn't waste time thinking about them.

Chapter 11
Seeking Advocacy

I received an e-mail from Norman on April 13, 2002, telling me he was seeking a canon law advocate to assist him in responding to the letter from Auxiliary Bishop Timothy M. Dolan. He had provided his personal profile and history, hoping the man would take his case. The fact he had sent such telling information via e-mail made me question how clearly he was thinking.

I read what he sent, which asked for advocacy support, along with the typed copy of Bishop Dolan's letter. I knew Norman was very upset, but it wasn't until I read what he said about the personal impact on his life, should what was stated in Bishop Dolan's letter actually happen, that I realized how terribly frightened he actually was.

I was taken by surprise two days later when I received a much happier e-mail from him. Norman was updating everyone who knew what happened that he had received good news. He felt the prayer support had been powerful and was most thankful.

Surprisingly, Bishop Dolan had done a complete flip-flop, indicating to Norman's former copastor from Saint William's Church that Norman had misinterpreted the letter he had received. I don't know if Norman knew what happened, but he didn't care. He was just happy someone had fixed things for him. He said he was more than ready to schedule an appointment to meet with the bishop in a week or so.

The following is the April 13, 2002, e-mail that I received from Norman:

> Subject: FW: I need an advocate
> This e-mail and attachment is being forwarded to you for your information. Thank you for your support, past and present. To my surprise I received my mid-month salary payment from the archdiocese, which was declared ended in the letter from Bishop Dolan (attachment). "Canon Law Professionals" is a website offering Advocacy. I await a response. Norm Christian
>
> ------Original Message-----
> From Norman Christian
> To: [name withheld]
> Sent: Saturday, April 13, 2002 7:14 PM
> Subject: re: I need an Advocate
>
> I am a priest of the Archdiocese of St. Louis ... Attached is my profile and history, prompting this need for your advocacy support. I ... was directed to ask you for advocacy by Father (name withheld). [His] workload is too heavy to add another case at this time. If I am away when you call, I will be able to receive your recorded message and respond after 11:30 a.m. Monday, April 15. Thank you.
> Norman Christian
>
> Profile/History (prepared April 13, 2002)
>
> Reverend Norman H. Christian, Archdiocese of St. Louis, Ordination: March 18, 1961
>
> Background:
> On or about October 26, 1995, Bishop Joseph F. Naumann, V G, Auxiliary Bishop, telephoned me that an accusation of sexual misconduct with a

minor was naming me as the perpetrator. The male victim would have been 13–14 years of age, when I was assigned to a rural parish in Crystal City, MO. The year was 1970–71. A possible civil lawsuit of $250,000 would name the archdiocese and myself for prosecution. The lawsuit was not filed. Through the archdiocesan lawyer, the victim agreed to accept $25,000 from the archdiocese (it recommended medical therapy but did not restrict its use in any way). The victim required that I personally pay the same amount of $25,000 in reparation. I agreed to this solution. I was able to pay $16,000 up front, and with a signed agreement prepared by our archdiocesan lawyer, I would complete the remaining $9,000 over 20 quarterly payments of $450 each. The payments began on May 15, 1996 and were completed on February 25, 2001.

Meanwhile, I was told to reside at a safe residence called 'Wounded Brothers,' located in the rural Franklin County area of the archdiocese. I began intensive therapy (3 group sessions each week) at the St. Louis Consultation Center. After nine months of the intensive treatment, a weekly group therapy program replaced the intensive treatment, along with individual private therapy as recommended by the Consultation Center's professional staff. I have now spent seven years of exact compliance with all of the discipline extended to me by the archdiocese. I have taken no new actions that should embarrass the church or otherwise give the church cause to reconsider their punishments previously instituted.

Currently, the archdiocese is undergoing strong scrutiny regarding 'pedophile priests,' and the local papers and national news have been feasting on the opportunity to increase their profits and audience ratings. On April 4, 2002, I received the following letter: [Norman disclosed the letter he received from Bishop Timothy Dolan.]

Action Taken:
Following a search for canon law advocacy, I received initial guidance from a qualified canon lawyer. He suggested that I immediately respond to Archbishop Rigali (not his auxiliary) with a brief request "seeking ... the revocation of this decree in accord with Canon 1734. The decree is invalid because it does not follow canonical procedure." I made sure that the letter was received as I asked for a return signed card from the post office. To date, I have not received a response from the archbishop.

Personal Impact on My Life
If my standing with the archdiocese becomes that stated in the April 2, 2002, letter, I will be financially destitute. There was no advance warning of any kind during the seven years since my removal from active ministry. I am 66 years old. I expected to be cared for by the church into my old age. Employers would see my age as less desirable for a salaried position than a younger man with a family. I am too old for a job with good medical coverage. I was expecting to reside in the retirement home for our priests when unable to provide rent for my apartment. I would have to depend on family and friends to reach out with help, and that is asking for more than they could provide. I fear I will end up in dire need.

The following are excerpts from an April 15, 2002, e-mail I received from Norman:
Subject: updating on Father Norm Christian

Today I received good news from my former co-pastor, [name withheld]. While he was visiting with Bishop Tim Dolan about his own future, once St.

William's Church (where we shared the rectory and parish's apostolate) closes on June 30, Bishop Dolan asked if he had been talking with me. [He] conveyed that I would not be able to live on the salary I was making ... without additional financial help from the archdiocese. ... He told me that Bishop Dolan indicated that support would not be necessary, that the archdiocese has no intention of abandoning me financially or medically and that the letter I received was a projection on their part that I might prefer to be laicized. ... Are your prayers being answered? WOW! I was anticipating the purgatory of a canonical proceeding, hoping for a reversal of the devastating directive of his signed letter to me. Now I understand a little better how important it is to remain connected in good times and in bad. I am convinced that I am loved by very many wonderful priests, religious and laity. I will carry all of you to the Alter of Sacrifice in thanksgiving and renewed hope. You gave your lives for me. Thank you all!
Norman Christian

Norman's saying he had to be within a canonical timeline in the procedure or he'd lose by default really made me think. He was in the same boat as his victims in having to act quickly. Strange how worried he was when the shoe was on the other foot.

I wrote him on April 21, 2002 (entire letter in appendix), saying I was surprised he'd sent such personal information by e-mail; I responded by regular mail. I said his mentioning having fears of losing by default prompted my writing and that it bothered me that I never heard him express remorse for all the damage he did to kids over the years. I felt angry, thinking of what he did to Sue. I explained that Sue's needs came before his and because she didn't want to be near him anymore, he would no longer be included in our family gatherings. He was welcome to come by to see Joe and me at other times. Norman never said anything about not being welcome at our family gatherings, and he did stop by occasionally to visit with Joe and me.

No Longer on Pedestals

In the April 14, 2002, *Post-Dispatch*, Kevin Horrigan wrote an article on pedophilia, "We Were the Good Kids." He had interviewed a licensed professional counselor, who specialized in men's issues. The counselor said when victims heard other men's stories in group therapy, it validated them. That's what happened for a young man named Steve, when his 1995 lawsuit was dismissed against a priest accused of molesting him in 1982, when he was a member of a youth choir and orchestra the priest directed. The Archdiocese of Saint Louis had successfully argued the statute of limitations had expired. Steve said no one ever believed him at the time; the only validation he received was at the SNAP (Survivors Network for those Abused by Priests) support meetings. He expressed how grateful he was to the support group for helping him get his life back.

That same article mentioned Barbara Dorris. Once this courageous and energetic woman acknowledged her own abuse by a priest in her youth, she jumped in with both feet to work toward making the church a safer place for children. Barb does all she can to encourage the church to remove predators from active ministry. She is currently the outreach director of SNAP and works closely with David Clohessy, the national director of SNAP. In Horrigan's article, Barb questioned why "the victims have to be the ones to leave the church and give up their faith. They didn't do anything wrong. They were being the good kids by obeying father."

The bishops had met with the Pope in Rome during spring of 2002, at which time they discussed the sexual-abuse scandal that had taken on a life of its own in the United States. After their return to the United States, I became frustrated upon hearing the rules they made for the church's first-time abusers of minors. The bishops were actually refusing to remove a priest from active ministry if it was *only the first time* he had sexually abused a child. After having just heard the Pope speaking on this matter, how could they even think of allowing first-time offenders to remain in active ministry? It most likely wasn't the perpetrator's first time abusing a child, just his first time getting caught. And even if it was the perpetrator's first time abusing a child, why was that any less a crime than if it was his second or tenth time? There are predator clergy sexually abusing children; it's that simple. The church must acknowledge that and do the right thing by immediately removing every molester of which they are aware.

I could not understand how our church leaders could think and act in such an irresponsible manner. I wrote Archbishop Rigali (entire 4-26-2002 letter in appendix) with my thoughts and sent a copy to Bishop Naumann. I said that hearing bishops say such sinful, criminal behavior was a problem in all of society was like a kid telling his mom and dad that everybody is doing it. The Catholic

Church is supposed to set the highest example of moral standards. I was ashamed of the bishops' statements. I hoped more Catholics also were writing letters, as I was far from being the only one upset. I had overheard many people—in malls, grocery stores, or wherever they met—who were obviously troubled by the bishops' statements.

Archbishop Rigali may have pitched my letter into the waste can, but if no one voiced an opinion regarding the hierarchy's refusal to remove first-time sex offenders from ministry, they could assume everyone was accepting of their decision. The bishops were setting a terrible example for their flocks by not following the Pope's direct instructions. If the bishops didn't have to obey him, why should anyone else? I wanted to know their justification for keeping sexual abusers in ministry. I also wanted them to explain their reasons for not informing parishioners about abusive priests assigned to their parishes. By not disclosing the truth, they took away every parent's right to protect children from possible clergy sexual abuse. I was becoming more discouraged and less trusting of the church leaders as time went by and had no idea what was happening with my brother.

The middle of May 2002 came around, and I hadn't heard anything from Norman since letting him know how I felt about his situation. I decided to drop a line to my friend, Bishop Naumann (entire 5-15-2002 letter in appendix). Maybe he could tell me how Norman was doing. I told him about the letter I'd sent Norman to explain my concern with not hearing from him. I asked if he could at least keep me informed on what was happening to Norman as far as the church was concerned. I wanted to know what to expect—would he end up on my doorstep, needing help? Not receiving any information from Norman or the church left me with nothing but unanswered questions and stress. I was used to being shut out of my brother's life but this time, I wanted to find a way to encourage him to apologize for the pain he'd caused so many throughout his priesthood. I didn't believe his therapist or the hierarchy was encouraging him to do it, judging from his being so worried about the truth of his behavior becoming public knowledge.

I was relieved when I heard from Norman on May 26. His e-mail seemed upbeat and never even mentioned my letter. He asked about getting together for lunch someday over the summer and said he was glad to hear from me. I assumed he was okay with what I had said to him.

I was pleasantly surprised to receive the following short letter from Archbishop Justin Rigali, acknowledging my letter to him.

> June 1, 2002
> Dear Mrs. Kuhnert,
> I received some time ago your letter concerning the present situation in the church. I know that you have been in contact with Bishop Naumann and that he has spoken to you at some length. I realize how personally you and your family have been involved in this situation and I want to assure you of my prayers. Throughout all of this we are confident that God's grace will bring the offenders to repentance, help the victims in their deep anguish, and preserve our innocent priests. At the same time we know that the prayers of all the people of God are so much a part of this healing process.
>
> Wishing you peace and strength in our Lord Jesus Christ, I remain
> Sincerely yours,
> Most Reverend Justin Rigali
> Archbishop of St. Louis

I expected so much more of him, the shepherd of our church. I believe God wants him to reach out and protect his flock, especially the children. How could he do so when he refused to meet with the clergy's victims? How was he protecting children when he refused to work with the victims' support groups in seeing that all known predator clergy are removed from active ministry?

I agree prayer is needed, but God must expect us to do a good bit of the work ourselves. That "work" applies to everyone—cardinals, archbishops, and bishops, too. We can't all just pray and expect God to fix everything for us. Those praying need to become part of the solution as well.

I received word from Norman in the first part of June; he'd be moving from his city apartment into the Priests' Retirement Home in Shrewsbury on July 1, 2002. He gave me his new address and phone number.

Moving into the retirement home meant Norman didn't have to worry about paying rent, utility bills, or shopping for groceries anymore. He was given private quarters in which to live and grew to love it there rather quickly, as he found the sisters catered to the retired priests in every way possible. He felt pampered there, and it was obvious he was quite content.

Since the scandal within the Catholic Church seemed to be the big topic of conversation everywhere for months, our pastor in Union, Missouri, wrote a long column on the topic of the sexual-abuse scandal for the July 21, 2002, Sunday bulletin. As I read it, I could feel myself tensing up. When he ended by stating the media was only publicizing the scandal because it hated Catholics, I knew I had to offer him my thoughts—he was way off base!

I read through his lengthy column as I wrote, covering each point he made. I typed several pages to explain my opinion. I gave him my reasons for feeling so strongly about what he had written.

I thanked him for looking at the problem from a layperson's point of view; I hoped he would read it.

The following is our pastor's article in the parish bulletin (Mitas, 07-21-02, Immaculate Conception Church, Union, Missouri):

> THERE'S NO PLACE LIKE HOME, especially when home is Union, MO! Last week I was on retreat in New Jersey. The Redemptorist Fathers have a retreat located right on the Atlantic. Very nice. Priests from all over the world come to this retreat, preached by Father Benedict Groeschel (a regular on Mother Angelica's EWTN). It's a great experience, especially having the opportunity to hear first-hand what's going on in the church today all around the world.
>
> The big topic of conversation, as you might imagine, was the big scandal that has dominated the media for the past several months. There were many thoughts. In addition to the hundred or so priests

who were there, there was also a panel of experts from many various fields, including psychologists, sociologists and social workers. Nobody was making light of the situation or even tried to make excuses for the crimes committed or the failure to deal with the criminals more forthrightly. Many interesting points, however, were raised and I'd like to share some of them with you.

First, deplorable as it is, the sexual abuse of minors is a problem that is found in every organization staffed by human beings; the Boy Scouts, the Armed Forces, corporate America, families, and every religious denomination.

Second, every organization that has had this problem in the past (namely all of them) has dealt with it in the exact same way the Catholic church did.

Third, the incidence of this kind of abuse is actually much higher in the other religions, whose clergy are almost all married.

Fourth, the third point surprises most people because they never hear of such misbehavior on the part of other clergy.

Fifth, the reason why nobody ever hears about the sexual misconduct of Protestant or Jewish clergy but why everybody hears about the priests is because of the tremendous and satanic anti-Catholic bias in the media. (Do you remember that day at the height of the scandal here when a full page and a half including the front page was given to one of our priests' misconduct from many years ago, while on the same page a small, two-paragraph story was given to a Baptist minister who committed the same crime the previous week and didn't even mention the man's name or church?)

Sixth, the reason why the media hate us so is because they're trying to push a totally different agenda from the Catholic Church, and they see us as the sole voice of strong opposition. A recent poll revealed that over 90% of those working in the media favor abortion on demand, homosexual "marriage," free and easy divorce, etc. In short, they're full throttle sexual revolutionaries. (They also voted for Bill Clinton by the same percentages; are you surprised?) They want to paint the nation in their colors. We stand in the way.

Seventh, since only 1 or 2 percent of the cases involved actual prepubescent children, the real problem is homosexuality, but the media insist on calling it pedophilia. Why? Because the media have no problem with homosexuality, and have, in fact, promoted it frequently, and because the word pedophilia still produces a sting. (I say still because part of the agenda of the more militant wing of the media is to lower the legal age for sexual consent, so that the perverts will have access to children without fear of recrimination.)

Eighth, there's no real war going on here. This sort of abuse is monstrous wherever it's found, but it is found everywhere. Why were the Catholics singled out? Is the crime less hideous when done by a rabbi, or an uncle, or a sergeant? Can the victim easily dismiss it because it was only done by a teacher? Are there no emotional scars decades later because it was just a scout master? Why do the media, the sudden safeguards of our national youth, never give these stories the same coverage as our priests even though they're much more common? You know the reason.

The media hate what you are and what you stand for as a Catholic. Every time you buy one of their newspapers, you make them wealthier and more powerful. Every time you patronize one of the advertisers of their programs, their influence grows.

When the *Post-Dispatch* kept piling on about the scandals, I quit my subscriptions. I haven't missed it.

Father Mitas

My July 26, 2002, letter of response to our pastor regarding his bulletin article (Kuhnert, 07-26-02, letter):

Dear Father Mitas,

After reading your column in the 7/21/02 Sunday bulletin, I felt the need to respond to the points you presented. I'd like to share my thoughts with you.

First, saying everybody else is doing it is something kids tell their parents. It's no excuse. I do realize sexual abuse of minors is, sadly, found in every walk of life and religion. I learned of some "problem" priests when my girls were in school in the '80s at high school and the one priest went to jail; the other continues to dodge complaints.

Second, the fact that other organizations have dealt with sexual abuse of minors the same way the Catholic Church did is unfortunate. The Catholic Church has always held itself way above the rest, and one would have expected it to set the standard for protecting the innocent children from pedophiles. Catholics so trusted the church, the thought of sexual abuse by clergy never entered their minds. Many had their children abused because of that trust!

Third, I don't know for a fact that such abuse is much higher in other religions. I believe celibacy has nothing to do with sexual abuse of minors. People making evil choices and acting out on them is the problem. I feel angry and betrayed when I think of how the leaders I so admired, trusted and respected all my life (61 years) were not practicing what they preached.

Fourth, I've seen cases in the paper and on TV over the years concerning sexual abuse of minors by clergy of other religions and various other occupations. It always upsets me to read about anybody doing it.

Fifth, I think the reason the scandal became such big news was because of the blatant and obvious cover-up that has gone on all these years by our trusted, moral church leaders. It appears they were more concerned about hiding the scandal than in doing the right thing. The offending clergy deserved to be removed from their duties and turned over to the courts for punishment, as any other evil person would have been. It is shameful to have hidden the ugly behavior all those years. No one can heal if they have to keep dirty secrets. People who choose to do evil things deserve punishment. The disgusting behaviors and cover-ups would still be going on if the news media hadn't made it public. I think the church earned the unfavorable publicity by its improper, immoral handling of policing itself. Something has to change before any change can occur. The public scandal may be the "change" that will bring about a change in how the church handles pedophiles.

Sixth, whether the media hates the church or not, it couldn't have had its feeding frenzy without the horrible behavior of our church leaders' way of dealing with sexual abuse of minors by the clergy over all these years.

Seventh, I think sexual abuse of teens is just as bad as that of prepubescent children. An older child, even age 18, 19, or 20, must really be messed up psychologically having been abused by clergy; someone who they had been taught from little on up to respect and obey, practically put on a pedestal. Being of a homosexual nature does not mean being a child molester. A child molester is a pedophile; a person who chooses to do evil to children and acts out his disgusting desires. What difference is it as to the age of the child when molested? It is sinful, no matter when! There is no excuse for clergy being abusive. They definitely must never think they had consent from their victims for the abuse.

Eighth, I don't think Catholics are being singled out by the media. I think Catholics are feeling betrayed and are super-embarrassed by all the cases that have been made public and are perhaps feeling like they are the center of attention and in shock that this could have happened. It's sad that there were so many cases to report. I don't believe for a minute that all of them have yet been made public. Every Catholic must live his/her life following God's commandments, from our church leaders on down. Those that do need not worry about the media.

There is a reason I have such strong feelings about this scandal. My brother has been a priest for 41 years and a pedophile for I don't know how long! It's a secret my brother asked me to keep after I learned about it 15 years ago. The archdiocese told my sister and me it wasn't ours to worry about; they would handle it. We trusted them to do so yet felt dirty for keeping the secret. Our church leaders knew of my brother's evil ways for at least 30 years. Their choosing to keep his secret allowed him to victimize many children over the years, including one of my own children. His own family wasn't even warned of his evil behavior. I find that revolting. I trusted and respected my brother. All the years of feeling blessed to have had a brother who was a priest have been shot down by disgust, not just in him, but in our church leaders who failed to act appropriately to protect all the church members. Thanks to their poor judgment in handling sexual abuse, many more kids were victimized, and that's just one of the evil clergy. I've learned from this not to trust anyone. I put my trust and faith in God alone. The religious, who I had highly respected, honored and trusted all my life, are now looked upon no differently than any other person on the planet.

I pray our church leaders will now adopt zero tolerance regarding sexual abuse of minors. No second chance, please! Offending clergy need to be turned over to the police. The Catholic Church must not, cannot police itself. Clergy offenders don't deserve special treatment. If anything, their crimes are worse because of the positions they hold.

I continue to pray for all the innocent clergy who are suffering from being painted with the same brush. Since trust is now gone, and one can't tell who is good and who is evil, the offending clergy must be removed for the good of the rest.

The leaders of our church have no one to blame but themselves for not doing the right thing all along. They knew what they were doing was wrong or they wouldn't have kept it secret. Keeping secrets allows no one to heal—the victim, the predator, or any of either's families.

Thank you for taking time to read this. I hope you will try to look at this problem from the layperson's viewpoint.

Sincerely,
Mrs. Carol Kuhnert

I was pleasantly surprised to receive a reply from our pastor (entire Mitas 8-05-02 letter in appendix). It gave me great hope when I read it, as it stated he couldn't disagree with anything I had written, even agreeing the church's sexual-abuse problems are self-inflicted wounds. While he didn't expect the media to say nothing, he didn't like their "piling on." Sometimes the truth hurts.

Chapter 12
Subpoena and Stroke

I started 2003 by writing to Bishop Naumann (entire 01-03-03 letter in appendix). I had become concerned while watching the evening news on Friday, December 27. Channel 2 in Saint Louis had shown a group of people picketing a Catholic youth vocal and musicians concert, which was performing inside the parish building at the time. A young man named Steve told the news reporter that the group's director had molested him when he was a member years before. I believed what he was saying because I knew of another accusation against the priest. A friend's daughter had made an accusation against the priest, and I went to Reverend Joe Naumann, who then was a young priest assigned at our parish at the time, to see what was being done about getting the accused priest removed from his position of working with children. He said the church had no plans to remove the priest. Reverend Naumann told me he was aware of what had happened, but since the girl wasn't willing to come forward and press charges, he said, "It wouldn't be fair to dirty the priest's name by removing him." I was disgusted with his response, even as he went on to assure me the priest would be sent for help. He claimed his hands were tied, because the victim wasn't willing to press charges. I don't understand how our church leaders can look the other way and allow a predator to remain in active ministry, working with children. This priest has yet to be removed. They will allow him to remain in his position, working with children, most parents unaware of any danger.

My letter to Bishop Naumann was meant to let him know how frustrated I had become over the years; I had lost all trust and respect for the church leaders. The church I had loved and from which I drew comfort all my life was gone. I was reaching out to him again in hopes he could influence others to bring about the changes needed to correct the shameful crisis in the church.

I found an article by Joseph Kenny in the February 7, 2003, *St. Louis Review* (a weekly Catholic paper) about another priest, Reverend John Hess, being sentenced for possession of obscene materials. Reading it added more fuel to my fire. I wrote a letter to Archbishop Rigali, with a copy to Bishop Naumann, along with a note expressing my doubt that Archbishop Rigali would pay much attention to my letter. I had greater hopes he would understand my frustrations

The *Review*'s article stated Father John Hess, the former pastor of Most Sacred Heart Parish in Florissant, Missouri, had been sentenced in February to three months in a halfway house, fined, and placed on probation after he had pled guilty to possessing obscene materials.

The article further stated this priest had pled guilty in federal court in May 2002 to a felony charge of possession of child pornography, but prosecutors later had to agree to let him substitute the obscene materials plea after his lawyer successfully raised an issue over a search warrant. Father Hess, age fifty-seven, got off with five years' probation and a $5,000 fine to go with a three-month sentence. He had faced a possible term of twenty-one to twenty-seven months in prison.

The article also told of FBI agents seizing a computer from Most Sacred Heart's rectory in March 2002 in a nationwide child pornography investigation, called Operation Candyman. The computer was found to have hundreds of images of child pornography on its hard drive; that information had come from the US Attorney's Office.

It aggravated me to see how the church agreed with Father Hess's attorney that accepting the lesser plea, which became available only because of an issue being raised over a search warrant, was the right thing for Father Hess to do, knowing he had already pled guilty to the felony charge of possession of child pornography. This is not what I had heard preached from the pulpit or in the confessional throughout my lifetime as the right thing to do when I had to choose between doing right or wrong. What had happened to accepting responsibility for what you've done and accepting the consequences? I don't remember it ever being suggested by clergy to look for a loophole.

In the middle of February, I received a very formally written letter from Bishop Naumann in response to my letter regarding Reverend Hess. Archbishop Rigali asked him to reply for both of them. He mentioned that some of the statements made about Hess hadn't been as clear as they could have been. It seemed he was defending this criminal.

Bishop Naumann thought I had misjudged the intentions of the bishops. He felt bishops had been very concerned for abuse victims and responsive in giving them assistance. I felt this seemed more like wishful thinking on his part, as I've seen no evidence of it, and I've been watching for the church's response for decades. When I asked the Survivors Network of those Abused by Priests in Saint Louis if there were many victims helped in such a way by the bishops, they couldn't name anyone.

I do agree with Bishop Naumann that accused priests are entitled to be innocent until proven guilty, like anyone else, but they must be held accountable for their crimes as well. If and when found guilty, they need to accept the punishment given by the courts, the same as any other criminal. They deserve no special treatment.

I do not see how the bishops have shown compassion to the needs of the victims, publicly anyway. From what I've observed, victims have been intimidated and further victimized by the church's attitude and its high-priced defense attorneys.

The manner in which Bishop Naumann's letter was written told me our longtime friend was now weighing his words carefully. It felt like yet another betrayal and loss and was quite unexpected. This letter was nothing like the casual notes we were accustomed to receiving from him. Only in the last paragraph did I see an indication of the supportive man we knew. I felt we had not just lost an ally; we had lost a good friend.

Excerpts from Bishop Naumann's February 17, 2003, letter of response (entire letter in appendix):

Dear Carol,

The archbishop and everyone in leadership in the archdiocese, since we first became aware of the investigation of Father Hess, have encouraged him to be honest and to cooperate fully with law enforcement authorities. ...

While the church recognizes and respects the right and responsibility of civil authorities to punish criminal activities ... we do not celebrate the necessity for anyone ... to be incarcerated. ...

The rehabilitation of offenders is premised upon their recognition and acknowledgment of the evil that they have done and remorse for the hurt and pain that they have inflicted upon others. ...

The church has consistently condemned all pornography. ... A person, who purchases child pornography, cooperates in the victimization of children ... but it is not the same sin as personally sexually abusing a child.

I understand your frustration ... However, I think that you misjudge the intentions of the vast majority of bishops. ...

Bishops have been very concerned for the victims of abuse and responsive in providing assistance for victims. ... At the same time, bishops have sought to protect innocent priests. ... Priests are entitled ... namely that one is innocent until proven guilty.

Finally, the church ... is about the work of mercy, not inflicting punishment. What the media has declared a "cover-up" was never that. The church does not advocate for public humiliation and punishment of anyone who has sinned. ...

Please give my regards to Joe and all your family. I remain grateful for all the kindness and support to me over so many years. ...

Sincerely,
Most Reverend Joseph F. Naumann
Auxiliary Bishop
Archdiocese of St. Louis

Nothing more has been heard of Father Hess since that time. This is frightening, because I would want to know if such perpetrators are living or working near me and my family. I think it is the bishops' responsibility to keep the public informed about them.

We received an e-mail from Norman on March 12, 2003, thanking us for a gift we sent in recognition of the forty-second anniversary of his ordination. He mentioned how painful it was for him to keep his profile as a priest invisible to everyone so as to protect himself and the archdiocese. Causing them more lawsuits was probably the worst thing Norman could think of happening anymore. The fact that he never mentioned one word of concern for any of his victims made me again question what kind of therapy he'd received all those years.

Norman mentioned his personnel file had been subpoenaed from the archdiocese by the Saint Louis County Prosecuting Attorney's Office, along with all the other priests ever accused of criminal abuse of a minor. He said, "There is nothing proactive that I can do to help myself. I can only be reactive if and when something happens in the legal arena. I do have legal counsel lined up, should that occur." He felt blessed to be living at the Regina Cleri Priests' Retirement Home and hoped to be able to spend the remainder of his life there.

Two months later, in May 2003, our phone rang as I was in the middle of washing my kitchen floor. I was surprised to learn it was a priest from Regina Cleri calling. He wanted to let me know my brother had suffered a stroke and had been admitted to Saint Mary's Hospital in Clayton, Missouri. One side of Norman's body was affected, and he would require a lot of physical therapy to recover.

When Joe and I visited him in the hospital, he seemed happy to see us. He was lying in bed, watching television, and told us, "I'm due in therapy soon, just waiting for someone to come get me. All this therapy is wearing me out. I get both physical and occupational, and they push me to my limits. Good news is that I'm expected to make a complete recovery." Norman was in good spirits, telling us about all the family and friends who had been by to visit. He seemed pleased so many had come. The only complaint he made was, "The meals are just hospital food, not all that great." We talked for about half an hour before someone arrived with a wheelchair to transport Norman to therapy. We walked with them to the elevator and then headed home.

He remained in the hospital for at least a month and eventually started walking again with the use of a walker. Norman continued physical therapy as an outpatient once he was released. He e-mailed me June 23, saying he was recovering but not as quickly as he would have liked.

My sister called, saying she had talked with Norman near the end of June. He told her the doctors had discovered a problem with his heart during a stress test and had decided to discontinue his physical therapy for a while. He had mentioned developing a new problem with his eyes, too, but he didn't go into any details as to what was wrong.

Chapter 13
Child Abuse Unit

It was the latter part of a morning near the end of May 2003. I was babysitting at one of my daughters' homes when my husband phoned and jokingly said, "Carol, what on earth have you done? The police just called here, asking for you!" He then went on more seriously, saying, "The detective said you weren't in any trouble; she just needed to talk with you." I glanced around my daughter's kitchen for a pen and paper to write the name and number I needed to call. I was to ask for a detective with the St. Louis County Child Abuse Unit. I couldn't imagine what it was about at the time, but I anxiously called the number right away. A very pleasant detective introduced herself to me and explained, "I am working on a child abuse case that happened in years past; it involved your brother, Father Norman Christian." A chill went through my body.

She went on, "We had subpoenaed your brother's personnel file from the archdiocese, and I came across the letters you had written him. I'd like to ask you some questions." Her politeness eased my nerves, and after we talked for a while, she asked, "Did you know your brother had been arrested?"

"No, I hadn't been aware of that," I answered. In fact, I was very surprised. "Norman failed to mention it to me." I was anxious to hear the details, so I quickly asked, "Where was he arrested, and when did this happen? Can you tell me how it all took place?"

"I arrested Father Christian on 'probable cause' earlier this month," the detective said. "I had gone to his workplace to arrest him, but he wasn't there. I went to his residence at the Regina Cleri Retirement Home several times, looking for him, but he was never home. After missing him so many times, I decided to leave my card for him, asking that he call me as soon as possible." She said he never called her, but that didn't surprise me. Norman never showed any signs of willingly accepting responsibility for the crimes he had committed. "Not hearing from Father Christian," the detective said, "I returned to the retirement home again; I finally found him home and arrested him."

"Did he have to post bail?"

"There's no need for bail on a probable-cause arrest. It's only needed after an arrest with a warrant. Father Christian was booked and processed and then released, pending a warrant."

I wondered what my brother was thinking while going through the humiliation of being arrested, booked, and processed for sexually abusing a child. Whatever grief he experienced couldn't compare to what his victims have suffered their whole lives because of what he did to them. I was pleased to learn of his arrest; he had finally been held accountable.

Luckily, my young granddaughter was at school and her little brother was napping when I made this call to the Child Abuse Unit, so our conversation went uninterrupted. At some point, I asked, "Did you know Norman had a stroke?"

"No, I hadn't been told."

I continued answering her questions the best I could. After a while, I told her, "I'll give you copies of all the papers I have pertaining to him. Maybe you'll find something that's helpful for one of his victims' cases."

"It must be difficult for you to talk with me about your brother," she said.

"The most painful thing was learning my brother was a pedophile," I replied, "and that he had even victimized my own daughter. Coming to grips with that was extremely difficult. Norman betrayed my family and many others throughout his priesthood. I think helping you is the right thing to do." I explained that I was as disgusted with the church as I was with him. "My brother committed countless crimes against children throughout his years as a priest, and the church has done nothing to warn anyone about him or remove him from active ministry. While it hurts terribly to know the truth about him, my concern is for all the children and their families he's hurt during his lifetime."

I wanted the detective to understand that I was relieved that a victim found the courage to tell the police what Father Christian had done to him. Finally, he and the church would be held accountable—at least for this one victim. I hoped others would find the courage to report their molesters, too, once they saw this victim was believed.

The detective graciously thanked me for talking with her and advised me that she might contact me again. I had just enough time to call Joe to let him know why the detective wanted to speak with me, before heading out the door with the baby to bring his sister home from school. I actually felt a sense of relief from having talked with that detective. I was glad she had called.

On March 1, 2003, the *St. Louis Post-Dispatch* ran an article by William Lhotka about Reverend Gary Wolken's receiving a sentence of fifteen years in prison for molesting a young boy over a three-year period while babysitting for friends. This seemed to me like a slap on the wrist for the damage the priest had done to that little boy and his family.

Reverend Wolken was removed from ministry at Our Lady of Sorrows church in March 2002 and was suspended from the priesthood. This pedophile pled guilty to statutory sodomy and child molestation. Even if he does serve the full fifteen-year prison term, however, he will still be a young man and a danger to children when he is released.

Joe and I were surprised to receive a card on September 13, 2003, from Bishop Naumann. He wrote that he had a practice of selecting a friend or coworker each day for which he would offer prayers and sacrifices of that day. He was letting us know he had chosen Monday, September 15, for our family to receive his prayers as a gift of our friendship. He mentioned his regret for "the personal pain" we were suffering because of the sexual abuse by clergy and the way it was being addressed by the bishops.

Though surprised by it, I really appreciated hearing from him again and especially appreciated his prayers for our family. I felt he had opened the door for me to again approach him with my concerns. I still held great hopes that he could influence the bishops to cease their cover-ups and remove molesters from ministry. After writing to thank him for his prayers, I expressed my aggravation about another priest abuse case that was reported by the media and then told him I'd be praying for him as well (entire 09-17-03 letter in appendix).

Norman e-mailed us on September 20 to thank us for an early birthday gift we had sent him. He seemed happy with plans for several days of birthday celebrating with friends and some old contacts from Saint William's.

He informed us that the hospital therapy he had been taking due to the stroke had ended, but he'd still be doing home therapy. He was quite happy to have passed the hospital's driving therapy test. Norman said he had decided to trade his stick-shift car for an automatic to make driving easier. He was satisfied with acquiring a 1992 Olds 88 with low mileage.

Norman mentioned playing cards with visitors in his room and getting to go to his first Cardinals baseball game, using the handicapped support. He said, "The service was excellent. They took me by wheelchair to and from my car to my seat at the game." He always loved the VIP treatment.

He would be returning to the monthly visits with the therapist who had been working with him regarding his sex addiction and would resume group therapy as well. It sounded as though he was getting his life back in order.

Upon reading the *Post-Dispatch* on October 5, 2003, an article titled "Rigali refuses to meet with abuse victims" jumped out at me. "Saint Louis Archbishop Justin Rigali refused one last time to meet with a clergy-abuse victims group, saying he was too busy before he moves to Philadelphia on Monday." SNAP had sent a letter to Archbishop Rigali, requesting a meeting on Sunday, but the Archbishop responded that his schedule was completely filled for the last two days he would be in Saint Louis before becoming archbishop of Philadelphia.

David Clohessy, SNAP's national director, expressed disappointment at Archbishop Rigali's response but wasn't surprised; neither the archbishop nor any other of the church hierarchy had met with any of SNAP's members in nearly a decade. Yet bishops across the country have made the time and found the compassion to meet with clergy-abuse survivors. Archbishop Rigali stated that other officials from the archdiocese could meet with them, and he would meet with the clergy-abuse victims in Philadelphia. It's sad that he never met with any of them here in Saint Louis. I hoped he showed more compassion to those in Philadelphia.

It was October 10, 2003, when I received another call from the St. Louis County Child Abuse Unit regarding one of their current investigations. The police officer asked if my brother had ever mentioned any of his victims' names to me. She hoped I would recognize the name of the young man in the current investigation. Unfortunately, I had to tell her he hadn't. "Norman was extremely careful never to reveal the names of anyone with whom he had been. He always was extremely private about his life and didn't spend too much of it with his family."

Norman had told me nothing of his sexual addiction until the time I learned of it from my daughter. Even when I asked him to tell me about it, he weighed his words very carefully. Actually, it was after he became so upset and angry over Jeanne's letter that Norman revealed certain facts to me that the hierarchy most likely would have preferred stay secret. The church continues to claim there have been no cover-ups in regard to the clergy sexual-abuse scandal, but I can't imagine what else to call its actions regarding predator clergy all these decades.

On October 13, 2003, I received upsetting news: Jeanne and her husband had been in an auto accident while on vacation. Their van was totaled, and they were in the hospital in another state. I thought Norman would want to know, so I called with the details. He wasn't too concerned; he hadn't even been aware they had gone on the trip. Soon after I related this news, he changed the topic of discussion to himself, saying he had gotten back to his sexual-addiction group-therapy sessions. I was glad to hear that. Norman also said that he'd discovered the therapy he'd received for the stroke alone had cost over $8,000, and he was very pleased the entire amount was covered by the insurance company.

Norman e-mailed us on December 3, 2003, while on retreat, to say thanks for a Christmas gift we had sent him. We knew he enjoyed eating at a certain pizza place not far from the priests' retirement home and had given him several of their gift certificates. He also mentioned getting to meet and shake hands with the new Archbishop of Saint Louis, Raymond Burke, who had stopped by Regina Cleri to pay a surprise visit to the residents. He thought Archbishop Burke was more personable than Archbishop Rigali, but that was his only impression of him.

A couple days later, I was sitting in the living room, crocheting an afghan while watching television. The phone rang, and when I answered, I heard Norman's anxious voice. "Carol, my name is listed as number thirty on SNAP's website!"

"What does that mean?" I asked.

"SNAP posts a list of accused clergy on the Internet. They've added my name to it. They've made my name public, but it's not as bad as if my name was in the newspapers or on television and radio. It takes special skills and equipment to access a website, and not as many people will see it. It's so much easier for people to get the news by picking up a newspaper or turning the television or radio on." Norman seemed to be trying to convince himself he had nothing to worry about.

"Norm, are you still going for your therapy sessions?" I asked.

He quickly replied, "Yes, I'm going for both group sessions and sexual-addiction therapy. I can go to my sponsor for help, as well as a woman I met on my trip to Israel. I'm doing okay." After we said good-bye, I discussed Norman's call with Joe. We realized it wouldn't be much longer before everything about Norman would appear in the media. It was just a matter of time, and the only control we had was how we would react when it happened.

I think Norman knew it was just a matter of time before his name, face, and crimes would be disclosed in the media, but he was doing a lot of wishful thinking in the meantime.

On December 5, 2003, the *Post-Dispatch* ran an article by Kim Bell about SNAP's planning to post a website that listed thirty alleged child molesters in the Catholic church clergy. Just the day before, members of SNAP had urged the Archdiocese of Saint Louis to release the names of all abusive priests, known or suspected. They said any number of such predators was walking around free, and it was extremely important parents knew about them so as to protect their children. The church claimed they didn't want to risk releasing names of innocent priests. Bishop Naumann said he would ask the archdiocese's sexual-abuse oversight committee about the proper way to handle releasing information about abuse allegations.

Each of the thirty persons listed on SNAP's website had worked in the St. Louis archdiocese and had been publicly accused of molesting a child, charged with a crime, or was the subject of a suit. It was possible that parents were not aware these men had been credibly charged or had served time if the church kept it covered up.

When Reverend Norman Christian was removed from his duties as the pastor of Saint William's parish, his parishioners were not informed that he was removed because he sexually abused children. Yet when Norman received mail or phone calls from old friends and parishioners, he took great comfort in the fact that many of them cared about him. Of course they cared about him; he was greatly respected, loved, trusted, and revered. His parishioners cared about the wonderful priest he presented himself to be. He carefully hid the shameful fact that he was a danger to their children, as did the church. Norman was deceiving himself as well. If he'd stopped the cover-ups and told the truth about himself, he would have seen everyone's true feelings for him.

I hadn't heard from Norman since that phone call, so I e-mailed him on December 17, asking if he had gotten any feedback from his name appearing on the SNAP website.

He e-mailed back the next day that "nothing has come of the public status." Again, he was thinking the website wasn't as public as a newspaper—back then, it was harder to access the Internet than just reading the paper.

Norman realized everything was out of his control at this point. He was simply waiting for the other shoe to drop. Still, his main concern was to protect the church from future lawsuits because of something he had done; nothing was more important. He made no apologies.

The year 2003 did not end peacefully for Norman, Jeanne, or me, as we worried and waited, wondering as we got up every morning if this would be the day news about Father Norman Christian's molesting children would be in the media. Through prayer, much thought, and all of what I learned through the years, I knew the shame was not mine. It belonged to my brother for what he had done and to the church for its extremely bad handling of the entire clergy sexual-abuse problem and their refusal to hold themselves accountable for any of it. Yet it was heavy on my heart, as thoughts of what my brother did ate away at me.

All my family and I could do was pray for strength and wait to see what was going to happen next. I especially appreciated my close friends at this time. Knowing they were just a phone call away was comforting.

Early in 2004, our pastor posted a question in his column of the parish Sunday bulletin in regards to a Gallop Poll that monitored church attendance of various denominations. He couldn't understand how Catholics' attendance could have slipped to an all-time low of 40 percent.

I wrote to him with my thoughts on what the problem could be, but I never received a response from him. He never called or mentioned it when he saw me at church; he just ignored my comments completely. He ended his bulletin column by asking, "What's going on?" I thought he was looking for feedback. Maybe I didn't tell him what he wanted to hear.

Our pastor's 01-11-04 parish bulletin article:

> BITS AND PIECES
> For what it's worth, the Gallup Poll has been monitoring church attendance of the various denominations in America since 1955, and its report for 2003 is in. For the first time, the Protestants have overtaken the Catholics in church attendance. In fact, the Protestants are at an all-time high (for them) at 47%, while we're at an all-time low 40%. When the poll started in 1955 it was 74% – 42% in our favor. What's going on?

Excerpts from my January 11, 2004, letter of response (entire letter in appendix):

> Well, Father Midas, when I was growing up back in good old 1955, all Catholics I know had 100% trust

in anything any religious said or did. ... Trust and respect were never an issue. With all that has come to light lately about how some of the religious took advantage of the trust given them over the years and how badly the church leaders dealt with complaints brought to their attention, the lack of people coming to church these days should come as no surprise to church leaders. The fact that it does tells me our church leaders still don't understand how big a hit trust in all religious took. ...

Now in 2004, many Catholics I know still have their faith in God; it's their trust in church leadership that is gone. ...

Catholics, maybe not all, but a large number, simply do not put much trust in what is coming out of our church leaders' mouths. ...

It's no surprise to me the church attendance is down. Maybe our church leaders don't want to accept the fact that trust in them is gone, just as some Catholics can't accept that these ugly things have really happened. In both instances, the truth is extremely hard to accept.

Sincerely,
Carol Kuhnert

Bishop Naumann was promoted and was moving to Kansas City. I wrote him a letter on February 12, 2004, letting him know how much he meant to our family and enclosed a monetary gift. I suggested he could take part of the credit for our children having developed into well-adjusted, happy, Catholic adults, happily married, and giving us nine terrific grandkids. That was just our family; he could multiply that by all the families he had encountered during his priesthood and get an idea of all the good he'd accomplished.

I also thanked him for letting me vent to him regarding my brother's addiction and my disappointment and lack of trust in the church leaders. I wished him much happiness and success in his new assignment.

CHAPTER 14
Media Exposes Father Christian

Joe and I had been away from home all day on March 3, 2004, and upon our return that evening, we found several messages on our answering machine. One was an emotional plea for support from Norman. He frantically told us, "There are bad things being said about me on the news! You can call Jeanne for all the details about the civil law suit against me and the church."

I thought it strange he didn't want me to call him back, but I guess he didn't want to answer his phone to anyone that night. We had several other messages on our machine from friends who were caringly reaching out to us, after having heard the news.

I called my sister, and she relayed the information Norman had given her—someone had filed a lawsuit against him and the archdiocese.

"He said they were saying horrible things about him through the media," Jeanne related. "He couldn't reach you and asked me to let you know. He really sounded scared."

We both had expected this day to come. I was glad his vile secret was finally exposed and hoped it would help comfort his victims.

I didn't sleep much that night. My mind kept replaying what my brother had done to the victim who came forward and so many others. And he still had not said he was sorry for hurting any of the kids while he served as a trusted and revered priest. I thought all night about how I could be of help to him. I hated what he had done, yet he was my brother. I wasn't going to turn my back on him, as long as he accepted the consequences for having sexually abused children throughout his life.

The following morning, I e-mailed Norman. I said, "I have determined the only way I can be supportive of you is if you do what you should have done the first time this ever happened; accept responsibility for your behavior, express sincere remorse to the victim and his family, turn yourself in to the authorities, and accept your punishment" (entire 03-04-04 e-mail in appendix).

I explained that I felt the church owned its own share of guilt for not dealing with these clergy sexual-abuse problems properly. I wanted him to think about the emotional turmoil he was experiencing, now that his name had been made public. I hoped that after thinking things through, he'd offer an apology to all his victims for what he had done.

The March 4, 2004 issue of the *St. Louis Post-Dispatch* ran an article, written by Peter Shinkle, on the suit filed against Norman and the Archdiocese of Saint Louis. It listed the plaintiff as John Doe TF and stated the police had arrested and questioned Father Christian the previous year, after a complaint had been made. It mentioned that additional information was still needed before going to the grand jury. The civil suit alleged the child was eleven years old when he was raped by Father Christian at Saint George Church in Affton, Missouri, in the early 1970s.

The Associated Press carried an article, written by Cheryl Wittenauer, on March 3, 2004, about a Saint Louis man suing a priest, archdiocese, and archbishop in a sexual-abuse claim in Saint Louis:

> The lawsuit, filed in St. Louis Circuit Court, alleged that the priest raped "John Doe TF" when he was eleven during an overnight stay in the priest's residence at Saint George Parish in south St. Louis County. ...
>
> In a written statement, the alleged victim, now in his 40s, said he filed the lawsuit "for the little boy who sat on the balcony at Saint George's crying for

his mother to hurry and pick him up" and for other children at risk of sexual abuse.

In a March 2004 written statement, the archdiocese said the priest was removed from active priestly ministry in May 1995, after church officials learned of an allegation of abuse of a minor against the priest that had occurred 20 years earlier. The priest, who was evaluated and admitted to a treatment program, now lives in a "monitored environment," forbidden to exercise any form of public ministry (entire archdiocesan statement in appendix). "The 68-year-old priest has not been defrocked," archdiocesan spokesman Jim Orso said. "It's only a matter of time."

He presumed wrong.

Chapter 15
Enlightenment

Our daughter Sue had told few people what her uncle was and what he did to her during her teens. When word of his being a pedophile became public, she decided to tell her in-laws that the reports in the news about her mother's brother were true. She knew they would be as shocked as everyone else and wonder if they should believe the news.

Sue e-mailed them on March 5, 2004, stating the accusation made against him was true and there probably would be more to come. She told them the church knew about his problem for much of his forty-three years as a priest and, after many attempts at therapy and finding it wasn't working, still chose to keep him in service, moving him around when problems arose.

She told them, "Unfortunately for me, my uncle befriended me during a very vulnerable and confused time in my life. He shared stories with me, took me places and told me and showed me things that were both disturbing and intimidating." Sue did not feel it necessary to share the specifics with them; it was bad enough that she was burdened with those memories. She explained that in 1987, after her son was born, "the protective mother in me took over, and I told my mom and dad about my uncle." Then she explained that the church always assured me it was taking care of the issue.

She told them my response to Norman's request for support and said she wanted them to know we were all right; they could talk with us about it. We felt blessed that they were and continue to be supportive. I say that because while many family and friends did stand by us, there were some who preferred to keep their distance.

I received a caring note from Bishop Naumann dated March 5, 2004: "I imagine the publicity surrounding the lawsuit against Norm has increased your pain. I pray the Lord, as only He can, eases your burden. I pray the Lord brings healing to all the hearts scarred by this tragedy."

He had always been there in the past for our family during stressful times, helping boost our morale. Receiving his note at this time was appreciated. We had been communicating for some time now regarding my feelings of the church's dodging responsibility when it came to the sexual-abuse scandal, and I thought he might choose to separate himself from me for becoming more publicly outspoken.

Bishop Naumann was the one church leader who reached out to me and my family with compassion and understanding throughout this ordeal, through his kind words and prayers.

The comforting, supportive phone calls we received from family and friends after word of Norman's crimes and the lawsuit against him and the archdiocese blared from the media meant so much to us during that painful time. We received a card on March 10, from some long-time friends, letting us know they were thinking of us, and we were in their prayers. I can't tell you how much it meant to receive their card at that very dark time. Knowing friends cared was a real blessing. No doubt there were many praying for our entire family during that extremely difficult time, and I'm grateful for everyone who did.

I started to wonder if my advice to Norman regarding the crimes he had committed was at odds with the advice the archdiocese gave him. I wrote Archbishop Burke a brief note (entire 03-11-04 note in appendix), asking what he advised Norman to do and enclosed a copy of my response to Norman's plea for support. I did the same with Archbishop Naumann (entire 03-11-04 note in appendix), as I wanted to hear the church's viewpoint from the both of them. I also wanted them both to read my advice to Norman, as Norman hadn't responded to me, and I hoped to learn something about what was happening to him. I couldn't understand why he would not plead guilty. As a priest, surely he wouldn't do anything but tell the truth. Again, I found myself questioning the therapy he received that programmed him so strongly to put protecting the church from future lawsuits as the most important thing.

I did eventually receive a response from Archbishop Naumann, but Archbishop Burke chose to ignore my letter.

Norman was about to mark the forty-third anniversary of his ordination the middle of March. In previous years, Joe and I had sent him a gift for the occasion, but we didn't know what to do this year. We decided to send him a card with a gift certificate to his favorite pizza place. I included a note, mentioning it was a horrible time to remember such a blessed event and prayed God would bless and keep him in His care as He guided him toward peace in his life.

Norman e-mailed us a thank-you on March 13, 2004, stating he saw "no reason to remember this anniversary in the future." He thanked us for the gift and hoped we'd all "find healing" in the life that remained for us. Not being able to serve as a priest anymore was quite painful for him. I wonder if he ever accepted his own responsibility for losing what he valued most in life: being a priest.

I received a response from Bishop Naumann dated March 13, 2004: "I have reviewed our files several times, and I find no indication that your judgment is accurate. I was not in archdiocesan leadership, but from everything I know of Archbishop May and everything that is in our records, there were no indications that Norm was not successfully living a chaste life."

I absolutely believe Bishop Naumann did review the church files several times, and he probably did not find indications that Father Christian was a danger to anyone. That's possible because of what Norman said about the archdiocese warning the therapists to be careful of what they put into personnel files. That being the case, there would have been no red flags in Norman's files for Bishop Naumann or anyone else to find. This practice leaves doors wide open for allowing predator clergy to serve in active ministry at unsuspecting parishes today and shows total disregard for vulnerable children's and adults' safety.

I sent a reply to Bishop Naumann (entire 03-18-04 note in appendix), thanking him for his note but asking again what the church was encouraging Norman to do regarding the current abuse suit. I wanted to know what our church leaders were advising Norman about making things right, now that he and the church were facing the lawsuit. I didn't see any reason why that information should be kept secret.

Archbishop Naumann responded April 18, 2004, apologizing for not responding more promptly, saying that my note got "caught up in the shuffle" of his recent move. He told me:

> The leaders of the archdiocese have always encouraged and counseled Norm to be honest and forthright about what he has done to injure anyone. He has been urged to disclose information about his conduct to anyone who would be helped by this information and/or to be able to receive the help to change his behavior. ... [Norman] is entitled to both civil legal counsel and canonical legal counsel. This is privileged information as I am not aware of what advice he received from civil lawyers or canon lawyers. ... There is only one person responsible for the hurt and pain that Norm's actions have caused, and that person is Norm himself; not his family, not any archbishop, not the church, etc.

I realize Norman caused the pain to his victims and their families, but the church enabled him to go on throughout his priesthood by keeping him in active ministry, moving him from parish to parish, thus allowing him access to new, unsuspecting families. The archdiocese sent him for treatment more than once for sexually abusing children—that alone should have told them he didn't belong in active ministry. I believe they must hold themselves accountable for contributing to the pain and destruction of these victims and their families' lives.

Church leaders would do well to give some serious thought to the huge number of people who left the church over the years because of the clergy sexual-abuse problem and how badly it was handled. Do they want to pretend those people don't exist?

Chapter 16
Criminal Investigator

One Thursday afternoon, I received a phone call from the Division of Criminal Investigators in Clayton, Missouri. The detective who phoned told me she would like to talk with Sue and me about Norman.

After checking with Sue, I scheduled an appointment for us to meet with the detective the following week. I gathered all my papers regarding Norman and made copies for the detective, hoping there was something that would be of help.

Sue and I were both nervous but that quickly diminished when we met the detective, a pleasant young woman who immediately put us both at ease. She took Sue to her office first to talk while I waited in the reception room. Afterward, the three of us discussed things together. It was not easy for Sue or me to talk with the detective, as old memories were stirred up, but it was obvious she appreciated our attempts to help her with the case. We cared about Norman's victims; helping the police seemed the right thing to do. Later, I learned that someone had questioned how I could "do that" to my brother, but I never turned him away. I was supportive of him to the very end. It seemed he just didn't want to hear what I was saying to him and chose to ignore me, never responding to any of my correspondence throughout the last year of his life. For my part, I felt he could not heal while keeping such a shameful secret and never apologizing to those he hurt.

In the first week of April, I left a message for the detective, asking her to call me—I hoped to get an update on Norman's case. My sister called later in the day, saying she had heard from Norman. He said that he expected the lawsuit against him and the archdiocese to end in a settlement, as previous ones had. I was surprised he believed that, as this lawsuit had been made public; it may have been wishful thinking on his part. He also told Jeanne that he was quite uncomfortable, as he was suffering from a case of the shingles.

On April 19, we received a letter listing new addresses and phone numbers for Archbishop Joe Naumann; his new residence was the Archdiocese of Kansas City in Kansas City, Kansas. I was still holding out hope that God had placed this good man in that position for a reason. He would be the one to help bring about change in the way the church was dealing with clergy sexual abuse.

Chapter 17
Sad but True

Through his column in the parish Sunday bulletin on May 2, 2004, our pastor had advised parishioners of a settlement the archdiocese made with a victim of a pedophile priest, the former Father Wolken, who had been convicted of child abuse. Our pastor's purpose was to assure parishioners that the archdiocese never had and never would use Archdiocesan Development Appeal money for such things.

I question that, because I do know that in January 1986, Norman told me how grateful he was to the Archdiocesan Development Appeal for helping to pay his huge bill for the program he was attending in New Mexico—it was going to cost over twenty thousand dollars just for him, and there were twenty-three other men there with him.

However, there was more about the column that I found disturbing.

Excerpts from our pastor's bulletin article (entire 05-02-04 article in appendix):

> SAD BUT TRUE
> Archbishop Burke faxed all the parishes with the sad news of the settlement in the case of the ex-Father Wolken, who was convicted of child abuse. He wanted to assure us all that the archdiocese

never has and never will use ADA (Archdiocesan Development Appeal) money for such things. ...

All I know about the case is what I heard via the various media, and since the charges were not contested, I can only infer they are true. In my opinion, the man should have been flogged, drawn, and quartered. Still, I have a hard time understanding why the archdiocese has to pony up for his crimes. ... Before a man is ordained a priest, he undergoes twelve years of intensive formation and testing. This was the case with the man in question. How was the archdiocese negligent? ...

I think we all know the answer. The man I question didn't have any money; the archdiocese does. Plaintiffs know that. Their lawyers know that. ... If the archdiocese can be proven negligent, that's different. But I disdain and deplore ... it's just taken for granted the diocese has to pay big bucks when one of its trusted priests commits an actionable offense.

Tort reform? Count me in!

Father Mitas

As I read his column, I hoped to read something that encouraged his parishioners to pray for this victim and the many others like him. He could have asked everyone to open their minds and hearts to all the victims of clergy sexual abuse, but he didn't.

It really is sad but true. The only things important to the archdiocese are its assets, image, and protecting its clergy. Nowhere in this column was there any care shown for the victim of this abusive priest. The article implied the victim only filed the suit to get money from the archdiocese. Very sad indeed to think the victim's plight was completely unimportant; the victim's concerns were ignored. Victims learn quickly that the church prefers to ignore them and that it may take a financial lawsuit to gain its attention. Victims I've met or learned about over the years mainly wanted to be believed and to see their abusers removed from ministry so others would not be harmed. They've expected an acknowledgment of wrongdoing and hoped for a sincere apology from the church for not having protected them.

Surprisingly, Father Mitas's column showed no care for the ex-priest who had committed the crime either. True, what he had done was horrid, but isn't the Catholic Church's position one of forgiveness? This priest had gone through all those years of training in the seminary. What might have been observed during his seminary years that was simply dismissed by those who were preparing him for the priesthood? Had he possibly been a victim of abuse there himself, as was the case with my brother? I believe the church is accountable for the men they present to us as trusted, reverent priests. There may be grace in ordination, but I don't believe it can cure molesters.

It was now the middle of June, and I felt as though Norman had deleted me from his life. It seemed that Norman was acting toward me as he had acted to our cousin's husband a while back. Surely if he had become ill and was unable to correspond, someone from the archdiocese would have let his family know. I decided to e-mail him again.

Excerpts from my June 17, 2004, e-mail (entire e-mail in appendix):

> Hi Norm,
>
> You are on my mind and in my prayers daily. I wonder if you have given any thought to what I suggested months ago that you do about the latest accusation. I imagine your canon lawyer and church leaders are encouraging you to admit nothing, so as to protect the church's assets from more lawsuits. I know it upsets you greatly when the archdiocese has to pay a victim because of your behavior.
>
> Norm, I am encouraging you to think about what has happened to your victims' lives. Please put aside your fears of what will happen to you by turning yourself in. While you may fear it, you have earned any punishment that's coming. Your victims didn't earn or deserve the misery they are living with. They were children, trusting someone they had been taught to respect and obey.

> The archdiocese has made mistakes with many priests and has its own problems to correct. ... I feel terribly angry with our church leadership. They still come across to me as trying to cover up what's happened over the years. I pray for God to guide them to do the right thing now. Meanwhile, I'll continue praying that God will bless you and guide you to do the right thing.
> Love and prayers,
> Carol

He replied June 25, asking that I not e-mail him anymore.

I wanted to keep Norman thinking of all the people he had harmed throughout his years as a priest. I hoped he might have a change of heart and make a general apology. I contacted him again on July 31, 2004 by mail, but I was starting to feel unsure of what I'd said to him. I turned to Joy and Charlie, old friends that Joe and I had met many years ago through a brain tumor support group when our youngest daughter was recovering from brain surgery. Sadly, their own beautiful daughter, Julie, lost her young life after many surgeries and years of fighting brain cancer. While Joy and Charlie are of another faith, I've never known more God-loving, faith-filled people than they and their family. I discussed my concerns with Joy, and she assured me I had been doing right by reaching out to my brother as I had been. As we talked and pondered some Scriptures, more ways occurred to me to try to reach him. Never once was she judgmental of anyone; she only shared my concern that Norman eventually would tell those he had harmed that he was sorry. I especially valued Joy and Charlie's friendship and support during this particularly difficult year with my brother. I feel very blessed to count them among our friends.

My July 31, 2004, letter to Norman:

> Dear Norman,
> I think about you and pray daily for God to help us both. I need help in my struggle to regain trust and respect in all church leaders. I pray He will impress

on your heart what you need to do to get peace for those you've harmed and for yourself.

As a priest, you let people down, and they need to know you understand how badly you hurt and misled them. They are broken and trying to put their lives back together. The church leaders also let them down. People turning to clergy for guidance in living their faith had their trust violated. They need to hear you acknowledge that you failed them and are deeply sorry. Then they may be able to reach out again with trust and respect for the church/clergy.

I believe God loves you and will give you the strength and courage to make things right. I hate what you've done, but you're my brother, and I love and care about you enough to say these things to you. Please put the needs of those you've hurt before your own or the church's needs, so they may begin to heal. God bless you and keep you in His care.

Love and prayers,
Carol

Another month went by with no word from Norman, so I decided to reach out to him again. I knew he was refusing to apologize for his crimes because he believed that would open the door to more lawsuits for the archdiocese. He didn't want that to happen. I was sickened even more to know that he continued to put the archdiocese above helping those he had hurt find peace.

My August 30, 2004, letter to Norman:

Dear Norm,
Again, I ask please give serious thought to personally apologizing to those you've abused. What you decide to do when you are in a difficult situation tells everyone who you are and what you're about much more than your behavior when things are going well. I'm praying you will do the right thing to help those you've hurt find peace.

I've always understood the church to say we were not to be concerned about acquiring material things; rather, be concerned about our spiritual lives. I thought that applied to the church and its leaders, too. God bless you and keep you in His care.

Love and prayers,
Carol

I had just mailed Norman my letter when I read another article in the newspaper about the archdiocese agreeing to help victims with their counseling expenses in response to their claims of sexual abuse; otherwise, the archdiocesan lawyer said, "The accusers would receive nothing because of the statute of limitations defense" (Tim Townsend, 08-26-04, *Post-Dispatch*).

While the church would be doing the right thing by helping victims with counseling expenses, I thought they needed to do more. Considering that we are speaking of our *moral* leaders, they must set the right example and work toward getting legislation passed to eliminate the statute of limitations completely on child sexual abuse so all evil perpetrators can be brought to justice. Too many victims see nothing happen to their abusers because of the statute of limitations. Why isn't the Catholic Church, with its moral philosophy, working along with those who have been trying hard to get that statute eliminated?

I wrote another note to Norman, relaying my disgust. The following is excerpted from that September 1, 2004, letter (entire letter in appendix):

Hi Norm,

I just read the 8-26-04 *Post* article stating, "The archdiocese has agreed to help people with their counseling expenses in response to their claims of sexual abuse." Archdiocesan lawyer Goldenhersh said the accusers otherwise would receive nothing "because of the statute of limitations defense." ...

The people I was taught to look to for spiritual and moral guidance are paying a lawyer to work the system in order to keep the Catholic Church from

going broke. ... Norm, don't you find it strange that a priest who recently admitted to stealing money from his parish publically apologized for what he did, but you and others like you are told to admit nothing? ... Please think about it, Norm; it's not just about the money. An "I'm sorry I did it. You trusted me, and I let you down. I am so very sorry" would go a long way in helping your victims. It may even help you find peace.
Carol

As I looked over the September 3, 2004, issue of the *St. Louis Review*, I came across an article by Joseph Kenny pertaining to sex-abuse settlements; the mediation process was explained. Bernard Huger, an archdiocesan attorney, said "The goal is to provide a means for healing for those whose allegations are found to be credible. ... We don't feel the archdiocese has actual responsibility, but since the priests don't have money and there is injury, somebody has to help the people or no one will. So the archdiocese steps up." Mr. Huger stated the mediation process was meant "as an initiative to pastorally respond to anyone who has been a victim. ... Rather than go into a public courthouse and present their case, which is very painful ... they have an avenue to use at a completely neutral office."

He explained that the mediator was assisted on a couple cases by a retired judge; both were picked by both sides in those cases.

He also said the process included some people specializing in mental health professions, to help assess the victims' needs, adding, "It's a very intense process." The victims usually come with family members, therapists, or attorneys. They have a difficult time telling of their abuse, even in a private office, "but we do think this is easier for victims. They tell their story once, and at the end of the day, it's resolved." Yes, the church can just cross these victims and their families off their list and move on to other things, but the pain lingers on for those who suffered the deception and sexual abuse by clergy. There is no easy time for them.

He further stated, "I have the highest respect for the committee members, all volunteers, who give an entire day to go through this."

His compassion seems greater for what the volunteers endured for one day than for the victims' lifetime of anguish. The entire day is full of testimonies reliving the abuse and its aftereffects. By the end of the day, the victim is a heap of raw emotion and completely drained. To give the impression that the mediation process somehow fixes everything by the end of the day is ridiculous. His remark lacks even the slightest amount of understanding or compassion for what these victims have been struggling with since the abuse.

As quoted above, Mr. Huger states the archdiocese does not have actual responsibility. Who, then, has assigned priests to parishes, sent predator priests to treatment programs, reassigned them to active ministry, and moved them around from parish to unsuspecting parish, putting children in harm's way?

Chapter 18
Norman on Deathbed

It was nearly the middle of October 2004. I hadn't heard from Norman since March, when I told him what he needed to do to have my support. While folding laundry one morning, I received an unexpected phone call. A woman introduced herself as a friend of my brother and said, "I'm sorry to inform you that your brother is extremely ill with kidney and liver failure. He is in the ICU at Saint Mary's Hospital." She gave me Norman's room number and added, "The doctors believe he may only have a week to live, and your brother gave me permission to call you about his condition."

Hearing that, my thoughts turned to all those he had abused. It saddened me that upon his death, the current case pending against him would have to be closed. That victim would never have the satisfaction of seeing Father Christian found guilty in court.

I had no idea what Norman had shared with this woman about his relationship with his sisters, but she seemed sympathetic in relaying the news. Letting her assume what she wanted, I responded, "I appreciate your calling to let me know, but you can tell him I won't be coming to see him. Please tell Norman he's in my prayers."

She said she'd tell him. I thanked her again for calling and said good-bye. Norman had ignored my correspondence all year, and I really had no more to say to him, but he was on my mind the rest of the day.

Jeanne called me a short time later after receiving a similar call, asking if the woman had called me.

"Yes, she said he didn't have long to live," I answered, "and that Norman had told her it was okay to call us. I had no idea he was sick, but then, I've barely heard from him since March, when that lawsuit against him became public."

"I didn't know he was sick either," Jeanne replied.

"He had sent an e-mail at the end of June, saying, 'Do not e-mail me in the future. I am doing the best that I can to take care of myself. Please respect my wishes.' He added that e-mail is insecure and remains in cyberspace forever, so I started mailing him letters instead. Norman didn't respond to any of them. Have you had any contact with him since then?"

"I can't remember the last time I've heard from him," Jeanne replied.

We talked a little about Norman's situation and both wondered if AIDS was a contributing factor to his approaching death. Once before when Norman was hospitalized, neither of us had seen him in quite a while and were shocked when we visited him. He had become extremely thin; he looked like a skeleton. Knowing what he had previously told us about his lifetime of seeking sex, even from strangers, we both feared back then that he may have contracted AIDS.

I told Jeanne I was not going to the hospital. "He's ignored all the letters I've sent him this year. I doubt he wants to see me now. I have nothing more to say to him."

"Al and I are going to visit him," Jeanne said.

I told her I'd talk with her later, and we said good-bye. I was still comfortable with my decision. Thinking about it now, my sister had little contact with Norman since the time he blew up at her for the letter she had written him. She may have had some things she needed to say to him.

On Monday, October 18, Jeanne got another call from the same woman. Norman had taken a turn for the worse. Jeanne called to let me know. I thanked her for the information but told her it didn't change my mind about going to see him. However, after that phone conversation, a thought popped into my mind. I quickly wrote Norman a short note and mailed it directly at the post office so he would receive it the very next day. It simply told Norman that the minute I heard a generic apology—just a simple admission that he had let people down as a priest and was sorry—made to all those he'd hurt during his years as a priest being broadcast in the media, I'd be right there at his side.

I figured he had completely shut me out of his life by ignoring all my letters that year. He had all that time to say whatever he wanted to say to me. Surely now, someone there with him could help him make any calls he wanted to make.

I had no need to see or speak with my brother now. I had forgiven him for betraying our family as he did. I said all I had to say to him. I knew he would soon be answering to God for the things he had done. There was nothing I could do for him. I was at peace in knowing the news of Father Norman Christian's death would help soothe many of his victims as they learned of it, knowing he wouldn't be able to harm any more children.

My cousin e-mailed me October 17, 2004, saying that her son visited Norman right after he was admitted to the hospital. He had met a number of Norman's priest friends there. She told me Norman had gotten discharged at the time her son was there, and he had helped with getting Norman into his friend's car for a ride back to the priests' retirement home. However, Norman had taken a turn for the worse after getting home and had to be rushed back to the hospital ICU. It was then that Norman gave permission for Jeanne and me to be notified of his condition; it appeared he was giving up.

My niece, Patricia, or "Pete," as she prefers to be called, was a flight attendant and happened to be in town on a layover when we were discussing the fact that her uncle was dying. She told me, "I will never forget receiving that phone call: 'Uncle Norman is on his deathbed.' The hollowness of the phrase echoed in my head. To say I was upset would be an understatement, knowing that his entire career as a revered priest of the Catholic Church was a sham. I was actually relieved to know he would never be able to harm anyone ever again."

We wondered about the many people Norman had abused, and we thought that the Survivors Network of those Abused by Priests would certainly want to have information about his being near death. Pete pointed out, "It would be the victims' last chance to confront the man who had stolen their childhood and wreaked havoc on their lives."

I asked her to contact SNAP to let them know, and I would pass the information on to the detective working on Norman's current abuse case.

I spoke with the detective on the phone the next day and told her Norman was near death. She informed me, as I had assumed, that her case against him would be closed once he died. We both felt bad for the victim; he'd be greatly disappointed that his chance of seeing Father Christian found guilty by a jury through the court system was gone. Sadly, it looked as though the predator priest was going to win again.

The detective called David Clohessy, National Director of SNAP, to give him word of Norman's being near death and was puzzled by the fact that they already knew about it. My niece had already talked with David, but while SNAP was grateful to have received the information, we learned later they didn't trust us. Pete and I were the priest's family, and they didn't understand our motives. Why were we reaching out to them? This kind of thing had never happened before, so they were not sure they could believe or trust us; they didn't know what to expect.

Pete described the call she made. "I urgently entered the phone number I found for SNAP, and David Clohessy answered the phone. I told him I was Father Christian's niece, and I advised him of Uncle Norman's declining health. Wasting no time, he thanked me for calling and immediately contacted the man that had brought the lawsuit against Uncle Norman. He told him that Father Christian was on his deathbed, and if he wished, he could take advantage of this final opportunity to confront the man who had abused him. After talking it over with David, the man had essentially concluded that his legs wouldn't support him at the bedside of his abuser. He simply could not bear to see that guy again.

"David called back to let me know that although the man was extremely appreciative to have received the information, he was going to decline the opportunity to confront Father Christian. My heart sank for this person as I thought of the inescapable pain that must have accompanied him throughout his life. It would be nothing short of a travesty if his feelings were never expressed to his abuser.

I thought, if he couldn't manage to do it, maybe someone could do it for him. It seemed imperative that I speak with him, so I asked David if I could call the man. Understandably, he was unwilling to give me the man's name and number without permission, but as soon as he got the okay, he gave me the phone number and told me his name was Tim. I wasted no time in calling him."

When she called and identified herself as Father Christian's niece, Pete said she didn't know it then, but Tim was worried that she had an ulterior motive for contacting him. His gut reaction was one of dread. A relative of his perpetrator was calling and probably wanted to berate him for daring to accuse her dying family member of wrongdoing. Still, he was curious and decided it was worth taking the call.

Gently, Pete said, "I understand you were a victim of Father Christian, and I just want to let you know that I am so very sorry for what he did to you." She detected a sigh of relief from Tim as she compassionately explained her reason for calling. "I want you to know that my aunt and I are truly sorry for what happened. If there is anything we can do for you, you have our total support."

"I appreciate what you're saying, but you don't have anything to be sorry for. You weren't responsible for your uncle's actions, but I am thankful you believe me."

Pete then said, "David explained that you didn't feel up to seeing Father Christian again, but how about having someone else deliver your message for you? Just tell me what you would like to say. I'll make sure he hears it."

Pete told Tim to think about it and call her later with his decision. He called her back that same evening, telling her the message he wanted Father Christian to hear. She realized how important it was to him when she had to promise him three times that his message would be delivered verbatim: *"You didn't get away with it. I told people about what you did, and they believed me, not you, the priest. You're dying in shame, and God will deal with you and all of those who have protected your kind."*

"That's perfect," he said.

She asked Tim if it would be okay if I delivered the message, as Pete was now living in Florida. He agreed, and Pete then promised, "I'll have Aunt Carol call you as soon as she can."

Pete told me later, "The thought of my uncle hearing Tim's powerful message made me smile as I hung up the phone." We both admired this young man for finding the courage to tell the police of Father Christian's abusing him.

"I was in tears listening to Tim's faint voice describing Uncle Norman's abuse," Pete told me. "He's married now, with two kids, and wonders if his son reaching the age when he was abused led him to report the abuse he suffered in his own childhood." Pete choked back tears as she continued, "I told Tim how truly sorry all of our family is for what happened to him. My heart was breaking. When he called back later with his message for Uncle Norman, I could tell he wanted so badly to do it himself but just couldn't."

Pete and I both understood the importance of Norman's hearing what Tim had to say, and then she asked me if I'd be able to deliver Tim's message to him.

Although I'd just sent Norman a note stating I would not visit him until I heard an apology to all his victims, I had second thoughts about that and told her, "Under the circumstances, I'll do it! It's important that Norman hears his victim's message."

I was barely finished speaking when Pete quickly responded, "No, Aunt Carol. I want to deliver Tim's message to Uncle Norman. It's an honor to do it for him. One way or another, I'll find a way to get to Saint Louis before he dies so I can deliver the message."

By Thursday, October 21, Norman had given permission for someone to use his computer to e-mail everyone listed in his contacts about his health issues. The e-mail stated, "Norm asked me to use his e-mail list to let people who care about him know his health situation. He is very, very ill." His current phone number and address were included, along with an invitation to join him for lunch or just visit with him at the nursing home, adding that complimentary meals would be available for friends and relatives. "I'm in the process of shutting down his computer (as per his wishes)," the e-mail went on, "so be advised that it's highly unlikely that a response to this e-mail would reach him. ... Please keep our dear friend Norm in your prayers."

That same day, I nervously called the number Pete had given me to reach Norman's victim. The man was expecting me to call, but I still felt anxious. After all the years of hoping and praying for a victim to report him to the police, why was I so afraid to speak to the one who actually did? I wanted to tell this man how sorry I was that my brother had molested him; our whole family felt bad for him and for everyone Norman had victimized.

My heart was beating rapidly as I entered each of the numbers on my phone to reach Tim. Though I wanted him to know how sorry I was for what Norman had done to him, I worried that talking with me might cause him more pain. The phone only rang twice before he answered. I identified myself and said that Pete told me it was okay to call him. I told him that I was open for any questions he might have. I described what the situation had been between Norman and Sue and said that I'd found out from her that Norman had been abusing children. I became less nervous as I told Tim what I'd experienced over the years in trying to get the archdiocese to do something about my brother's sexual addiction and that of other clergy like him.

"I'm so disgusted with how the church has dealt with its clergy sexual abuse, protecting its assets, image, and predator clergy, while ignoring the victims," I said. "It is completely immoral and unacceptable. The last time I heard from my brother was back when your lawsuit against him and the church hit the media. He was scared and had called me looking for support."

Tim seemed pleased to know that Father Christian was scared that day, telling me, "He should have been scared."

I then told Tim about my decision not to support Norman any longer unless he turned himself in, confessed his crimes, apologized to his victims, and accepted his punishment. "After that time," I said, "I heard little from him."

Tim listened intently as I told him of my getting word that my brother was dying. "Even then, I was determined not to see him, and I quickly wrote him a short note, reiterating that I wouldn't visit him until I heard his apology broadcast over the media."

Tim seemed pleased that I had sent Norman that message, saying, "That's great. It just amazes me that my abuser's family would stand up for me."

"Over all these years, I never heard my brother say he was sorry for having hurt children," I said, my frustration causing my voice to rise. "Tim, my family and I are very sorry he caused you so much pain."

I thanked Tim for talking with me, and then Tim softly stated, "I've come pretty far in letting go of my anger and getting on with my life."

"Tim, you did the right thing in reporting Father Christian," I responded. "You're a wonderful role model for your own kids. Know that Father Christian's family believes you and supports you, not him. You told the police what he did, and they believed you. Thanks to your courage, he and the church will finally be held accountable. They can't cover up for him anymore."

Tim had listened patiently to all I had to say. At this point, he slowly began to give me a sketchy picture of what had happened between my brother and him. I'm glad I planned ahead, having a large box of tissues nearby, because what I heard was heartbreaking.

Tim began by telling of an unusual break he had at work one day. "This guy I worked with was reading the newspaper and suddenly he looked at me and asked, 'Were you ever Catholic?' I wondered why he asked but told him, 'I used to be.' I expected he'd ask why I left the church. I've been asked that a lot and was ready to fend off any ideas of coming back. But he didn't say anything; he just kept on reading. Minutes later, he looked back at me and asked, 'Were you in Sacred Heart Parish in Festus?' That question threw me, but I told him I had been. With that, he asked if I'd known Father Christian. That scared me! I didn't know if I could trust talking to this guy, but I said that I did know him. The next words out of his mouth were, 'Father Christian was weird.' And I said, 'Father Christian was a child molester!' The guy looked at me with this shocked look on his face and asked, 'How did you know?' I just told him, 'Me too.'

"Then he asked if I'd ever gone to the police. I told him those guys don't ever get in trouble, so why would I go to the police? This guy hadn't gone to the police either, but he showed me the article he was reading. It was about some priest getting arrested.

"I immediately thought of Father Christian's telling me, 'Who do you think they'll believe—you, a kid, or me, a priest?'"

Hearing Norman's warning to Tim stunned me, as he had used the same intimidation tactics with Sue.

Tim continued, "My coworker asked if I'd ever heard of SNAP. He explained it was a group of people who have been sexually abused by priests. They support each other and work together in trying to get molesters removed from ministry. He showed me SNAP's contact information, and as soon as I got home, I looked up SNAP's website. Still, it was weeks before I found the courage to make that call. I was so glad when I finally did. That was the beginning of getting the help I really needed."

Tim spoke quietly as he told me how my brother had entered his life. "My parents were divorcing when I was about eight years old—that's when Father Christian got friendly with me. We took bike rides, saw movies—he just made me feel special. I worshiped him, and I felt awful when he was moved from our parish. I missed him so much. Then one day, he called my mom and invited me to spend a weekend with him at his new parish in Saint Louis. I couldn't have been happier or more excited! Father seemed happy to see me, too, but after my mom headed back home, his mood changed, and he started making me feel stupid and ashamed by the things he did and said. He kept it up, and I couldn't understand why he was acting that way. He had never done that before."

Tim did not go into details, but he managed to give me a good idea of the abuse he endured. He spoke of "something horrible happening in the middle of the night." Father Christian had done "something he had no business doing to me. I was scared to death and ran to call my mom to come get me right away! It seemed she'd never get there. I was so glad when she finally arrived. I cried the whole way home, unable to talk about what had happened. Father was following us home in his own car, so I sobbed to her, 'Just ask him.'"

I loathed my brother for his depraved behavior, and my heart broke for this young man. Tim then brought up his message to Norman, saying, "Pete told me you would deliver my message to Father Christian if she couldn't make the arrangements to do it herself."

I assured him, "Don't worry; your message is going to reach Father Christian one way or another." If Pete couldn't make it happen, I would.

I thanked Tim again for talking with me but mostly for having the courage to tell the police what Father Christian had done to him. I knew the church required that a victim be willing to face his abuser in court before they would give any consideration to removing the priest from ministry. Tim was a courageous hero in my eyes. Since he had come forward and pressed charges, my brother and the church were finally being held accountable. Father Christian's cover-ups were over.

Norman was moved from the hospital to a comfortable room at a nursing home located in North Saint Louis, near the airport. His move proved to make Pete's anticipated visit a lot easier for her flight to Saint Louis from Florida that coming weekend. Our biggest concern now was if Norman would live long enough for Pete to make her visit at the end of the week. I prayed all week long that God wouldn't take him before Pete could pay that visit.

On Sunday evening, October 24, I received a call from Pete.

She had delivered Tim's message.

"Aunt Carol, I just came from Uncle Norman's room. I'm in my car in the parking lot. He seemed stunned when I gave him Tim's message, but he never said he was sorry. He told me that I didn't understand. I've let Tim know his message was delivered, and now, I'm drained and need to get to my hotel and try to get some sleep."

Pete called the next morning, excitedly telling me that we were invited to meet with David Clohessy, the national director of SNAP, along with Tim and Bill McClellan, a *Post-Dispatch* newspaper columnist who wanted to interview all of us. Pete had told them everything would have to come together quickly, as she was scheduled to work a flight out of Florida in a couple of days. With such short notice, we didn't have time to get nervous.

Pete, Sue, and I arrived at David's home early Monday evening, where the meeting was to take place, just as Bill McClellan was arriving too. We were told at the door that Tim and his wife had already arrived and were waiting inside. I felt very uncomfortable walking into the room and coming face-to-face with the man my brother had sexually abused as a child. What could I say? Hello? It's nice to meet you? I'm sorry for what happened to you? Nothing seemed right. I wanted to hug him but thought he might not want me to touch him. I don't remember exactly what I did say, but I nodded a hello to the young man in jeans and a sweatshirt, sitting quietly with his wife beside him. I tried to hide the tears that were rolling down my face as I quickly walked past them to a chair. Thoughts of the pain this man and his family had endured for decades weighed me down. Everyone sat around the coffee table in David's living room, and his two delightfully talented children lightened the mood a bit by playing a few selections on their musical instruments. We all enjoyed their entertainment, but once they were sent off to do their homework, our serious conversation got underway.

We all took turns speaking that evening. It still brings tears to my eyes as I remember it now. It was an evening of mixed emotions, to be sure. I was very angry and disgusted with my brother for having betrayed so many parents' trust. I felt so bad for this young man and for his keeping such a horrible secret for decades—an innocent, trusting kid who was raped by my own brother, a priest.

It was heartbreaking to realize that decades of closeness and love that should have been between Tim and his mother was destroyed because of Father Christian's lies and betrayals.

Tim's wife sat quietly and calmly beside him that entire evening. Her concern for him was obvious, and I admired her strength in supporting him all those years, especially when he had courageously decided to report his abuser to the police.

I spoke of how I had learned that Norman was a child molester and what I experienced with him and the church leadership from that point. My niece spoke about the visit with her uncle in the nursing home, where she delivered Tim's message. We were all eager to hear the details.

She began, "Uncle Norman was expecting me, as I had called the nursing home to advise them when I would arrive. For much of the previous two days, I pushed away recurring thoughts that the Grim Reaper would deny me this final visit with him. I desperately hoped I would get there to deliver the message before he died. On October

24, I was in flight to Saint Louis, and it felt as though we had just taken off when the captain announced we'd soon be landing—I had spent the entire two-and-a-half hour flight pondering the myriad ways my uncle's self-serving actions had affected not only his victims but also those with whom his victims had loving relationships. As my thoughts turned to the upcoming face-off, my mind raced, and my anxiety peaked. I've never been the type who enjoys verbal showdowns. I'd sooner walk away than get into a heated debate.

"As I made my way off the plane, it hit me that what mattered was not my uncle's reaction to hearing Tim's words but only that he heard them. I don't recall picking up the rental car, and I don't remember what the weather was like. The car practically drove itself as I pondered the mundane goings-on of those with whom I shared the road. Surely their days would contain nothing of significance when compared to the profound event that was about to unfold in mine.

"Upon reaching my destination, I took a moment to rehearse once more the words Tim had dictated to me. Then, with one deep breath, I was on my way up the driveway to the entrance of the nursing home. My palms were sweating, and I cursed the trembling in my legs. I passed a nun who was leaving, and I wondered if she knew what I was about to do. There were three other nuns meandering in the foyer, and one of them softly asked if she could be of assistance. I told her 'I'm here to see my uncle, Father Norman Christian.' With a look of pity in her eyes, she told me his room number and pointed down the hall.

"I hadn't seen him in years, and I hoped he wouldn't be suspicious of my visit. Most likely, the only family members who had come to visit would have been those whose unconditional Catholic faith dictated steadfast support, even in the aftermath of his admission to having sex with little boys. I opened the door to his room and entered. The nun standing at his bedside turned and greeted me. I wondered how much this nun knew of my uncle's career in pedophilia. Surely she knew, but did she emphatically support the church's protection of him? I didn't want to be thrown out of his room until I had delivered Tim's message and gotten some sort of response from this despicable man, so I altered my demeanor from woman on a mission to that of a sweet, loving niece—and the nun excused herself from the room."

We were all eager to hear what happened next. Pete continued, "As I approached my uncle's bed, it occurred to me that his gaunt, gray face seemed a more accurate warning of the monster that lived within than the smiling face of deception he had previously worn. He seemed glad that I had come, and his smile might have been bigger if he'd have had the energy to invest in it. It was obvious he thought I was there just to bid my final farewell. *What an arrogant son of a bitch*, I thought.

"I said, 'Hi, Uncle Norman.' He quickly responded with 'Hi, Patty,' making me cringe. Only a few family members refer to me by my given name. I wasn't accustomed to hearing it. Still wearing the same innocent smile I had put on for the nun, I said, 'I came to deliver a message to you.' My smile disappeared as I asked, 'Does the name Tim Fischer ring a bell?'

"The expression on his face went flat as he quietly answered yes. I asked, 'Do you remember Tim Fischer?' Again, he solemnly said yes. I told him, 'Tim really wanted to be here himself, but he just couldn't make it. I have a message he wanted me to give you.' I took the paper from my pocket and said, 'Let me read it for you. *You didn't get away with it. I told people about what you did, and they believe me, not you, the priest. You're dying in shame, and God will deal with you and all of those who have protected your kind.*'

"My uncle turned his head away from me and looked at the floor. I couldn't tell whether this was done out of shame for what he had done or disappointment that I had forsaken him on his deathbed. He said nothing, so I asked, 'Do you have anything to say to Tim?' He merely shook his head and said no. I told him, 'I fear for your soul when you die, Uncle Norman. Aren't you at all concerned about what will happen to you when you die?' This time he only shook his head but said nothing.

"I asked, 'What do you have to say about all the boys you've hurt during your priesthood?' I was stunned when he answered, 'I never hurt them; you don't understand.' I responded at once, 'You did hurt them! What you did was horribly wrong. You need to think about what's going to happen to your soul when you die. Take this opportunity right now, Uncle Norman, to make an apology, at least to Tim. I will write down whatever you want to say to him.' My uncle stayed silent, so I said, 'Please help Tim heal. Acknowledge that you let him down as a priest, and tell him you're sorry, before it's too late. Ask him to forgive you for the appalling things you did to him. Your soul will end up in hell if you don't make things right with everyone you abused.' He seemed unconcerned and remained silent.

"I pleaded with him, 'Please explain it to me, Uncle Norman. Help me understand.' I stood looking at him through my tears, waiting for a response, but he said nothing. I sensed he wasn't going to say any more, so I chose to end my visit, but before leaving him alone with his thoughts, I jotted down my phone number and placed the paper on his bedside tray. I offered, 'Please think about apologizing to Tim. Just call me at this number, and let me know what you want to say.' He said nothing; he just stared blankly at the floor. I slowly turned and quietly left his room.

"I'm sorry to say that Uncle Norman never called. I tried my best to put the fear of hell in him, sincerely hoping he would be able to think of nothing but his victims' devastated lives until he took his last breath.

"My legs now felt absolutely vigorous as I came back down the steep driveway to the parking lot. I felt elated! I had left my uncle's room in tears, but any of the staff most likely thought I was emotional due to his being near death. I took a deep breath and cleansed my lungs of the stale, oppressive air that hung like an invisible fog inside the building.

"Suddenly, the overwhelming fear of angry nuns caused me to look back, but I was relieved to find that none were coming after me. I questioned myself as to why I credit them with an innate ability to sense everything. I made it quickly to the car, got in, and immediately entered Tim's number into my phone to let him know I'd delivered his message, just as he'd said. I told Tim that my having done for him what he found impossible to do for himself was not only an honor but a gift.

"Our family had trusted that the Catholic Church was taking care of things, as they had continually assured my aunt. Uncle Norman had admitted to my mother and aunt that he had been molesting kids throughout his priesthood. My delivering Tim's message made me feel that I had taken a stand against the church's lack of action. I held

Father Christian accountable for what he had done to at least this one young victim. I knew I could never mitigate a lifetime of pain for my uncle's victims, but I am grateful to have had the opportunity to bring at least one of them another step toward healing." Pete took a deep breath and then looked at Tim, saying, "Tim, I am very sorry for all the pain you and your family have endured because of my uncle and the church."

I think listening to Pete tell of how she delivered his message was music to Tim's ears, and I am proud of her for doing it. Had I delivered Tim's message, I think Norman would have quickly tuned me out and not heard a word. I believe he was so caught by surprise to hear his niece saying those words to him that it really stuck in his mind.

Tim seemed comforted by all Pete had said. After she finished speaking, he told about the relationship that had developed between him and Father Norman Christian when he was just a kid and what happened on that frightful night in Father's bedroom at St. George's rectory. Tim told us it was not an easy thing for him to talk about at any time. He explained that he feared that with us in the room, it might be even more difficult.

Tim told his story quietly and slowly, having to stop at times. He said he knew now that Father Christian had spotted a vulnerable child and had taken advantage of him. "With my parents divorcing, it didn't take me long to look at Father Christian as a father figure," Tim said. "He and I hung out, riding bikes, seeing movies, and just spending time together having fun. I was so happy; he just made me feel special. My heart was broken the day Father Christian got moved all the way to Saint George's in Saint Louis. How could someone who was doing so much for kids get moved? I cried. After he moved, he still came to see me, even though it was a thirty-mile drive. He'd take me to a secluded swimming hole a friend of his owned. He called it the "blue hole" and said we could go there anytime. My mom took me to visit him in Saint Louis, too, for the day. We'd ride bikes and just hang out. I missed him something awful, so you can imagine how happy I was the day he called my mom with an invitation for me to spend a weekend with him at his new parish. In retrospect, my mom and I both realize there was a red flag waving when Father made the remark that he wanted me to visit, but it would have to be a weekend when the 'grumpy old bastard pastor' was away. Regrettably, we didn't think anything of Father Christian's weird comment at the time; we both thought he was wonderful."

Tim's mom certainly trusted this priest with her son. So an excited, happy, innocent little boy was taken to spend a fun weekend with the person he looked up to as a father figure, only to leave there a broken child, terrified, raped, and told that no one would believe him if he told.

Tim's horror story continued. "It took my mom a long time to drive to Father's parish in Saint Louis. I was eager to get there, and he seemed really happy to see me. Mom helped me bring my things to his room, and then she headed back home with my siblings. I was more than ready for the fun to start when, suddenly, Father's friendly mood changed. He controlled an uncomfortable conversation for a long time about a friend of his. He claimed the guy was so weird he wouldn't use a public restroom. Father told me that was just stupid and then asked me if I didn't think it was stupid. When I told him that I didn't like using them either, he made fun of me. He kept it up, and I didn't think he was ever going to stop. When he finally did, I was left feeling like there was something really wrong with me; I had never felt so dumb. After that, he seemed like he was mad at me, but finally, he groaned, 'Let's go for a bike ride.' He sort of smoothed things over, and I felt better after the ride, but we had ridden in the heat of the afternoon and were really hot and sweaty when we got back. Father said we both needed to shower and told me I could sit on the couch and listen to music while he showered first.

"I didn't know what to think or do when Father Christian came strolling out stark-naked in front of me after his shower. When I turned my head away, he laughed loudly at me, saying, 'This bothers you? I thought you wanted to be an artist.' Frightened, I lied to him and said it didn't bother me; he had just surprised me. He kept laughing really loud. I guess I looked scared because he kept asking in the midst of his laughter, 'What's wrong, Tim? What's wrong?' I was trying to look away from him, but he continued walking back and forth in front of me, laughing and yelling, 'The naked body is natural! You should be comfortable with it!' He seemed angry with me again and finally hollered that I should go take my shower. I was glad he told me to do it so I could get away from him. I didn't understand why he was acting that way, and I was scared.

"Like most eleven-year-olds, I had forgotten to take my clothes into the bathroom with me. So after my shower, I came out with a towel around me to find them and get dressed. Father was in his bedroom, fully dressed by then, and asked if I'd want a back rub. That sounded good, so I answered, 'Sure, just a sec,' planning to throw my clothes on first. But Father said, 'Oh, just come over with the towel and lie on the bed.' Being the innocent kid I was, I did as he said, and he started rubbing my back, and then my legs, and then he told me to roll over. Again, I did what he said, but unexpectedly, Father Christian pulled the towel open and touched me where he had no business putting his hands. I rolled away as quickly as I could and felt terribly ashamed as I ran and threw my clothes on as fast as possible. Father never said anything about what he had done. We just went out to eat supper as though nothing had happened."

We could see that Tim was having difficulty talking about the abuse he suffered from Father Christian, but he continued. "It was still very hot outside, and when we returned, it was really hot inside his apartment too. The only air-conditioning he had was in his bedroom. It was getting late, so I asked him where I was going to sleep. Father told me, 'If you want air-conditioning, you'll have to sleep in my bedroom, in my bed with me.' I was too young, innocent, and trusting of him to sense any danger, so I just told him sure and asked where I could change into my pj's. With that, he frowned and started shaking his head and shouting at me, 'I sleep in the nude, unless that bothers you too!'

"The thunderous tone of his voice had made me feel stupid again, so I timidly replied that it was okay. He had already succeeded in making me feel like everything was wrong with me in just the short time I had been there. I wasn't going to let him know it bothered me to sleep in the nude. I'd obey him, like my mom had told me."

While Tim had been struggling to contain his emotions as he told of Norman's despicable behavior, our tears flowed freely as we grasped the reality of the horrors this little boy had endured. After some pause, he began to tell us what happened next.

"We went to bed, and I eventually managed to fall asleep, but at some horrific time during the night, I woke up with fear sweeping over me. I couldn't move! Father Christian was on top of me, doing things he had no business doing. I was scared and wondered what was happening to me. I pretended to be asleep and can remember thinking, *Jesus, this can't be happening*, but it was! What on earth happened to all the fun I was supposed to have with Father?"

We all sat there stunned as Tim paused again, finding it difficult to go on. "When he was done, I jumped out of bed, grabbed my clothes, and ran into the bathroom screaming, 'You stay away from me!' Dressed, I ran to the phone to call my mom. I was sobbing, 'Mom, come and get me right away! Please, come now!' She asked what was wrong, but I could only say, 'Come get me now!' As I hung up the phone, he came into the room and asked, 'What's going on, Tim?'

"I shouted at him, *'Get away from me!'* He calmly asked, 'What? What's wrong, Tim?'

"'Stay back!' I yelled as I made my way to the door of his balcony overlooking the street below. Only that door was between me and Father as I waited the long time it took Mom to arrive. As young and frightened as I was, I still realized it was going to take my mom a long time to get there for me because she'd have to wake my siblings, get them in the car, and then make the long drive to Saint Louis from Crystal City. I was really scared!"

The terror this little boy had experienced was seizing us all. Our hearts were aching for him as Tim continued. "It had stayed really hot all night inside that rectory apartment. It was somewhat better out on the little balcony porch. I don't know how long I waited out there, crying and anxiously watching for my mom's car to pull up. It seemed as though she was never coming. When Father would look out or say something to me, I'd scream at him, 'Stay away!' He probably didn't want me yelling at the top of my lungs outside, where people could hear, because he finally did stay away and leave me alone.

"I remember seeing Mom's car come around the corner, but I don't remember how my bike got put back into her car. We left, and Father Christian followed us all the way home in his own car. Mom kept asking me over and over what had happened and what was wrong, but all I could do was cry the whole way home. I just couldn't bring myself to talk about what had happened."

Back then, that little eleven-year-old boy most likely didn't even know the word for or have any knowledge of what Father Christian had done to him. Tim said, "I finally told Mom to just ask Father what happened."

Again, this little kid trusted the priest he looked to as a father figure. Young Tim honestly expected Father Christian would tell his mom the truth of what had happened in the middle of that terrifying night, in a trusted and revered priest's bedroom.

He continued, "It was nearly daybreak when we got home. Being tired, my siblings and I headed straight to bed, but Mom and Father Christian sat talking for a while. I don't remember the rest of that day except for Father calling my mom again that evening and asking how I was doing. After talking a while, Mom called me to the room and, with the phone in her hand, told me, 'Tim, Father Christian is hurting, and you need to tell him that everything is okay. Tell him that you still love him!'

"I did not want to do it and I didn't understand why my mom wanted me to say those things to him, but she kept insisting and shoved the phone at me. When I screamed, 'No,' she said again, 'He loves you and he is hurting.'

"I stood there with Mom shoving the phone up to my head and finally said it, just like she told me to, but I never forgave her for making me do it."

My heart pounded as I listened to all he'd endured. I was again thankful my parents were no longer living, so they would not have to learn the shameful truth about their only son, their pride and joy.

Tim went on with his story. "Now, several decades later, I feel terrible that I hated my mom all those years. I had thought she knew because I thought that Father had told her what he had done to me, and she didn't care. It never crossed my mind that he might have lied to her."

Eleven-year-old Tim couldn't imagine a priest telling lies, but Father Christian had indeed lied to Mrs. Fischer that night. Tim's mom told him that Father's explanation was that he had frightened Tim by accidentally rolling over on him in his sleep, and he thought Tim had become homesick as well. Thanks to Father Christian's lies and criminal behavior, Tim lost his relationship with his dad and his mom.

Then, thankfully, in 2003, Tim said he noticed a SNAP article in the newspaper and finally decided to call their number. "After making that initial call, I found the support I needed from members of the group, and before long, I was talking to a detective and reporting what Father Christian had done to me. When the detective asked me what Father Christian had actually told my mom about that night, I realized I didn't really know. I had just assumed he had told her the truth. I called my mom right then and asked what Father Christian told her about the happenings of that awful night I spent with him in Saint Louis. That was the first I realized that my mom never knew what really happened. Father Christian had lied to her!"

One simple phone call to his mom and a simple question helped Tim discover the truth—and his mom too. It was also the start of their rebuilding the loving relationship Father Christian had taken from them. "Mom had made a very bad mistake, but I was finally able to forgive her. I had never told my dad what Father did to me because I was afraid he'd kill Father and have to go to prison."

I sat in David's living room that evening with a heavy heart as I listened to Tim's story. It all seemed like a horrible nightmare. As my eyes overflowed with tears, I knew I wasn't going to wake up and find it all to be a bad dream. This young man and his family had been living with this haunting nightmare for thirty years. I thanked God he could finally speak of this brutality that had happened to him as a child, the painful secret he kept inside for so long.

It seemed Tim had done an amazing job with his life in spite of the horrible problems resulting from Father Christian's raping him. It was easy to see how much he loved his family. He and his family share a strong faith in God but attend worship in a different denomination. Tim wants no more to do with the Catholic Church.

Tim told more about Father Christian in blog entries on his website March 6, 2006 (no longer available online) stating, "When Father Christian had returned from a retreat in New Mexico back in the 1980s, he invited me to visit him. Still out of politeness to clergy, I went. He seemed thrilled in telling me that he had discovered he was gay. I asked him 'What about celibacy? You're not supposed to have sex with anyone.' Father laughed and said, 'Things are going to change with that ancient and archaic rule! Archbishop John May is going to set up a parish that has all gay priests and nuns here in the Saint Louis community to serve our needs.' To my knowledge, this was never done."

My blood pressure was high the following morning when I was given a physical in preparation for a scheduled cataract surgery. I explained to my doctor what had transpired the night before and told him to watch for Bill McClellan's column in the newspaper. He didn't seem concerned about my blood pressure. I wondered, since he was Catholic, if he just didn't want to hear about it.

I called my sister later that day and told her how proud I was of her daughter for delivering Tim's message to Norman. She didn't say much, but I could sense she was proud of Pete too.

Chapter 19
Family Speaks Out

Bill McClellan's column about Father Christian appeared in the October 27, 2004, *Post-Dispatch*, which just happened to be Joe's and my forty-second wedding anniversary—what a way to celebrate. The article spoke of Father Christian being an "ex-priest," but that was incorrect, as he was not laicized. Mr. McClellan really brought the problem of priests sexually abusing minors to the public's attention, as his article contained comments from the priest's family in support of the victim.

In Norman's forty-three years as a predator priest, the church had failed miserably in dealing with the sexual-abuse problem. I talked with Tim several days after the column appeared in the paper. I knew he was nervous about how people would react to him after reading it. He told me how happy he was with all the support he received from people at his church that weekend and then asked how it had gone for me. I had received the opposite reaction. It seemed people were avoiding me at my Catholic church that Sunday; there was no show of support. I did get calls at home, though, and I knew I was doing the right thing in holding my brother and the church accountable.

The article explained that Father Christian had been moved around from parish to parish and in 1986, he told me he was going on a sabbatical to New Mexico.

"His return address [on a letter he sent] was in care of the Servants of the Paraclete," the article read. "Later, the Servants would gain certain unhappy notoriety for their efforts to cure pedophilia, but at this time, the name meant nothing to Carol. Her brother wrote that he was dealing with an addiction. He said he did not intend to discuss it and hoped the family 'will have the kindness not to ask too many questions.' Whatever the mysterious addiction was, he was soon cured, and he returned to the Saint Louis area to resume his priestly work."

The article went on to note that Sue had told me the "disturbing news"—that while I had thought my brother was counseling her through her difficult adolescence, he had been taking her to "gay and X-rated movies" and "telling her of his own sexual exploits. Later, Carol would hear from other relatives that her brother had been sent to New Mexico only after eight boys had come forward with allegations of sexual abuse. In 1995 he was removed from the ministry and sent to a center for 'Wounded Brothers' in Robertsville, MO."

The article also told of my receiving a letter a year later, addressed to my brother at my home.

"Norman explained it was from a victim," the article said, "a young man who had reached an out-of-court settlement with the church." It went on to say that just ten days before the writing of the article, "Carol received a phone call. 'Your brother is dying.' Carol had long felt a need to reach out to her brother's victims. She did not know how many there were. Dozens? Hundreds?" The article then described how we contacted SNAP and met the person my brother had abused and that my niece delivered the victim's message, which was quoted in the article, to her uncle.

After Bill McClellan's column appeared in the newspaper, I received many supportive calls but an especially surprising one came from a retired nun who had taught Norman as well as my children in elementary school. How much her call meant to me that day is beyond measure. I will be forever grateful to her for reaching out at a time when so few were doing so. We had been talking for quite a while when Sister said, "Carol, you are doing this for the victims, aren't you." It wasn't a question. What a comfort it was to know that she, of all people, understood. I had gone on and on about the shameful way the church had handled the entire sexual-abuse problem over the years. Sister compassionately said, "Carol, I am so sorry this has happened to your family. I understand why you didn't tell me about your brother. I'm as upset as you with how the church leaders have been dealing with this serious problem. I am behind you 100 percent."

I emphasized, "Sister, the church leaders must stop covering up for these predator clergy. They need to remove them from ministry and reach out compassionately to their victims. The church must give victims the help they deserve and desperately need. After Norman had been removed from ministry and you were asking me about him, I wanted to tell you the truth, but he had instructed me to say nothing; and I trusted the church leaders were taking care of everything as they had told me."

Sister responded sadly, "I know." Then she told me, "A good friend of mine, who had been in one of Father Christian's parishes, called me this morning. She had read Bill McClellan's column in the newspaper, and it had upset her terribly. She went on and on, saying it just couldn't be true. Father Christian was the most wonderful priest she ever knew. Carol, my friend refuses to believe he would do those things."

I knew exactly how difficult it was for her friend to believe the priest she had placed on a pedestal was a child molester. I suggested, "Sister, you might want to call your friend and tell her that as hard as it is to believe, it is absolutely true. Explain to her that's how pedophiles gain access to children in the first place. They earn people's trust and respect, and parents willingly hand their children over—in this case, to the most unlikely pedophile imaginable."

I was so aggravated with our church leadership at the time, I had thoughts of leaving the church, but Sister helped me realize the Catholic faith itself was still good. My faith in God was strong. She asked me to stay and fight for change in how the church deals with its abusive clergy and their victims. I gave it some thought after we talked and decided she was right. Besides working toward the removal of predator clergy from ministry and helping their victims, church leaders needed to be prodded to help all members of the faith understand and cope with their own sense of betrayal, to show them, by example, to be compassionate toward all victims.

The church's policies must stop protecting its reputation before they protect children. Many younger parents, who have been paying attention to the church's poor handling of clergy sex-abuse cases for the past decade, are not willing to put their families at risk. Church membership has been dropping.

Sister asked if I ever talked with Archbishop Burke about my concerns. I told her about the two letters I'd sent him and that he never acknowledged receiving them. I then told her none of my family would be going to Norman's wake or funeral. She said she fully understood why, and we would all be in her prayers. I thanked her for that, as I am always grateful for anyone's prayers.

This nun has been another of those special people in the Kuhnert family's lives. She just happened to have been our youngest daughter's teacher the year she faced her brain surgery. Joan had to miss her entire second semester of school that year and had tried to stay caught up with her classmates by being tutored at home. Sister kindly made sure Joan wasn't forgotten by them. She had her classmates making special cards or crafts every week and would send different kids by our home to deliver them and visit with Joan for a while. Those visits and little gifts were the best medicine ever. This nun knew the meaning of encouragement and support; it's a side of her most people didn't get to see. Our family definitely counts her among our blessings.

I wrote Sister after we talked, thanking her again for having called (Kuhnert, 10-29-2004, letter). I wanted to make sure she knew how much I appreciated her reaching out to me and my family as she did. I said again how my heart went out to the victims; that the church I once cherished and turned to for comfort and guidance had turned into a house of horrors. I asked her to pray God would restore it and that it would take a long time for Catholics to regain their trust in its leadership.

While it must have been very hard for her to accept, I told Sister that when confronted, Norman admitted to my sister and me that he did those horrible things to children. He and the church managed to successfully cover up his crimes of sexually abusing minors throughout his years as a priest. Clearly, that was not and never will be the right thing to do.

Although Sister passed away in 2013, I am not using her name in this book. She informed me that the hierarchy ordered the nuns to remain silent and not to take sides on the clergy sexual-abuse issue—remain obedient and just stay out of it. She asked that I not use her name. Sadly, still today the church is silencing its "religious" on these matters. That's certainly not the image that's put forth to its membership and the media.

Shortly after Bill McClellan's column was published, one of my relatives called, and we talked at length about the awful way the church was handling its clergy sexual-abuse problem. When I emphasized that my sympathy went out to all the victims, that the church leaders and Norman and all those like him needed to hold themselves accountable for the crimes they've committed, she agreed. Then she mentioned that another family member, who had read McClellan's column, had commented to her, "How could Carol talk about her own brother like that? How could she do that to him?"

It stunned me to realize this Catholic mother would choose to protect a molester simply because he was a relative. She ignored the fact that Norman raped and molested countless children and betrayed the trust of their families, as well as my own. Relative or not, he needed to be held accountable.

I told her, "It doesn't matter that he's my brother. The fact that he's a priest makes his sexually abusing children all the more evil. Norman betrayed parents' and children's trust and respect in priests and the Catholic Church in general. For decades, I've read or heard various reports of clergy sexual abuse and spoke with many victims. As hard as it is, Catholics must accept that there are people in the religious life capable of betraying their trust and causing great harm. After twenty-seven years of watching the church continually covering for its clergy molesters as long as possible, it's obvious that parents need to be vigilant of their children's relationships with anyone in the religious life, as they would for any adult who would seek access to their child."

I've forgiven my brother for betraying our family as he did. My daughter also has forgiven him for what he did to her. We know since his death that he is answering to God for all the pain he caused to so many. I care very much for all who were hurt by my brother and hope they can find some peace in knowing that the shameful truth about Father Norman Christian became known before he died. He went to his death as a known child molester—a pedophile priest.

On October 29, my sister called to tell me that the archdiocese had phoned her with the news that Norman had died that morning.

She'd been given no details, only that someone would call her later with the funeral arrangements.

After we had said good-bye, I realized how relieved I was that he was gone. I felt sad for the victim who had hoped to see him found guilty in court, but there was no feeling of sadness that my brother had died. I grieved for all the children, vulnerable adults, and families whose faith and lives were destroyed by him.

We eventually learned that Father Norman H. Christian had died in his room at the nursing home, Friday morning, October 29, 2004, just four weeks after happily celebrating his sixty-ninth birthday with clergy companions at the Regina Cleri Retirement Home.

A memorandum was sent that day from the Vicar General's Office, Saint Louis, Missouri, informing all bishops and priests of his death and funeral arrangements. It stated:

"It is my sad duty to inform you of the death of Reverend Norman H. Christian. Father Christian died this morning, October 29, 2004. Visitation will be Sunday, October 31, 2004 from 3:00 p.m. to 9:00 p.m. at Collier's Funeral Home, 3400 N. Lindbergh Boulevard, St. Louis, MO 63074. The funeral mass will be celebrated at 11:00 a.m. on Monday, Nov. 1, 2004, at St. Richard Parish, 11223 Schuetz Road, St. Louis, MO 63146. Please remember Father Christian and his family in your moments of prayer."

Jeanne called me once she received the church's finalized funeral arrangements. While giving me the information, she mentioned that Norman's friend had called her, requesting pictures of him to display at the funeral home. Jeanne was going to go through old snapshots and find some to give her.

We both found it very strange that the church had not placed his death notice in the local newspaper for the general public's information. Only the memo was faxed on the day he died to all bishops and priests from the Vicar General's Office. Information about his funeral arrangements was given to select relatives and friends through phone calls made by some cousins. I learned from parishioners that the parish where Norman spent his childhood, attended school, and later said his first Mass, Our Lady of Sorrows, merely announced he had died; no further information was given. Anyone from that parish who may have wanted to pay their respects or attend his funeral was left waiting and watching the papers for funeral arrangements long after he had already been buried. Father Christian's wake, funeral, and burial all happened quickly and quietly.

Joe and I and our children did not attend Norman's wake and funeral. It didn't seem appropriate to celebrate the life of someone who betrayed and hurt so many children while serving as a priest, especially knowing he had refused to ever say he was sorry. I said prayers for him at home, along with the many I said for all his victims and their families. Jeanne felt the need to be there; she and her husband attended his wake, funeral, and burial.

Over time, I learned there were relatives and friends who had chosen not to attend any of it. I received an e-mail from a relative who had attended the funeral, stating, "He was buried from Saint Richard's in Creve Coeur to Calvary Cemetery and there were forty to fifty priests in attendance. Archbishop Burke was the celebrant; it was a great tribute to Norman."

After reading that, I knew I had made the right decision in not going. I had forgiven Norman long before he died for betraying our family and knew it was up to each of his victims to forgive him for what he had done to them. I found peace in knowing Norman was now answering to God, as we all will. It's disgraceful that after being removed from active ministry for having sexually abused children throughout his priesthood, Norman was given a glorious funeral as a priest in good standing, with Archbishop Raymond Burke as the celebrant, especially considering the fact the church had been talking about laicizing him not that long before his death.

One of the good sisters who had been caring for Norman at the priests' retirement home had come across a picture taken of him the day he celebrated his sixty-ninth birthday, and she mailed it to me. I was surprised to receive the picture but glad to get it since it was taken shortly before his death. I sent a note thanking Sister for her kindness in sending it to me.

It's hard to say what I feel when I look at that picture of him. A jumble of emotions rushes through me, all tangled together as I realize how little I know about my own brother. I will never understand his choosing to live such an evil and destructive life. While I was aggravated and deeply disappointed that he refused to apologize to those he'd hurt, I was no longer angry with him. Holding onto hatred would only make me ill. It's sad that Norman remained a self-centered individual to the very end, protecting the church so they would continue to support him. He obviously hadn't paid attention to anything I had said to him throughout that last year. I don't know if he even read any of my letters. He might have just thrown them away unopened, considering I never received any responses.

I received a call from the detective at the Child Abuse Office shortly after Norman's death. She just wanted to thank me for helping with the case against him and the church. It saddened me, knowing with his death, the case would close.

It was uplifting that she had taken time from her busy schedule just to say thanks. I thanked her for doing what she does in helping victims find some kind of justice. I wished I could have been of more help to her.

Since the church had kept my brother's death and funeral arrangements from the public, I took it upon myself to inform our own family and friends of his death. Very few were aware that Norman had recently become extremely ill. The few who had learned of his frail condition were most likely watching for a death notice.

On November 6, 2004, I wrote an informational letter and made many copies, which I then personalized by dating and writing each person's name and on some, adding a personal note before signing.

The purpose of sending these letters was to let our relatives and friends know Norman had died and where I stood regarding him and the crimes he had committed against children. I felt this was his and the church's shame, not ours, and I hoped that uncovering what they had been hiding with just my brother's crimes alone would get people thinking about this huge and dangerous problem within the church. Maybe others would start holding the church accountable in protecting not only its followers physically but also in upholding the integrity of its holy name and demand that such priests be removed from ministry.

The following is excerpted from my November 6, 2004, letter (entire letter in appendix):

> Most likely you've heard that my brother, Father Norman Christian, died October 29, 2004. The archdiocese did not run his death notice in the paper, and my sister and I had nothing to do with his funeral arrangements. ... I learned about sixteen years ago that Norman was a pedophile when Sue told me what he had told her and places he had been taking her years before. She had since been avoiding him, and I didn't understand why. I confronted him after that and he admitted his lifestyle to me. He

was angry with Sue for breaking his confidence in telling me about him. ... I have spent the last sixteen years trying to get Norman and the church leaders to do the right thing for all sexual-abuse victims and to protect against there being any more victims. ... I am not mourning the loss of a brother, but I am mourning the loss of the church I loved, trusted, and looked to for comfort and guidance all my life. My faith in God is strong, but in the church leaders, it's completely gone. ...

Their number-one concern has always been to protect the church's money from future lawsuits. Norman went to his death never apologizing to our family or any of his victims for what he had done. ... He said it would open the door for more lawsuits for the archdiocese. ...

Norman was given a burial as a priest in good standing. To me, it was the ultimate slap in the face to all his victims. He *never* expressed remorse to me for the pain he caused to so many children and their families. Maybe the archdiocese had second thoughts about it, since they didn't run his death notice, nor did they announce funeral arrangements at any church. ... More cover-up; we didn't go.

It was November 10, and I was recuperating from cataract surgery from the day before when I received a phone call from Bill McClellan, the columnist from the *Post-Dispatch* newspaper. He gave me the name of the person who wrote story articles for the obituary section of the paper, Denise, suggesting I contact her. Mr. McClellan was aware the church had not placed Norman's name in the paper's regular obituary column at the time of his death. He suggested I could request a belated story article announcing his death. I was grateful to have that option available to get word out to the public, not only that he died but also to alert people of the fact he was a pedophile. Maybe it would give others he abused the courage to report what he did to them—now they would be believed.

The next day, Denise e-mailed her rough draft of Norman's

obituary to me, saying I could make any changes I wanted. I did make some changes to what she had written, one being to send memorial donations to the Survivors Network for those Abused by Priests, and returned it to her. I received a call from her the following day. My version had gotten edited quite a bit before making it to the printing presses. She told me she had never written an obituary like that one.

Norman's belated story-obituary appeared in the November 13, 2004, *Post-Dispatch*, with the headline "Reverend Norman H. Christian, Controversial Priest." The church's decades of covering up for my brother were over. The unedited version was posted on the *St. Louis Post-Dispatch*'s website. I hoped any clergy-abuse survivors reading of his death found comfort in seeing that this predator priest would no longer be a danger to anyone.

The following is the belated obituary that was published:

> Reverend Norman H. Christian
> Controversial priest
>
> A funeral mass was celebrated Nov 1 at St. Richard Catholic church for the Reverend Norman H. Christian. Father Christian died Oct 29 from kidney and liver failure; he was 69.
>
> Father Christian was born in St. Louis. In 1961 he was ordained by Cardinal Joseph Ritter and began his ministry at St. Peter Catholic Church in Kirkwood. He then went to what is now Ascension/St. Paul Parish in Normandy. Later, he was at Sacred Heart Catholic Church in Festus, and St. George Catholic Church in Affton. From 1978 to 1981, Father Christian was at the former Nativity Catholic Church in St. Louis. He was at the former St. Adalbert Catholic Church in St. Louis until 1986 and then St. William Catholic Church in Woodson Terrace, until being removed in 1995.
>
> The archdiocese said Father Christian was removed after an allegation that he had abused a minor 20 years earlier. He was sent to Wounded Brothers

Project, south of Robertsville in Franklin County, according to a *Post-Dispatch* news article in March. An October 27 column by Bill McClellan described how Father Christian's sister, Carol Kuhnert, of Union, and other family members had reached out to his victims.

The family requests that any memorial donations be made to the Survivors Network for those Abused by Priests, 7234 Arsenal, St. Louis, MO 63143, or to masses.

On November 3, 2004, I received a rather interesting phone call from an eighty-year-old woman saying she was a parishioner from St. William's parish, where Father Christian last served as pastor. She was calling to ask for my sister's name and address, but we ended up talking about Norman for quite a while. It was clear she was having a very difficult time believing any of the dreadful things she'd read and heard about her revered Father Christian in the media. Our conversation seemed hard for her to swallow too.

It seemed even more difficult for this woman to believe there were other priests, like my brother, still serving in active ministry, and unless their victims found the courage to report them to the police and were willing to face the church's intimidating defense attorneys, they would be allowed to remain working with unsuspecting children, with absolutely no warnings given to parents that accusations were ever made against them.

It must have made her think, as she mentioned several priests' names to me, asking if she should be concerned about them. I told her I didn't know but suggested she and other parishioners should hold the church accountable by writing letters to their pastors and bishops, asking questions of them. I suggested she ask what they were doing to help all the abuse victims and especially ask why such priests weren't removed from active ministry as soon as their criminal behavior first became apparent. Why did they wait to be forced to remove them by lawsuits and court orders?

I believe this lady was trying to comfort me when she said, "Archbishop Burke kept it short" at Norman's funeral and that he mentioned something about Norman's sins. Maybe she thought I would be less upset with the archbishop's celebrating a glorious funeral Mass for an unrepentant predator priest if I knew he had at least mentioned the priest's sins somewhere during the beautiful tributes. I knew then this woman didn't understand why I had not attended my brother's funeral. I hope she has done some serious thinking about what we talked about that day and has posed some questions of her own to the church leaders since then.

The church's public-relations people continue to do great work in convincing the faithful that they are doing everything that needs to be done. Actions speak louder than words, but sadly, many of the faithful are content to look the other way and ignore how little action there's been on the church's part.

The *St. Louis Review* ran a belated death notice for Norman in the November 5, 2004, issue (entire article in appendix). It seemed strange that the Catholic paper made a mistake listing Sacred Heart parish in Florissant, Missouri, instead of Festus, as one of the parishes Norman had been assigned. His assignment at the Festus parish was where he first befriended young Tim and his family and began grooming that vulnerable little boy and his mother for his own evil intentions.

The death notice they published also failed to mention that he had been sent for treatment more than once and then reassigned to unsuspecting parishes when the treatment sessions had ended.

After my brother's death, I noticed how few sympathy cards we received. I recalled when Dad died and again, years later, when Mom died, our family received many cards and notes from family and friends. I imagine under the circumstances of my brother's death, most people were at a loss for what to say or do, so they said or did nothing, making the cards and calls our family did receive all the more appreciated. I thought it strange that our family hadn't received any form of condolence from the church either.

After Norman died, I felt nothing but relief. I no longer needed to worry about him; his life with its secrecy was over. After sending my letter regarding his death and surrounding circumstances to our family and friends, we began to receive phone calls and cards. What a blessing it was to know family and friends did care and were reaching out to us during that painful time. We weren't being abandoned because of my speaking out against the church's shameful handling of the clergy sexual-abuse crisis.

One sister-in-law had written me an exceptionally comforting and understanding note. While I thanked her that day, I doubt she understood just how much her supportive words really meant to me.

Several longtime friends were very encouraging over the years as they'd listen to me venting my frustrations. They were just as outraged that the church kept sexual abusers in active ministry, protecting them instead of children.

I was happily surprised by two supportive cousins. I hadn't heard from them since childhood. One, a Catholic nun in a cloistered order, began praying that the church would remove all clergy molesters and help their victims. The other, an ex-nun, had left "the unbelievably abusive treatment in the convent community." Having made reports of what was happening to her and others to the Convent Mother General and even writing to the Pope, nothing was ever done to help her. Fran left the convent and the Catholic Church and now feels deeply for the clergy abuse victims. Reconnecting with these cousins and learning they too believe the church needs to be held accountable helped bolster me more.

Amid decades of communicating with church leaders about their shameful mishandling of clergy sexual abusers, I sometimes wondered if speaking out mattered. The many who are speaking out today have convinced me it does. With public awareness, more people are holding the church leaders accountable. Progress is slowly being made in ridding the church of its abusers. Those involved in the cover-ups are beginning to be disciplined instead of promoted.

I had noticed the name of still another of my cousins, also a nun, listed on some of Norman's group e-mails. I wondered how honest he had been about himself with her over the years and decided to send her a copy of the letter I sent to family and friends regarding Norman's death. Realizing she had been in communication with him, I was interested in getting her perspective of his situation and the church's way of handling it (Kuhnert, 11-12-04, e-mail).

She responded the next day by saying she wasn't aware of all I had written about Norman. She looked for the McClellan article in the *Post-Dispatch* and read it, finding it all terrible and heartbreaking, and she was praying for us.

I wrote back, telling her my faith in God couldn't be stronger and that I prayed daily for His guidance. I felt strongly that the church needed to own up to its complete mismanagement of the clergy sexual-abuse problem. I realized it was all in God's hands, not mine, but I felt that we all needed to do what we could to help heal our deeply wounded church.

Chapter 20
Another Victim

One beautiful autumn day, having just come inside from taking a walk, I answered the phone to a pleasant-sounding man asking, "Is this Carol?" Then he introduced himself, adding "I was sexually abused by Father Christian when I was a kid. Tim gave me your number, suggesting I call you. He said you would believe me" (11-14-04 phone call). I immediately choked up and could only respond, "I am so sorry."

"It took until I was forty-six years old to finally get the nerve to tell the authorities how Father Christian sexually abused me when I was a kid," he said.

"I am sorry!" I repeated. "I didn't know. His behavior was inexcusable. Nothing I can say can make anything he did okay. But I'm very thankful you found the courage to report your abuse."

The man continued to tell me more. "I read Tim's story in the paper, and I recognized Father Christian's name. It didn't take me long to call SNAP, and they've given me the support I needed to begin healing by reporting him. It's lucky I noticed Tim's story in the newspaper. He's been such a huge help since we've met. I wish I had learned about SNAP sooner in my life. Everyone there understands what I've lived through. I was just a kid, happily riding with Father Christian as he drove somewhere that we could swim. Father told me, 'Oh, we're going to have a great time, a whole day of fun in the country.' We went to the country all right, but I didn't have any fun.

I ended up being sexually abused by both Father Christian and a volunteer fireman who lived in the area."

My heart ached for this man, and though I didn't think it was possible, I was even more disgusted with my brother. He was truly a repulsive piece of filth to have joined another predator to share in sexually abusing this child. This man's mentioning the volunteer fireman reminded me of a time in Norman's life when he had excitedly told Joe and me about being made a chaplain for a fire department. He had seemed very proud and excited about it.

The horror story wasn't over. He told me, "As soon as I got home, I told my dad what had happened, but he didn't believe me. He punished me severely for saying such horrible things. My father said that a priest could never do such terrible things to a boy." The man sighed deeply and then continued. "When my own dad wouldn't believe me, I decided there was no point in telling anybody else, not even my mom. I didn't want any more punishment. Father Christian had warned me that no one would believe it if I told. My dad convinced me he was right."

That horrible secret had eaten away at this man throughout his life until the day he saw that another victim had reported Father Christian and was believed. I hope he's found some peace in his life since reporting his own abuse. He did share some happier news with me. He was overjoyed about the arrival of a new grandson. Most likely this grandpa will keep a watchful eye on that little guy growing up.

I was able to meet this brave man when I joined him and other SNAP members at a press conference that was held in his behalf. I admired him for bringing Norman's crimes and the church's cover-ups to the public's attention.

The November 16 issue of the *Post-Dispatch* published a letter to the editor, accusing the paper of bashing the Catholic Church by dredging up "old news" for its front page. The writer wanted the paper to focus on sexual abuse in other religions and in the public school system as well. I wrote a response that made it into the November 21 issue of the paper. I commented that the *Post-Dispatch* was "helping people who were victimized by the church a long time ago to begin to heal and, at the same time, open the eyes of today's parents to the dangers that lurk within their parishes. Church leaders are still protecting problem priests from prosecution and keeping them in service until forced to remove them. Compassion belongs to all those who have been victimized, not to those who have been covering it up."

Another woman's letter appeared in that column the same day, stating the abuse was made worse by the church's cover-up tactics. She wrote, "The repeated deceit by the highest Catholic officials gives these stories 'legs' and elevates them to justifiable outrage." I thought she was right on target.

I was still recovering from the previous week's eye surgery when my sister and brother-in-law stopped by, bringing us one of her delicious home-baked apple pies. Along with it, she brought a copy of Norman's funeral liturgy booklet and four cards bearing his picture with dates of birth, ordination, and death on the front (Archdiocese of St. Louis, 10-31-04, Christian's funeral liturgy). On the reverse side of the card was the following verse:

> I have only one spouse on earth, Jesus.
> Crucified and forsaken.
> I have no God outside of Him.
> In Him is all of Heaven
> With the Trinity
> And all the earth with humanity.
> So, what is His is mine,
> And nothing else.
> Chiara Lubich

Funeral Liturgy

Rev. Norman Christian

Born: October 1, 1935
Ordained: March 18, 1961

Died: October 29, 2004

Since I hadn't attended Norman's wake or funeral, Jeanne was being thoughtful in bringing me these things for remembrances. I assumed the four cards were meant for each of my children. I thanked her and laid them aside, and we talked for a while. They said nothing about Norman's funeral, and I didn't ask. It wasn't long before they were on their way home.

After they left, I began reading the liturgy pamphlet and cards. The verse seemed so inappropriate to have been placed on a pedophile priest's memorial card. I found myself becoming upset at the thought of my sister giving them to people as a remembrance of him. Later, when I told our children that Jeanne had given us the funeral cards with Norman's picture, I asked if they wanted one. None was interested. I wasn't surprised.

As time passed, the thought of my sister's attending Norman's quietly held wake and funeral bothered me more and more. I felt by doing so, she gave her approval to this fraudulent celebration of his life as a priest in good standing. In fact, Archbishop Justin Rigali had signed the letter that removed my serial child-rapist brother from ministry because they couldn't trust him. Yet here he was, his priestly life being celebrated, with Archbishop Raymond Burke presiding at the funeral. I felt betrayed again, this time by my sister. It appeared to me she was looking the other way and pretending everything was okay in the presence of all attending Norman's funeral. She learned the truth about Norman when I did, and she was as upset as I was that the church did not do the right thing the moment they knew he was a danger. Though my sister often told me she felt as strongly as I did, she could not bring herself to get involved toward bringing about change. She assured me she was praying for everyone involved. I was troubled even more; if people who actually knew what the church was doing were not willing to help change things, what could be expected of those denying the possibility of clergy committing such crimes?

Feeling as I did, it had become too painful for me to visit with my sister or even speak with her on the phone. On November 16, 2004, I decided to risk writing my feelings out to her in hopes she would read and reread it, giving some thought to my concerns. I explained that until she and others like her stopped looking the other way, child-raping clergy would never be stopped, and children would never be safe.

Jeanne had been a good sister to me throughout my life, and I loved her. She had joined me in watching what Norman and the church were doing when we first learned he had been abusing children. Things changed after Norman angrily yelled at her regarding the letter she sent him following our talk with Monsignor Naumann. Norman must have frightened her terribly at that point, and she just backed away and washed her hands of everything regarding him and the entire clergy sexual-abuse scandal. I told her it didn't matter what anyone thought or how something looked; we needed to stand up for what was right, not for what looked right.

I received a reply from her within a couple of weeks, telling me she was "truly sorry for any hurt" caused to my family (Meyer, 11-27-04, letter). She hadn't realized her actions had been hurtful to us. I knew she hadn't gone to the funeral with the intention of causing us pain, but since then, I found myself wanting to communicate with her as little as possible. I didn't like that and felt I needed to let her know what was bothering me before it destroyed our relationship entirely.

She said she still shared my feelings about Norman and "the powers that be," adding she did care about all those who had been hurt. It was just that she had to deal with all of it in her own way; she wasn't a "knock-down drag-out fighter." She would write letters and express her feelings in that way. I hope she has been doing that and encouraging others to do the same—and often.

She also said she could not have found peace if she had not attended Norman's wake and funeral and thought it brought consolation to many who were there. It didn't seem she had considered his victims' and their families' pain in learning he received a glorious funeral from the church. As for the little cards with his picture, she said the verse hadn't appealed to her either. She had been told it was one of Norman's favorites and suggested I could throw away whatever I didn't want. She was right about that, but missed my point about giving those cards with that particular verse printed on the back as an appropriate remembrance for a pedophile priest.

After telling me of her prayers for all the innocent priests suffering because of the scandal and for her own ability to say and do the right things, she agreed the church had not done all it should in making things right, and she prayed that was changing. My sister then asked me to try to understand her need to be at the close of our brother's life. I have given what she asked a lot of thought—I still am. I don't understand why the need to be at her betraying pedophile brother's funeral was stronger than the need to stand by her betrayed sister's family and thereby help give the church hierarchy and Norman's sexual-abuse victims a strong message as well. There was nothing more she could have done for Norman at that funeral but pray for him, and she could have done that at home, as I did. Most likely, Jeanne never truly considered my feelings and what I was standing up for. She probably felt that being Norman's sister, her presence would be expected by all of those in attendance.

While my sister was sure of her need to be at our brother's funeral, she told me she understood my family's not attending any of it. I think if she truly understood, she would have realized that her attendance demonstrated acceptance and support for how the church dealt with Norman's crimes against children. I know Jeanne didn't intentionally set out to hurt us. What she doesn't seem to understand is that while her attitude and actions hurt us back then, they continue to hurt abuse victims today, coming from many others who share the same attitude. Many Catholics still refuse to reach out to the clergy's victims with compassion and understanding, because the church fails to hold itself accountable for its own wrongdoing. It's easier and less painful for such Catholics to stay in denial about the whole shameful problem.

It's very sad that same attitude still exists in many Catholics today. Church leaders' continued cover-ups and refusals to speak honestly and openly about abusive priests doesn't help. Their failure to show compassion for all the victims has brought about the same response from parishioners, especially those who adamantly refuse to believe priests would do such things, even after the priest has admitted guilt.

A week or so later, in the middle of December, Jeanne and Al stopped by again on a Sunday morning. She and I spent most of the time discussing the priest scandal, and she seemed to share a lot of my feelings. I told her I thought a big part of the problem lay with the bishops. She agreed but gave no indication of being willing to help try to convince them to change their ways.

Jeanne was well aware of how various clergy talked badly about SNAP, merely a group of sexual-abuse victims supporting each other and working to get predator priests removed from active ministry. Any victims who resorted to lawsuits did so most likely because it was the only way to get the church's attention. I pointed out to my sister how I had been ignored by the church during the sixteen years I'd been trying to communicate with them after I learned of Norman's pedophilia. I hadn't asked them for a penny, yet my letters were usually ignored. Jeanne said she had written Archbishop Burke twice herself, and he never answered her letters either. She started making excuses for him, but I told her to stop; there were no excuses. His ignoring our letters as he did spoke loudly of his choosing to ignore the problem and us.

"I've come to the conclusion," I told her, "that Catholics are brainwashed from infancy to do as they are told, not to think for themselves or ever question anything when it comes to religion." She didn't agree with me, but I saw that behavior in her, and I could see it in myself in the past. We did agree the church was mortally wounded, and something needed to be done to restore its trust and respect. I hoped my sister would do more than just pray about it.

In late November I received a call from Tim. He mentioned his lawyer had asked who he would be bringing to his mediation hearing with the archdiocese. This hearing would give Tim the opportunity to speak to representatives of the church along with a mediator, who would be listening as well and making a judgment about what had happened to him. Tim would be allowed to report all the details of what Norman did to him and his family when he was an innocent child and explain how his life has been affected by what Norman did, as well as by the church's poor handling of it. He had great hopes of finding some form of justice and healing at this hearing, especially since his rapist had died before he could be taken to trial.

I asked him, "How soon is your hearing coming up?"

"It's scheduled for December 14, and I'm still trying to decide who to bring with me," he answered. "So far, my wife, brother, and my mom and dad will be coming. Of course, my lawyer will be there." Then he caught me by surprise when he said, "I was wondering if you would consider coming with me too."

I knew I wanted to be there to offer moral support, if Tim wanted me. I told him, "Yes, just let me know when and where."

It was many weeks later when I realized that not only was I to be there, but I was to speak at the hearing as well. At first, that thought frightened me, but then I saw it as an opportunity—an enormous gift. All those years of trying to be heard and getting ignored by the church had been very frustrating. This time, I would be heard—by them and a mediator as well. I owed Tim a big thank you.

Tim's lawyer called me after he learned Tim wanted me to join him at his hearing. He said he thought it would be helpful to Tim for me to join them that day, and I felt all the more comfortable with the thought of doing so.

I started jotting down things I wanted to say to the mediation board. When it met my satisfaction, I typed and printed everything in large print, as I was still having difficulty reading since my eye surgery. I wanted no problems reading from my papers the day of Tim's hearing. Once I was satisfied with what I put together, I called his lawyer and asked if he would care to hear what I prepared. I wanted his opinion on its appropriateness. He listened as I read through it and when I finished, he simply said, "Wow, that's fine. Now I understand why Tim asked you to join him."

I felt as prepared as I could be for the mediation hearing, but it was unnerving to think about facing those intimidating people who would represent the archdiocese that day. We had the truth on our side, however, and I knew what I knew—and that's what I could speak about for Tim. He deserved an acknowledgement of wrongdoing, an apology from the church, and some form of justice to be decided by the mediator. If I was feeling nervous, I could only imagine how Tim must have been feeling. I prayed for him and his family to make it through the long, stressful day they were facing.

Joe drove me, and we arrived before eight thirty in the morning at the Laclede Gas Building in downtown Saint Louis. Joe eventually would settle himself comfortably into a recliner in the reception area on the twenty-third floor of the US Arbitration and Mediation offices, where he could relax and watch TV while I addressed the mediation board inside the conference room.

Tim told me his lawyer, Ken Chackes, had advised him and his family to dress comfortably that day, as the mediation process would take quite a while. He had worn his jeans with a denim shirt and navy blue sweater, along with his favorite New Balance tennis shoes. He told me, "I plan on being as comfortable as possible when I tell the church representatives and mediator about Father Christian." His wife, brother, parents, and I all thought the same and arrived in nice but casual clothes as well. His lawyer, though, arrived looking very businesslike in his suit.

Upon arrival, everyone was directed to one large waiting room with many comfortable chairs. After greeting us, Tim introduced Joe and me to his parents and brother. As we shook hands, I told them, "I'm glad to meet you but wish it was under different circumstances. I'm so sorry for all the pain my brother brought to your family."

After sitting by them, Tim's mom began telling of Norman's involvement with their family. She told us, "Father often stopped by unexpectedly to see Tim. I thought it was odd when I'd tell him it wasn't a good time because the boys were in the bathtub, but he'd tell me, 'It's okay; that won't bother me any.' He'd go right into the bathroom with them, knowing the boys were stark-naked."

I could sense her pain as she told me, "After I had turned to Father Christian for help with some marital problems, he encouraged me to divorce my husband. Looking back now, I believe he wanted my husband out of the way so he could have easier access to Tim."

It didn't surprise me when she said, "Father was inappropriate at times with me, too. I didn't understand a priest 'coming on' to me like he sometimes did. He even brought me gifts from his trips and sabbaticals."

I told Mrs. Fischer that Norman never brought any souvenirs back for his sisters; he rarely even told us when he was going on a trip.

Obviously troubled, she told me, "I can't forgive myself for not recognizing what Father was doing to Tim."

Tim's dad added, "It hurts that Father Christian destroyed my relationship with Tim. He damaged our whole family. Now, thirty years later, we've finally learned the truth. Tim and I are back in each other's lives; but Father took so much from us."

The more I heard how Norman had destroyed their family, the

more disgust I felt for my brother. I was just as disgusted with the church leaders' lack of compassion for the many victims. I had spoken only briefly with Tim's brother when things began, promptly at 9:00 a.m. A gentleman entered the room and quietly called our names, asking that we follow him. My husband then headed to the reception area.

Tim, his wife, lawyer, and I quickly followed our escort down a long hallway into a very small, windowless room. He directed us to take seats on one side of a beautiful, highly polished, extended wooden table, while he took the seat at the end of the table to our left. I realized then that he was the mediator. Our seating was not very comfortable, as the chairs were cramped against the wall. Next, those attending for the archdiocese entered the room, all dressed very businesslike, and there were double the number I was told to expect. In all, there were three lawyers—Bernard Huger, Lucie Huger, and Ed Goldenhersh—in addition to Dr. Susanne Harvath, a mental health professional; Peggy Henderson, a volunteer; and Monsignor John Shamleffer, JCL, Judicial Vicar of the Metropolitan Tribunal, Archdiocese of Saint Louis.

After all were seated, the mediator started by introducing himself as Mr. Geigerman. I was the first person called upon to speak. He introduced me to the church representatives as Father Christian's sister, Carol Kuhnert, and then asked me to begin.

I remained seated and began reading from the papers I had prepared (entire statement in appendix), looking up at the emotionless faces and cold eyes staring at me from the other side of the lengthy table to emphasize what I was saying. Their stern stares didn't frighten me; if anything, I was strengthened by them. I began, "I've been in contact with Norman, various priests, and bishops for the past sixteen years regarding sexual-abuse cases. Mostly, I've been told it's none of my business; they were taking care of it."

There was no warmth of friendliness radiating from anyone on the other side of that table. Tim told me that a young female lawyer in the group never would look at him. He said he was later informed she was the daughter of the lead lawyer.

Disgusted, I told them, "All I saw was cover-ups and the church avoiding victims and their families. I saw no reaching out to victims, no apologies, no compassion, and no change over all these years in how they deal with sexual abuse. It bothers me yet that the archdiocese didn't even warn my sister or me about our brother being a danger to our children. I've forgiven my brother. He's answering to God now that he's dead. But until the church leaders start holding themselves accountable for the harm they've done and continue to do to sexual-abuse victims, I cannot trust nor respect them. They continue to keep priests just like Father Christian in active ministry now.

My brother told all his victims that no one would believe them if they told; they were just kids. They'd believe the priest, and he was right! The church's cover-up is so good, if Norman hadn't victimized his own niece, and if she hadn't found the courage to tell me about him, I never would have known what he was. I believed my daughter when she told me her uncle was a child molester." Still feeling their intimidating stares penetrating me from across the table, I told them, "I feel betrayed by the church leadership. Stop making the church the victim in all of this. The bad publicity is all your own doing."

While more was said, my main point was they needed to take appropriate action regarding the molester/priest; if guilt is acknowledged, he needs to be turned over to the police. "His crime is worse because of his position of trust and respect in the church. He deserves no special treatment from anyone."

I thanked Tim and Mr. Chackes for inviting me to join them for the mediation hearing. I appreciated the opportunity to speak with the archdiocesan representatives along with the mediator. After decades of written letters and talks with clergy, I assumed the hierarchy had disregarded me, as I received few replies and never saw any real change in how the church was dealing with its abusers and their victims. I finished what I had to say by telling them the church needed to show compassion for all the victims. "They must stop being silent about one another. Their cover-ups are as bad, if not worse, than the sexual abuse itself."

Once I had finished speaking, several of them questioned me. While I don't recall specific questions, I answered them and also mentioned that Jeanne and I were stunned the day Norman explained to us that the archdiocese instructed the therapists to be careful of what was written in his personnel file in case it was subpoenaed for a court case. They gave no response to that.

Mr. Geigerman listened intently the entire time I spoke. The tension in that room could have been cut with a knife, and I was relieved when he told me I was excused; he personally escorted me out of the room. When doing so, he handed me a business card and said, "Thank you for coming today. If you would like to discuss your concerns further, you can call Monsignor Shamleffer and make an appointment to talk with him and the Archdiocesan Sexual Abuse Review Board. His information is on this card."

I thanked Mr. Geigerman for listening to me; then he turned and reentered the mediation room to listen to the next speaker.

The Sexual Abuse Review Board he mentioned had originated as the Gennesaret Committee in the late 1980s to review allegations of clergy sexual abuse against minors. The board's purpose was to ensure that persons sexually abused by clergy or others working for the Archdiocese of Saint Louis were taken care of by the church and that their abusers were removed from active ministry or would no longer work near children. This all sounded good, but unfortunately, there's been little action on the church's part, except when it is court-ordered. Even then, they often must be reminded to do it.

Once I left the mediation room, it was Tim's brother's turn to join him in facing the church representatives and tell what he knew about his brother and Father Christian's relationship. He was looking forward to speaking up for Tim; no one in that room would intimidate him. Earlier, in the waiting room, he had told me, "Tim hadn't said anything to me about Father raping him back when it occurred, but I always had a feeling that something bad had happened because Tim wasn't the same happy kid. He seemed so down all the time, and I couldn't figure out why."

I sought out Tim's parents to let them know I was leaving. They were still waiting for their turns to address the archdiocesan representatives and mediator. They would tell their own horror stories of how Father Christian preyed on their family. Their hearts ached badly, and they blamed themselves for not realizing his intentions back then—but he was a priest! They had only the utmost trust and respect for him. It was going to be a long, emotionally draining day for their entire family. The pain my brother and the church caused just this one family has been devastating. Yet the hierarchy continues its hesitancy to acknowledge wrongdoing, apologize, or offer help for what has happened to such victims. They shouldn't need to be forced to do these things.

At least the room where they sat waiting was welcoming. Bright sunlight gleamed through the many large windows along the one wall, providing a beautiful view of downtown Saint Louis. Various snacks and beverages were provided on a large table in the middle of the room. The large cushioned chairs offered some comfort during that long day. Tim later told me they had all been given lunch, as they were not dismissed until late afternoon.

As I said my good-byes to Tim's parents, his mom held my hand and said, "I'm worried about Tim in there." She wouldn't have had to say a word; the look on her face said it all. The lifelong pain that Norman and the church had inflicted on this family was obvious. After brief hugs good-bye, I went to find Joe, who still was resting comfortably in that recliner. We headed home, but Tim and his family were on my mind the entire day.

What an experience that memorable day was for me—to stand with Tim, who I greatly admired for his courage, on the day he faced the church and told what Father Christian did to him. Tim placed the guilt, blame, and shame where it belonged—on Father Christian and the church leadership for keeping him in active ministry.

An acknowledgment by the church that something was done wrong or an apology would mean so much to those suffering from having been betrayed, molested by trusted and revered clergy. From what I've observed over the years, victims have been left to fend for themselves. Many have found strength in turning to each other through the Survivors Network of those Abused by Priests (SNAP). This organization works hard to get known pedophiles removed from active ministry in hopes of protecting unsuspecting children in today's parishes. It is strictly "a volunteer organization—a 501C3 charity registered with the federal government" (Dorris, 12-06-04, e-mail). They must "comply with all the rules and regulations and face an audit once a year." SNAP "has no lawyers or therapists on staff." They "do have four full-time staff and the same expenses as any business—rent, phone bill, postage, printing, travel expenses, etc." Leaders often pay their own travel expenses to take part in special meetings and events.

Most of SNAP's money comes from small donations, twenty-five dollars being typical. Many donations are from people who are frustrated with how the church is mishandling the problem of clergy sexual abuse of minors. I was told some victims do make a donation if they receive a settlement, but the vast majority of them never get help of any kind from the church. Lawyers have helped SNAP too, but many of them have taken cases without ever settling one, so they have not gotten a dime either. SNAP never gives money directly to a victim. Its donations are only used to help finance the process of getting molesters removed from active ministry.

Many Catholics blame the victims and SNAP organization today for giving the church and predator priests the bad press by talking to the media about what happened to them. The church leaders make it worse by their silence.

Many believe these victims' lawsuits are only about the money. I disagree. Lawsuits may be the only way to get the church's attention. Abuse victims are mainly interested in an acknowledgment of wrongdoing and in receiving an apology for what happened to them. They also want their abuser removed from active ministry so he can't hurt others. Many victims have incurred much debt over the years on medical bills, while trying to pull their lives together. The stress of keeping the secret can cause physical ailments that plague them for a lifetime.

A Google search of "health effects of childhood abuse" has shown that abuse survivors are sick more often and go to the doctor more. They are not "winning a lottery," as my brother once said, if the church finally helps them out financially.

Catholics need church leaders to show them by example how to reach out with compassion, understanding, and prayers to all the victims of predator clergy. This could be done so easily at every Mass, and it could help bring about a change in everyone's attitude toward the abused.

With all the thought given to Norman's sexual-abuse crimes during his priesthood, I began questioning the screening process for anyone who is admitted to the seminary. What would it take to turn someone away?

Knowing SNAP watches everything the church does, I asked Outreach Director Barb Dorris what was known about the seminary's screening process. She told me the church claimed "to have a tight screening process but that it didn't seem to be very effective" (Dorris, 12-06-04, e-mail). Quite a few pedophiles had been ordained since 2000, and a known molester was ordained as well, with the archdiocese claiming there was "grace in ordination."

I was also told those who did the evaluating at the seminary were part of the seminary staff. That didn't present a picture of objective evaluation. Plus, it was not unusual for facts to be hidden from the evaluators if it was known a person was a molester. With such red flags, why even consider such men for the priesthood?

The mediator at Tim's mediation hearing had suggested I take my concerns to Monsignor John Shamleffer, with the church's sexual-abuse committee. I started 2005 by writing Monsignor Shamleffer a letter on January 10, explaining my disappointment and frustration (entire 01-10-05 letter in appendix). I wondered why the church refused to take immediate action and remove molesters from ministry and how they intended to fix the problem; I had been waiting patiently for over sixteen years for some glimmer of hope that things were changing.

I didn't understand how priests like Norman could feel okay with God when going to their deaths when they never once apologized to their victims for the pain they'd caused.

I told Monsignor Shamleffer that I had always expected much more of clergy in respect to morals and integrity than I do of politicians or the general population, and I don't think I'm alone in that expectation. It's an enormous disappointment to realize they are no different from the average person—and many of them are worse. There were bishops who knew of clergy offenders but after sending them for treatment, they reassigned them to unsuspecting parishes— over and over! How can one trust or respect such decisions? I believe it is that realization that has been causing church pews to empty.

CHAPTER 21
Archbishop Naumann Transferred

It was January 16, 2005, when I read about Archbishop Joseph Naumann, the caring priest who had become our good friend over the years, being transferred. He was taking over the reins as head of the archdiocese in Kansas City, Kansas. I wrote to congratulate him on his new position, asking that he use his powers to bring healing changes in dealing with sexual-abuse cases within the church. I believed if anyone could do it, this man would be the one (entire 01-16-05 letter in appendix).

It brings me great sadness to think our friendship may be a thing of the past, but from the time I began speaking out in trying to get Norman to apologize and accept responsibility for the pain and suffering he caused so many children and families and for the church to do the same, I noticed a change in the archbishop's relationship with our family.

He used to write friendly little notes on his Christmas cards and enjoyed kidding around with my husband, Joe, calling him his "number-one man." They had chaperoned together for various teen functions back when he was a young priest at our parish. Father Joe was easy to talk with and proved to be very compassionate and willing to help anyone with difficulties. I completely trusted and respected him. There were times while raising our family when Joe and I needed advice. Sometimes, I turned to Father Joe, and he'd patiently listen and offer his thoughts on what was troubling me.

Father Joe attended Joe's fiftieth birthday party in 1987 and wrote some humorous recollections of Joe for the memories album we put together for him. He wrote:

> It is almost impossible to confine to one page the crazy events that Joe inspired. I recall the many quotes that Joe would attribute to me. Whenever I heard him begin a sentence with 'Father Joe said,' I would hold my breath and hope that all his listeners would know not to believe him. Usually, the quotes put in my mouth were an insult directed at another member of the CYC Adult Advisors, for example:
> Father Joe says that you have chicken legs.
> Father Joe says that you are too fat to ride in the boat.
> Father Joe says that you are operating a quart low.
> Most of all, when I think of Joe Kuhnert, I think of one of the most caring, generous, and selfless people I have ever known ... He's my number-one man!

Bishop Joe did surprise us in September 2003 with a short note, writing:

> I hope and pray that you and all your family are well. September 15 is the Feast of Our Lady of Sorrows, so it is the most appropriate day to remember you in prayer. I regret the personal pain you have suffered from sexual abuse of minors by clergy and the way it has been addressed by the bishops. I ask for your prayers for those of us entrusted with leadership in the church to have the wisdom and courage needed for our responsibilities. Thanks for your personal support and friendship over many years.
> —Bishop Joe

I greatly appreciated another caring note he sent on March 5, 2004, when the lawsuit against Norman became public. "Dear

Carol," he wrote. "Just a note to let you know you are in my prayers. I imagine the publicity surrounding the lawsuit against Norm has increased your pain. I pray that the Lord, as only He can, eases your burden. I pray the Lord brings healing to all the hearts scarred by this tragedy. Bishop Joe." He seemed to be the only one from the church giving any thought to me and my family.

A letter from him on April 18, 2004, responding to mine that asked about Norman, had a post script. "I still have my two hand-painted bowling pins!" He was referring to pins I had painted for him many years ago. It was a hobby I enjoyed when I was young. I painted hundreds of the pins as caricatures of many people. I had even painted one of Archbishop May for Norman to give to him. The archbishop liked it and sent me a note of thanks.

Back then, I had the highest respect and greatest trust in all clergy. They were up there on those pedestals, right where they belonged, according to my strict Catholic upbringing.

Except for a Christmas card stamped with his name, we no longer hear from Archbishop Naumann. I pray the humble, caring pro-life priest I've known and respected for so long still exists and is using his position as archbishop to bring about the needed change in the church, especially in recognizing that being pro-life includes protecting the life of these innocent children whose lives have been and are being destroyed by clergy.

I received a response from Monsignor Shamleffer (entire 01-25-05 letter in appendix), but instead of answering my questions, he suggested I meet with his committee to better understand things. I was to make an appointment with the Episcopal vicar, but the thought of doing so ran chills up my spine. I would have to give that matter a lot of thought.

Chapter 22
Persistence

I read an article in the Associated Press by Jim Suhr on January 28, 2005.

> Three priests, accused of sexual abuse years ago, have been defrocked, including one blamed in the alleged suicide of an ex-marine he was said to have molested in youth, Saint Louis archbishop announced Friday "with deepest regrets to all who have been harmed."
> Archbishop Raymond Burke said he "launched the proceedings, what the Roman Catholic Church calls laicization, last year against Michael McGrath, Donald "Father Duck" Straub and Robert Yim in light of credible allegations of sexual abuse of a minor against them. ... All three men, who each served in several Saint Louis area parishes, have been notified they have been "dismissed from the clerical state." None of the men has been criminally charged.

I found what he mentioned last extremely disheartening.

The article also stated that "a spokeswoman for the Survivors Network of those Abused by Priests called the defrockings 'a baby step'; it 'doesn't absolve Burke of the Christian duty to protect innocent children from these men.' ... The group pressed Burke to post on the archdiocese's website the names of all known, suspected, and admitted abusive clergy in Saint Louis."

I decided to write the archbishop again (entire 01-29-05 letter in appendix). I asked why he continued to ignore my sister's and my letters. I told him it was good he launched proceedings to laicize three priests for abusing minors but he needed to go further and help get them criminally charged, so they could end up in prison, thereby protecting children.

I mentioned the needs of clergy-abuse victims and how my brother had threatened his victims that if they told anyone, no one would believe them. I said I didn't understand why he wouldn't meet with those of his flock who had been victimized.

I asked him to stop protecting pedophile priests and rejoicing when they won by a technicality. I thanked him for urging anyone harmed by clergy to contact the archdiocese or authorities. I told him that many Catholics discuss their disappointment and complain to each other about what is going on; the ones who have given up on any change have just stopped going to church.

It was the beginning of a very cold February in 2005 when Tim called, expressing his frustration from not yet receiving the expected letter of apology from the archdiocese. Why should it take two months to mail the simple apology he was promised? Tim asked if I would join him at a press conference SNAP was holding to call attention to the bishop's inaction in this matter; of course I would.

On February 3, 2005, I drove to David Clohessy's home. I was riding with him to the press conference. While there, a reporter with the metro networks called to speak with David. In learning I was there, she asked for a phone interview with me as well. Sitting on the couch, I nervously took the phone from David; my anxiety waned as I realized this was another opportunity to make people aware of the church's lack of concern for clergy-abuse victims. After introducing herself to me, the reporter asked, "As Father Christian's sister, this must be difficult for you to speak about, but can you tell me how you feel and why you are doing this press conference today?"

I answered, "I no longer trust that the church is taking care of things, not for the victims anyway. I feel badly for this man and everyone else my brother abused, as well as the many others sexually abused by any religious. All have been terribly betrayed by someone they greatly revered and trusted. It takes enormous courage for victims to come forward and report their abusers. They fear not being believed. My brother told his victims no one would believe them. Everyone would believe him, the priest. I hope that, seeing this victim was believed, others will find the courage to report their abusers to the police.

"I hope to make people aware of the church's lack of empathy for these victims. The archbishop protects his priests incredibly well, covering up for them, but he ignores the rest of his flock. Victims, their families, and all parishioners are left to cope for themselves in healing and trying to understand any of it. It's shameful that the archbishop has yet to give Tim what he wanted most of all—his promised letter of apology from the church. Not receiving it has made Tim doubt the hierarchy's sincerity. It doesn't reflect well on the archbishop's empathy for these victims. They seem to be insignificant to him."

I let the reporter know it was time for us to leave. She thanked me for talking with her, and then David and I hurried off to meet the others in front of the Archdiocesan Headquarters. The press conference was to begin at 1:30 p.m., on the sidewalk in the bitter cold.

Bundled in winter coats, scarves, and gloves, we all shivered, bracing against the strong, frosty winds that wintry afternoon. Our group of ten or so SNAP members and supporters huddled together, waiting for the TV reporters to arrive. I was meeting most of the group for the first time. Tim's wife and young children had come with him.

Several reporters from various TV channels had arrived, so David started the press conference by stating why we were there. He waved me to the microphone, introducing me as Father Christian's sister, and pointed out that I and my family supported Tim, not Father Christian. That day was the first time Tim or I talked publicly about Norman's abusing him. Tim stood silently behind me as I spoke.

"It's extremely difficult for Catholics to believe priests would sexually abuse children," I said. "It's unthinkable our church leaders would continue covering for such priests; sending them for therapy and afterward, keeping them in active ministry. Often, they are reassigned to other parishes, where they can groom more unsuspecting parents and children. Victims of these abusive priests deserve everyone's compassion. They are the innocent ones.

"Priests who sexually abuse disgrace themselves and the church by callously misusing their positions of reverence and trust to take advantage of vulnerable children, and they destroy many lives in the process. Maybe if everyone voiced their concerns to the archbishop, deluged him with letters holding him accountable for keeping sexual abusers in ministry, he'd be more inclined to protect his flock and remove the predators.

"My family and I are very sorry for all the pain my brother caused to all his victims and their families. I encourage all abuse survivors to come forward and report whoever abused them to the authorities. All guilt, shame, and blame belong to the abusers and the church."

Tim came to the microphone next and bravely spoke. "I've been waiting nearly eight weeks for the letter of apology promised to me in December at my mediation hearing. The church has never tried to help, console, or apologize to me without lawyers or now, the press being involved. It makes me wonder if they really are concerned about protecting kids. If it takes eight weeks or more to say I'm sorry, how long does it take them to say stop the molesting, to the priests? It's taken at least thirty years that I know of. They told me in front of my lawyer that they believed me, but I guess it's too hard for the archbishop to send me my letter. Preventing the abuse of children must not be on his front burner."

Tim briefly mentioned his appreciation for my and my family's support. He had e-mailed February 1, 2004, before we held this press conference, saying. "Carol, if I haven't told you lately, thank you for all you have done to help heal my wounded soul. You are someone I look up to. Thank you for believing me." His message was heartwarming, not because of his gratitude but because I knew from my own daughter's fears of not being believed that it took courage for him to come forward and report Norman's crimes. I was proud of him and my daughter.

Once the press conference was over, we all walked inside the chancery with Tim as he delivered a stamped, self-addressed envelope for the archbishop's use to mail his letter of apology. In accepting it, the receptionist told Tim there was no one available to speak with him at the time. Even Tim's young son saw through her comment. They then went home to continue waiting for the letter promised Tim months ago. I wondered how many people would be disappointed by the archbishop's failure to give Tim his promised written apology. I hoped that many watching the news that night would let their feelings be known to the archbishop.

Besides TV, Internet, and radio coverage, our press conference was covered by various newspaper reporters. Kevin Lavery (http://news.stlpublicradio.org) wrote: "The sister of an accused child molester is calling on Saint Louis Archbishop Raymond Burke to make a formal apology for the abuse. Last December, the archdiocese settled a lawsuit against Father Norman Christian, who was accused of molesting victim Tim Fischer in 1972. The settlement required Archbishop Burke to write Fischer a letter of apology."

Mr. Lavery wrote that the letter hadn't been received, and I wanted the archbishop to be more compassionate toward these victims. He quoted me: "You would think he would be reaching out and protecting his flock, and I don't see him doing that ... He protects his priests very well, but he does not reach out to his priests' victims."

He further wrote that "church officials say an administrative snag is holding up the court-ordered apology." The archbishop's spokesman at the time, Jamie Allman, said, "The archbishop has had this letter [of apology] ready to go for two months now, but Mr. Fischer's attorneys and the attorneys for SNAP simply haven't bothered to give us Mr. Fischer's address."

That statement was incorrect, as they had already mailed their settlement to Tim; the apology letter could have accompanied it. Seems the archbishop found it more difficult to give Tim what he wanted most—that written admission of the church's wrongdoing in the letter of apology.

Tim's press conference received a lot of publicity. I could only hope that Catholics were taking note and contacting the archbishop about his lack of compassion for these victims.

Tim was extremely disheartened with the church hierarchy. Before the press conference began, he had told us, "I was refused a meeting with Archbishop Burke if I had my lawyer along, as it wouldn't be a pastoral meeting, and I couldn't bring any SNAP supporters along with me either. I wasn't about to enter a snake pit without my charmer along. I refuse to meet with them alone." It was obvious that Tim felt no welcoming or any form of compassion from the church after he reported that Norman had abused him.

Returning home that evening after the press conference, I received many supportive phone calls from friends and family who had seen or heard me on the news. Even our children received calls from their friends and neighbors. One of the calls came from another cousin of mine. She is a little younger than I am, and I couldn't remember when we last saw each other. She called to congratulate me on my courage in speaking up for the victim. Then she went on to tell me how her parents often called upon my newly ordained brother to counsel her in her early teens. I wasn't aware of it, but she said she had been difficult to handle during her teens, and her dad would frequently call Norman to step in and control her. She said she didn't give Norman an easy time, but as I listened, it sounded like he did the same with her as with my daughter. Sadly, my cousin never told anyone about his behavior with her; she just continued to rebel against authority. I truly doubt anyone would have believed her back then if she had reported Norman's behavior. She would have been seen as a troubled kid and he as the wonderful, revered priest, trying to get her on the right track.

The early years of my cousin's life were very difficult. It took her decades to find her way, and now I have a probable understanding as to why. It wasn't until after many years that she found a way to break free of Norman and all he drew her to; then she began to live a happier life. I wonder how many people's faith and lives he destroyed during his priesthood. How many people left the church because of just this one priest's criminal behavior and the way his crimes were hidden?

Tim e-mailed me in the middle of February, rather upset about something he read in the February 12, 2005 *St. Louis Post-Dispatch*. The church had released a statement made by Archbishop Raymond Burke that read, in part, "When a member of the church has knowingly, deliberately, and publicly damaged seriously the unity of the church, his or her bishop has the duty to impose a sanction, in order to call the offending person to repentance and to restore the unity of the church."

Tim wondered, "Has a Catholic priest raping an eleven-year-old boy knowingly, deliberately, and publicly damaged the unity of the church?" One would think so, yet Tim's perpetrator, Father Norman Christian, received a beautifully celebrated funeral and burial as a priest in good standing, with Archbishop Raymond Burke as the celebrant.

It was a long time in coming, but the archdiocese's promised letter of apology dated February 18, 2005, finally arrived in Tim's mailbox. Other than knowing Father Christian was no longer in active ministry, the apology and an acknowledgment of wrongdoing was what he had wanted most of all.

Following are excerpts of the letter:

> Dear Mr. Fischer,
>
> Through reports of members of the Gennesaret Committee of the Archdiocese of Saint Louis, I have been made aware of the painful experiences you described to those who attended the mediation of your report of sexual abuse by Norman Christian, which you reported occurred during the time when he was serving as a priest of the Archdiocese of Saint Louis. I understand that you have brought those painful experiences forward to the archdiocese in an effort to seek healing at this time in your life and to receive funds to assist you with healing.
>
> For my part, I want you to know how sincerely sorry I am for the suffering you have experienced for so long from the abuse of Norman Christian that you have reported. It pains me deeply ... that your trust in a priest ... was betrayed, with ... great consequences in your life.

The archbishop didn't refer to Norman as "Father Christian" at any point in his letter, yet he gave Father Christian that glorious funeral as a priest in good standing. He mentioned in the letter that "Norman Christian was removed from priestly ministry a number of years prior to his death. ... The archdiocese ... will do everything possible to protect children and young people in the parishes, schools, and other institutions. I seriously regret that the archdiocese was not able to provide that protection to you." He merely hinted at the church's wrongdoing when he expressed, "I sincerely regret the archdiocese was not able to provide that protection for you."

In closing, Archbishop Burke said he would welcome the opportunity to meet with Tim in the future, if he thought it would be helpful, and that he'd remain in his prayers.

The letter was signed, "Most Reverend Raymond Burke, Archbishop of Saint Louis." Though strangely worded, Tim was happy to have finally received the written apology.

The church's taking so long to send Tim his promised apology posed a question to many, who wondered why the hierarchy found it so difficult to admit to misconduct and to say I'm sorry. Do Catholics who donate on a regular basis realize that part of those donations go toward paying high-priced defense lawyers? These lawyers work to allow the church to escape accountability for the sexual-abuse crimes committed by predator clergy, many of whom are allowed to remain in active ministry. How many people have ever thought about that, and if so, are they comfortable with it?

The church seems to see everything from a lawyer's eyes. They really do not seem to care about a person who has been abused by clergy during childhood. If the statute of limitations is past, the church can simply excuse itself from any responsibility toward that abuse survivor. No compassion, no concern. This clearly is not the moral or Christlike thing to do.

Tim Townsend wrote an article in the *Post-Dispatch* on February 22, 2005, "Abuse Victim Gets Apology from Burke" (section B, page 1). Among other things he wrote, "The archdiocese has repeatedly said it will do everything in its power to help heal victims ... Nevertheless, it seems the simplest and perhaps the most meaningful thing a bishop can provide—a note of apology—is surprisingly difficult to obtain."

Chapter 23
Editorial

I read an editorial in the February 25, 2005, issue of the *Saint Louis Review*, titled "Healing Wounds and Preventing New Ones." It reported that the 2004 audits of the US Catholic dioceses showed nearly complete compliance with the safeguards to protect children from sexual abuse. The article went on to refer to the Gennesaret Committee, which is made up of laity and clergy, saying their work to help clergy sexual-abuse victims is "not a matter of throwing cash settlements at victims and their lawyers but an attempt to find the best way for the person who's been wronged to heal from the ordeal." How nice that sounds.

The editorial went on to say, "Abusers will never again be allowed to masquerade in Roman collars and give a bad name to the dedicated and holy men of the priesthood." I wondered how that could be said, as there are still such men in active ministry.

That editorial seemed so convincing; it was certainly what Catholics wanted to believe. However, having watched how the church dealt with sexual-abuse victims and the clergy who molested them over decades, the editorial came across as all talk and no action. There was little, if any, evidence the church was actually doing what it claimed.

My husband and I, both feeling strongly that the church's actions did not mirror the words in that editorial, made a decision regarding our monthly parish donations. We sent our pastor a note (entire 03-03-05 note in appendix), informing him that we decided to cut our parish donation in half, starting that month; the other half would be sent to SNAP every month thereafter to help with its efforts in supporting the victims of clergy sexual abuse in trying to get clergy molesters removed from active ministry. We still do this to this day. SNAP is a strong support system for all clergy-abuse victims and their families. I urge everyone to help support them in any way possible.

I felt a bit ill, wondering how many Catholics might believe what they read. After giving the matter a lot of thought, I got the idea to ask a friend of mine, who was president of the Women's Guild at the parish where my brother and I had grown up, to look into the possibility of allowing David Clohessy, Tim Fischer, and me, along with some members of the Survivors Network of those Abused by Priests, to come to speak to the women about the clergy sexual-abuse issue.

On February 26, 2005, I wrote my friend, explaining the need for victims to tell what happened to them at the hands of a priest when they were just kids and the importance for parishioners to hear it directly from the victims. I told her how people tended to victimize them again for reporting what the priest had done, blaming them for giving the church and predator clergy a bad name by talking about it. I stressed that the attitudes people have toward these victims needed to change; what had happened to them in their childhood was not their fault. I felt educating the parishioners with accurate information would help raise awareness of the wrongs being done, thus creating a change in behavior toward the victims.

I had hoped since it was my and Norman's home parish that many of the older parishioners would remember us and be more willing to listen to what we had to say. The idea to call upon my friend for assistance came after spending a sleepless night wondering what to do and praying for direction. I was filled with hope, and as it turned out my friend did help in making my point; just not the way I originally thought.

I explained to her that SNAP was not the demon organization out to destroy the church that many had been making it out to be. It was a large group of people—and still growing—who have had the misfortune of being sexually abused by a priest or other religious as a child. Some reported it when it happened, only to be punished for saying such a thing. They weren't believed. The church manages to cover things up, not wanting the facts to be known, and most Catholics don't want to hear them. If they knew the truth, they'd have to deal with it. It's easier to stay in denial and blame the victims. Why else do so many people look the other way?

Many SNAP members and supporters gathered on March 2, 2005, in the dark, on a cold, windy corner in front of the bishop's mansion, for a candlelight vigil. It was held in memory of all the victims who had taken their lives because of the abuse they suffered. There were no reporters, no attorneys, nothing to be gained, only offering love and support to the families grieving the loss of their loved one. That is what SNAP is about—people who care and support one another. This vigil is an annual event.

It was the second anniversary of the death of one such victim of clergy sexual abuse, and I sent his parents a note, expressing my sympathy and letting them know they were not alone in their struggle with the church. My heart truly ached for them. While I didn't know them or their son and could only imagine the pain and sorrow they were experiencing, I wanted to express to them how sorry I was that this had happened to their son and family.

I explained the one thing we shared was disappointment and anger with the Catholic Church leadership for its uncaring and disgraceful way of ignoring victims and protecting the pedophile priests. I briefly told how I learned of my brother's pedophilia. I told them that the church continued to protect my brother over the next seventeen years, while I believed they were taking care of things. While I never noticed any changes in how the church was dealing with its pedophiles and their victims over the years, I trusted they were handling things as they had said. I explained I decided to turn my attention to supporting victims of clergy after my brother was given a celebratory funeral as a priest in good standing. I hoped this family would find some small comfort in knowing they were not alone in holding the church accountable for what had happened to their son.

Chapter 24
Grief

The March 4, 2005, issue of the *Saint Louis Review* ran an article from the Archdiocesan Office of Laity and Family Life, providing tips for Catholics when they talked with someone grieving the loss of a closed parish. The Archdiocese of Saint Louis had been closing quite a few parishes at the time, and many were upset by it. The article listed ways of "showing an authentic concern for the grieving person."

As I read that article, I wondered why something similar couldn't be done to show that same concern for victims of clergy sexual abuse. I wrote the committee, suggesting the possibility and listing simple ways, similar to what they had done, that people could show concern and compassion for the clergy sexual-abuse victims and their families (entire 03-08-05 letter in appendix). I hoped they would agree there was a need for such help, but I was disappointed again, as I never received a response on my suggestion. I was ignored, which seems to be the church's way of dealing with people addressing the topic of clergy sexual abuse.

My cousin Fran, the former nun, called in March, asking if I wanted a picture of Norman she came across in her things. If not, she was going to pitch it. I had enough pictures of him; he had his picture taken every year at various parishes where he was assigned, and that was one thing he always gave to Jeanne and me. Plus, I had snapshots of him taken during family events.

I suggested Fran could contact SNAP and ask if they wanted it. She had told them a bit about herself after Norman died, saying that they could contact her if she could be of help to them. It is taking her a lifetime to recover from the abuse she suffered during her years in the convent. She could definitely relate to the victims of clergy abuse. "We have all been violated and abused. Finding peace within ourselves is our goal, forgiving ourselves for not knowing, and also forgiving others who know not what they do. We have to let go of the anger and move on."

It's heartbreaking when I think of how she endured so many years as a young girl in convent life, suffering abuse and reaching out for help, only to be sickened by the church's refusal to address any of the "horrible issues blaring at them in the face," as she referred to it. "It is like a huge volcano erupting, and they just look the other way, as if it doesn't exist."

Following a write-up in the *Post-Dispatch* March 20, 2005, by Tim Townsend, regarding abusive priests living at Regina Cleri, the priests' retirement home, the Wounded Brothers Center in Robertsville, and the Vianney Renewal Center in Dittmer, I e-mailed Mr. Townsend, thanking him for helping uncover some of the secrecy and getting the word out to the public. He did a great service, especially for all the unsuspecting families living near the three centers. None knew pedophiles were housed in those residences, free to come and go as they pleased. At least now parents had been made aware and could protect their children from having contact with them.

That same article explained how abusive priests from all around the United States often ended up living in Saint Louis facilities available through the archdiocese. Bishops and judges across the country could send them here permanently, but questions persisted regarding the facilities' security. The fact that families living near them had not been warned is another shameful example of children being put at risk, while predator priests are protected and cared for by the church. The assumption is made that these predators will not act out again. That is dangerous. My brother lived at all three of these facilities during different periods of his priesthood. He was well cared for and extremely happy while living at each one of them.

Regina Cleri is a retirement home for priests located in Shrewsbury, which is in south Saint Louis, Missouri. Norman enjoyed his comfortable rooms there, as well as the delicious food and royal treatment. He told me he hoped he could live there until he died.

Chapter 25
More Victims Come Forward

After months of contemplating the invitation to meet with the church's sexual-abuse committee, I made my decision, sending a response of "no, thanks" (entire 04-02-05 letter to Monsignor John Shamleffer in appendix). I didn't feel comfortable meeting with any of the committee members. Actually, I didn't think I could believe what they would say to me.

In April 2005, the world was saddened by the death of Pope John Paul II, who had become for many Catholics an example of compassion and integrity. In the spring of 2002, he had told the Catholic Church leaders in America there was "no place in the priesthood for those who would harm the young." He also said such abuse is "rightly considered a crime by society; it is also an appalling sin in the eyes of God." Sadly, it appeared the bishops completely ignored his words.

In April 2005, Joe and I were blessed with the arrival of another cute granddaughter. The other two granddaughters were delighted to finally have another girl in the ranks, as the boys outnumbered them. Our whole family was excited about her arrival. Again, we were blessed with happier things to think about.

I received a response to the letter I'd sent to the church's sexual-abuse committee (entire 04-11-05 letter in appendix). I was told to find copies of the committee's policies for handling sexual-abuse cases on the archdiocesan website or by contacting the vicar for Child Protection and Welfare. I was pleased the letter ended with Monsignor Shamleffer asking that I "continue to do all you can to support victims of abuse."

Monsignor did agree it was an issue for the entire church to reach out and help all the victims. He claimed the archdiocese "has removed anyone who has any substantiated allegations of sexual abuse," but from all I had been observing since learning my brother was a child molester, I didn't find those words believable. I've seen the church protect and defend predator clergy, even after being found guilty in court. In 2005, the Archdiocese of Saint Louis posted a $500,000 bond to keep a convicted priest out of prison, while they appealed his guilty verdict and prison sentence (Patrick, Robert, "Priest's sodomy conviction is reversed," 11-08-06, *St. Louis Post Dispatch* article).

It takes an enormous amount of courage for those who have been abused by clergy to report the crimes and press charges against their molesters, as they must face the wealthy church and its intimidating defense attorneys. These victims come armed with truth on their side but financially, they are no match. While taking that step is frightening, their decision to let go of the painful secret that's been haunting them all their lives may give them some peace. Hopefully, they can come to accept what happened was not their fault.

SNAP e-mailed me on April 11, inviting me to an upcoming press conference regarding two more of Norman's sexual-abuse victims. They had come forward to press charges. A Law and Order article in the April 14, 2005, *St. Louis Post-Dispatch* stated that victims were filing lawsuits, claiming Father Norman Christian had molested them on church property and at a Festus swimming hole in 1970 and 1971. They claimed the church knew he was a pedophile while he was at Sacred Heart Church in Crystal City, Missouri, and failed to protect children from him.

It was difficult holding back tears at this press conference as I listened to the victims' statements read, telling what my brother had done to them.

One of the men talked with me before that press conference and said that his eighty-year-old mother, who hadn't been told at the time he was molested by Father Christian, suffered a stroke upon learning about it now. His mom told him she felt terrible for not being able to help him when it happened. He explained to me that when he told his dad at the time of the abuse, his dad refused to believe him. How frightened and alone that little boy must have felt. I expressed my sorrow for all the pain that man endured.

Many long years had gone by, and this victim's dad was deceased, but after reading that another victim had spoken out about what Father Christian did to him, this man decided it was time to tell what Norman had done to him too. He told his mom the painful secret he had been keeping since childhood, and I imagine, with her heart aching for her little boy, she believed what her grown son now told her. With his mom's and SNAP's support, this man was finally able to go to the police and report the crimes Norman had committed against him when he was just a young boy.

It's sad, but this is what happened with many of the young victims who did tell a parent or other adult that they were molested by a priest. They were not believed, or even worse, they were punished for saying such things.

On March 7, 2005, Tim e-mailed Pete, Sue, and me: "What are you doing April 14? I will be speaking at a forum on justice at the library in University City at 7:00 p.m. I'll be talking about the great peace the three of you gave me with your real apology. I would love to see you all again! You don't have to speak, and I won't tell that you are there if you don't want me to."

I asked Tim how this came about. He responded, "Ken, my lawyer, is a friend of this woman lawyer. She read our story in the *Post-Dispatch* and called Ken, asking if I would do this. She just sent me a flyer this morning. Hope you can make it."

The flyer stated that Restorative Justice was a set of principles that guided the justice process. The public was invited to come to "learn about addressing crime through a new method that focuses on both victims and offenders." They would also "listen to crime victims share their experiences of healing and wholeness obtained through Restorative Justice principles."

I felt nervous for Tim that evening as we entered the large, crowded room. We were directed toward some long tables along one side of the area, where various informational papers and pamphlets were available. Recessed ceiling lights fully illuminated the room, and we noticed the many rows of chairs were filling quickly. A long table full of snacks stood against one wall, while several more tables, with chairs for the speakers, were stretched end to end in front of the room.

We spotted Tim and his wife but could only talk briefly with them, as we had to find seats before the event got underway. Each of us whispered "good luck" to Tim. I added, "You're going to do a great job."

It was National Crime Victims' Rights Week, and the evening was meant to help the public learn about addressing crime. For us, it was about seeing Tim come to life. How far he had come from the quiet, monotone-speaking young man we first met at David Clohessy's home when we gathered to do the interview with Bill McClellan. Tim was now able to speak about his experiences in public, and it appeared to be a bit more bearable for him.

We fought hard to hold onto our emotions. Still, tears trickled down our faces as we heard Tim telling of Norman's raping him when he was only eleven. I doubt Sue, Pete, or I will ever forget hearing the listeners' gasps at the horror of what Tim disclosed. He spoke with great composure that evening.

Our hearts ached as we were reminded of what Tim and his family endured because of Norman's and the church's poor judgment and cover-ups all these years. It's unthinkable and shocking that a priest would rape a child. It's absolutely heartbreaking to realize that a member of your own family is that evil monster.

I've gone back over the years in my mind, looking at old snapshots of family gatherings for signs, something that would have given me a clue that my brother was this dangerous, evil person, but there is nothing. I always noticed he paid more attention to his nephews than his nieces, but I didn't read anything into that, because he was uncaring toward me, too, for most of my life. I just figured that being a priest, he didn't want to bother with girls. I had always faulted myself for his disinterest in my life.

Tim had mentioned his gratitude for our reaching out and supporting him against our own family member, adding, "Never in my wildest dreams did I ever expect anything like that to happen." We knew we had been of some help to Tim, but it never occurred to us that our actions would have meant that much to him. We just felt it was the right thing to do.

Attending that forum took an emotional toll on all three of us; we felt bad for everyone who had shared a personal story that night. Everybody there offered encouraging words to the victims. Conversations could have continued for hours, but the room had to be vacated before the library closed.

Tim's wife e-mailed me shortly after the event (Fischer, 04-16-2005, e-mail): "Carol, thanks for coming to the forum to hear Tim speak. He has come a long way in being able to speak about his experiences, and it has been very healing for him. He has improved a lot emotionally. This is in large part due to the support he has received from you and your family. Kim."

On April 19, 2005, I received an e-mail from Survivor's Network of those Abused by Priests, informing me that Senate Bill 17 was stalled in the House of Representatives. The biggest opponent to the bill was the Ohio Catholic Conference. They had more resources, experience, and members than SNAP.

While abuse survivors do not have the clout, lawyers, and wealth that the Catholic Church holds, they come together to speak the truth about their pain as the SNAP organization. Their biggest goals (both past and present) are to prevent more children from being abused and to help victims heal. They knew Senate Bill 17 would do both.

On April 21, 2005, I wrote to our state representative, Michael Vogt, explaining why I felt so strongly that he should do all he could to help pass Senate Bill 17. I received a belated reply from him dated September 6, 2005, assuring me of his support in this matter (entire letter in appendix).

Chapter 26
Not Welcome

I was waiting patiently for an answer from my friend as to when some members of SNAP and I could expect an invitation to speak to the Women's Guild at my old parish. She had told me she was waiting for the pastor's permission to allow us to speak to the women on the subject of clergy sexual abuse. Then came the day of my big disappointment; my request had been turned down. That was the least of it, however; my friend actually made the decision for the pastor.

In her May 3, 2005, reply to me (entire note in appendix), she explained:

> I have to clear speakers with Monsignor, and he was gone, then busy; he asked for time to think on it, and I said okay. In the meantime, I tried to feel out quite a few of the ladies, and I was quite shocked when every single one I approached told me that they did not want to listen to any speaker about this and would probably leave if I had one. When Monsignor finally got back to me, he asked me what I thought and felt and I had to say that after speaking to the ladies, I felt I would turn your request down. He agreed. I hope you won't hold it against me, but there's no use getting the ladies any more riled up.

My first reaction was complete surprise, followed by feelings of hurt, disappointment, and anger from what she had done. I couldn't understand why she had taken it upon herself to make that decision, but after dwelling on it for a few days, it finally occurred to me that she and the ladies from the guild actually helped me make my point about the bad attitude Catholics show toward those who have been raped or sexually abused by clergy. My friend's negative response was actually a blessing in disguise.

The ladies' behavior provided a good example for the pastor as to how Catholics victimize abuse victims further—they blame victims for giving the priest and church a bad name by telling what happened. When I sent my friend a note, thanking her for getting back to me, I told her just that: that she and the ladies helped prove my point. I said I would take it up with the church leaders myself, and I asked her to keep all the victims and their families in her prayers.

I decided to write the church's pastor (05-06-05, Kuhnert letter, entire letter in appendix) and sent copies to Archbishop Raymond Burke and Monsignor John Shamleffer as well. On May 6, I wrote my letter to the three of them, calling attention to my friend's turning down my request to speak. I wanted them to address the attitude of most Catholics toward abuse victims, something that church leaders have never done. I was hopeful they would see the need to address this subject with church members.

My cousin had sent me newspaper clippings from California (Pepper & Galvin, 05-07-05, The Orange County Register, CA, article) showing the archbishop in Orange County hugging clergy-abuse victims as he apologized to them for the church's wrongdoing. Newspapers ran the Orange County archdiocese's sincerely worded apologies and the victims' expressions of gratitude. I wondered why the St. Louis Archdiocese couldn't publicly express sorrow for what had happened to its victims. I asked that they give serious thought to my concerns and suggestions.

Chapter 27
Monsignor Visit

Monsignor Telthorst phoned one day to tell me he had received my letter and would like to chat, his place or mine. My thought was that Archbishop Burke, Monsignor Telthorst, and Monsignor Shamleffer had talked among themselves after receiving my letter, and he was told to respond to me. I realized then that my hope of getting a response from each of them with his own opinion was foolish.

I was not comfortable meeting in Monsignor's office, so I asked him to come to my home. We agreed on June 1 for the meeting, and as it would be late in the morning when he would arrive, I invited him for lunch.

My husband, Joe, would join the discussion, but I wanted someone familiar with SNAP as well, someone who could readily answer any questions. A woman whose teenage son had been abused by a priest and later had taken his own life accepted my invitation. Mary Ellen had great public-speaking skills and could give her perspective of what victims and their families suffer because of the church's shameful handling of its clergy sexual-abuse problem. I admire her patience, strength, and determination; she's a very caring person and strongly supports all clergy-abuse victims.

The weather was hot and humid on the day of our meeting. Mary Ellen was comfortably dressed in a cotton blouse, skirt, and cool sandals. She smiled as I opened the door, inviting her to come inside our air-conditioned home.

After introducing her to Joe, we went into our living room, and Joe brought some cold beverages in for the three of us as we sat discussing the things we wanted to talk about with Monsignor. Besides being an impressive speaker, Mary Ellen is attractive and gracious. Her striking facial features would later seize Monsignor's attention as they distorted in grief while speaking of all she and her family had endured since her son's sexual abuse by a priest.

I told her, "I intend to ask Monsignor if he is willing to help rid the church of its pedophile clergy and help him understand the importance of reaching out to the victims and their families. I want him to realize that he needs to inform his parishioners of what is happening when their parish priest is removed because of sexual abuse. They deserve to know the truth. He's going to hear what I've experienced with my brother and the church since learning about his crimes."

I realized Monsignor's meeting with us might be the church's way of appeasing me—maybe I'd stop speaking out publically. I'm sure the hierarchy was bothered that a priest's own family talked of the diocese's negligence. Still, I had to hold on to hope that Monsignor's willingness to listen was a step in the right direction.

I told Mary Ellen, "We need to make Monsignor understand that the days of covering up are over, and I'd like to hear him explain why molesters are kept in ministry. I want to hear his thoughts about the church's appalling mishandling of its clergy sexual-abuse cases."

Mary Ellen nodded. "I'm anxious to hear what he has to say, too, and I'll gladly answer any questions he may have about SNAP. I intend to tell him about my experiences with the church. I want him to know what happened because of Father Funke's sexually abusing my son. Thank God, that priest was found guilty, but he only served ten years in prison for the crimes he committed against Steve."

Nearly an hour passed since Mary Ellen's arrival, and we were beginning to think Monsignor wasn't coming when our phone rang—he had gotten lost. I gave him further directions, and it wasn't long before he was at our door. He sheepishly apologized. "I'm so sorry to be late. I didn't check the directions you mailed me. I hope my being late hasn't ruined the food you prepared."

"It's okay," I said. "I'm just glad you were finally able to find us."

All was fine. I had prepared a large pot of homemade vegetable beef soup, along with bacon, sliced tomatoes, crisp lettuce, and toast for making BLTs. I put all the food, condiments, crackers, chips, and pretzels on the kitchen table and let everyone help themselves. It was lunch as I would normally do for Joe and me—very casual, using our everyday dishes, utensils, glasses, and paper napkins.

Our conversation remained lighthearted as we ate, not touching on the subject for which we had gathered. Monsignor glanced out the sliding glass doors to our deck and noticed the river flowing by at the bottom of the hill. Sunlight reflected from the rippling water. He remarked, "It's beautiful in the country. Have you been living here long?" Before I could answer, he asked, "Are there many fish in there?"

I told him, "We moved out here after Joe retired. It's been five years already, and there are oodles of fish in that river, waiting to be caught. It's relaxing, rowing the boat up the river and sometimes tossing a line in to fish. Our grandkids love fishing and swimming in the river. Norman liked coming out to fish too." Our conversation remained mostly about the joys of life in the country.

When we finished eating, Mary Ellen, Joe, and I cleared the table. Once the food was put away, we rejoined Monsignor at the table and began the serious discussion that brought us together. Joe made sure coffee, iced tea, soda, and water were offered throughout the afternoon.

I must admit that Monsignor listened patiently to all we had to say and seemed to show concern. Mary Ellen provided him even more insight on clergy sexual-abuse victims from having worked closely with SNAP. She had experienced so much—her son's sexual abuse by Father Funke, the church's poor handling of it, and her son's later suicide in 1991—that she could answer some questions for Monsignor I couldn't.

He listened closely as I spoke about Norman, starting with his early years growing up in Our Lady of Sorrows parish school. I explained how many of his present parishioners knew my brother well—or at least they thought they did.

When I brought up the attitude of many Catholics toward clergy-abuse victims, Monsignor responded that he wasn't aware of that problem. I saw that as a big part of the problem. Pastors don't seem interested in how the clergy-abuse problem affects their parishioners or how they act toward the victims. If anything, pastors encourage those negative attitudes by not reaching out to the victims. They need to lead by example and pray daily with the parishioners for the victims during Mass. Reminders ought to be placed in the parish bulletins to pray for these victims, including a short prayer. I continued telling Monsignor what I had been doing since learning of my brother's pedophilia.

"I am disgusted with the archbishop for not even acknowledging my correspondence to him since he became the archbishop of Saint Louis," I said. "It seems to me that he's spending all of his time and energy protecting pedophile clergy and church assets. I see no signs of his reaching out to the victims and their families or his flock in trying to help them understand and cope with the turmoil."

I gave Monsignor a condensed version of what had transpired over the past eighteen years in my family, but he got a good idea of the toll it took on me and my family's faith in the church's leadership.

It was obvious that my patience with the church leaders had worn thin as I told Monsignor, "I learned about my brother's criminal behavior seventeen years ago. The church's answer to me then was they were taking care of everything; it wasn't mine to worry about. In all that time of watching not only Norman but many other accused clergy that surfaced over the years, and trusting that church leaders would remove molesters from ministry and help their victims, I saw no change in their actions." I explained to Monsignor what troubled me about Norman's and the hierarchy's behaviors, and then I became emotionally choked up, finding it difficult to go on.

I was extremely grateful that Mary Ellen had joined us that day, as she placed her hand on mine and softly said, "Monsignor, I have been involved with SNAP for many years. I turned to them for support after my son was sexually abused in the '80s by Father Funke. The Catholic faith had always been very important to me, but then I found that the people who told me how God wanted us to live our lives weren't living that same Christian life. They were doing some of the most un-Christian things I had ever known."

Monsignor listened intently as she continued. "When my son told me he had been sexually abused by Father Funke at our parish rectory, I held him. He cried and I cried." Mary Ellen told Monsignor of the emotional upheaval her son and all their family endured in trying to find healing and justice, while trying to get his abuser removed from ministry and punished for what he had done. They wanted to be sure he wouldn't be allowed to hurt anymore children.

"I think what upset me most was that the police had two previous accusations against Father Funke," she said. "They had interviewed the parents and the children, but the parents refused to let their children testify. Part of me can understand that as parents, the first thing we want to do is protect our children. But if just one of them would have come forward and testified, my son would not have been abused."

Mary Ellen answered Monsignor's questions pertaining to the abuse victims and SNAP, and after some time, he asked her how her son was doing since he suffered the abuse. It was obvious he was startled when she said, "I no longer have my son. On January 25, 1991, Steve took his own life." Wiping her tears, she added, "It's still very difficult to talk about."

Monsignor seemed uncomfortable and immediately offered Mary Ellen his sympathy for her loss. I know it was the natural thing for him to do, but it was the first time I had heard a priest in the Saint Louis Archdiocese express compassionate words to someone in pain because of clergy sexual abuse. I wondered why it took a young victim's suicide to make it happen.

Monsignor suddenly seemed to think of something and completely surprised us when he abruptly stated, "My parish is a victim too. The parishioners are extremely distressed with our school's name being changed."

The archdiocese had closed a neighboring parish school, and its students joined his parish school. He was referring to a decision to rename the school for the blended students. Mary Ellen and I just sat there, dumbfounded by Monsignor's total lack of understanding. He actually had compared the parish's displeasure of a school's name change to the grief of a family mourning a young man's suicide.

We had been talking for hours when Monsignor asked, "What is it you want me to do?" I quickly responded, "We would like to speak to your parishioners to let them hear the victims' stories. David Clohessy, Mary Ellen, a few clergy-abuse victims, and I would be glad to address some of your parish organizations. Maybe if they hear what's actually happened, they'll change their attitude toward these victims. It could open the door to a healing process for your parishioners in dealing with the sexual-abuse scandal, and it would really help the victims in healing by being heard. Your parishioners would gain understanding as to why victims wait so long to report the abuse from their childhood. Monsignor, how soon do you think we could speak to your parishioners?"

The expression on his face could only be described as "deer caught in the headlights," as he seemed to think for a bit. Then he told us, "It would be at least in the fall before I'd even be able to think about that happening."

"That would be okay!" Mary Ellen happily responded.

Monsignor quickly added, "You know I can't make people come to anything."

"We realize that," I replied, "but you can surely help by making the meeting possible. Plus, you can encourage your parishioners to attend. Examples of your showing compassion for these victims would make all the difference. You could start tomorrow, by praying for these victims with your parishioners at daily Mass. Please help them realize these were innocent children who were betrayed by the very priests they were taught to obey and trust."

"I could probably do that," Monsignor replied, but he didn't really commit to anything we asked of him. He just left us with false hope.

We had asked him to pray with parishioners daily for all the victims and their families, as well as for the priests, and to ask the archbishop to request such prayers be said at every parish in the diocese.

As he was leaving, he thanked us for talking with him, adding, "I have a better understanding of the abuse victims and their families after hearing all you had to say." Monsignor did seem patient while listening to us that day, but in retrospect, I think he was only trying to placate us.

I'm sorry to say that in all the years that have passed since we talked with Monsignor, I still haven't heard prayers during Mass specifically for clergy-abuse victims. I do not know if the archdiocese doesn't care about them, or if it simply doesn't want to acknowledge them.

I hope Monsignor continues to think about the things Mary Ellen told him. Father Funke was sent to prison for ten years for his crime against her son but has since finished his prison time and is now a free man again.

I sent a note to Monsignor the next day, thanking him for making the time to come to our home and listen to what we had to say (entire 06-01-05 note in appendix). I also asked him to request that the archbishop instruct all pastors to lead by example in showing compassion and understanding for victims by inviting victims to speak of their abuse at their parishes. That step could help parishioners feel comfortable in reaching out to these victims themselves, and they wouldn't be afraid to open their minds and hearts to listen. Since Monsignor's parish had experienced the removal of two molesters from ministry within a short time, I thought it would benefit the parishioners there to listen to some of the abuse victims. I think it's important that Catholics know how the victims' and their families' lives have been affected because of the abuse and the church's treatment of them since reporting the abuse. I reminded him I'd be willing to come with members of SNAP to speak at his parish whenever he could schedule us in.

Members of SNAP have yet to be invited to speak at that parish. It seems the church doesn't want parishioners to hear what victims have to say. Perhaps they think the less information parishioners know, the fewer questions they'll have to answer.

Chapter 28
And Yet Another

When another victim came forward to report that Norman had sexually abused him, I was again invited to join members of SNAP at a press conference in front of the Archdiocesan Office. I was more than willing to speak out in support of this victim and let him know my family and I were very sorry for the pain my brother caused him and so many others during his lifetime. I felt uneasy and somewhat shaky standing there. As I listened to the victim describe how my brother had destroyed his young life, it was hard to contain my emotions, and I found myself once again swallowing my anger (and terror) as I thought about how many children might have been harmed by my own brother. I took peace in knowing this particular victim finally managed to free himself of the painful secret that had tormented him for so long. I hoped others still suffering in silence would hear his story and find the courage to report their abusers as well.

Since another of Norman's victims came forward publicly, I decided to send a letter to the editor of the *Post-Dispatch* in hopes of encouraging others to think about what these clergy-abuse victims have gone through.

My May 20, 2005, letter to the editor of the *Post-Dispatch*:

> The sexual abuse of children is a crime that will be repeated over and over again throughout a pedophile's

lifetime, until he or she is discovered and stopped. It's good that some of Father Norman Christian's victims are now finding the courage to let go of the ugly secret they've been keeping since they were kids. What happened to them was not their fault. It was their love, trust, and respect for a priest that made them easy prey for such an unlikely pedophile.

Years ago, parents taught their kids to respect, trust, and obey all religious. It was unthinkable that one would ever harm a child. I ask those who refuse to believe the reports of sexual abuse by clergy to please open their hearts and minds, and listen to what the victims have to say. Father Christian threatened his victims by telling them that no one would believe them, that he'd be believed, the priest!

My family and I are very sorry for the pain my brother caused to heaven knows how many during his priesthood. Those abused by clergy deserve our compassion and understanding, and they need to be remembered in everyone's prayers.
Sincerely,
Carol Kuhnert

Tim called toward the end of May, saying a man had called him from Tucson, Arizona. He had come across Tim's website, telling his story of abuse, and in reading it, he recognized Father Christian's name. He told Tim that he and his brother were also victims of Father Christian. Sadly, the man's brother had taken his own life. He said he'd thought of calling SNAP several years prior but didn't follow through. Tim suggested he call David Clohessy right then, as he would find the support he needed through them.

It's sad to realize how many people there may be like this man—hurt so badly by my brother or other clergy but still too frightened to report their abuse.

Three lawsuits had been filed by former Sacred Heart Parish altar boys from Crystal City, Missouri, saying the late Reverend Norman Christian sexually abused them in the late 1960s and early 1970s, when he was a priest at that parish. The men claimed he abused them at the church rectory, in his car, and at a swimming hole on a creek owned by the Festus property owner, also named in the lawsuit (Peggy Scott, 05-13-05, the *Leader* article).

The defendants' attorney, Ken Chackes, said, "In records we've obtained from the archdiocese, it shows Father Christian admitted abusing a number of boys from 1963 to mid-1980s. But it didn't come out until Tim Fischer sued. If they had acknowledged what happened, it would have made a huge difference in Tim Fischer's life. If they had reached out to victims years and years ago, it would have made a big difference in these men's lives. They lived with the secret all these years."

Monsignor Telthorst must have reported to the archbishop after his chat with us, as I received a letter dated June 2, 2005, from Archbishop Burke shortly thereafter (entire letter in appendix), acknowledging the May 6 letter I had sent him, Monsignor Shamleffer, and Monsignor Telthorst.

Archbishop Burke explained that he understood my pain but said, "With respect to your letter of May 6 last, it is not possible for me to respond to it in detail. A number of the assumptions and assertions, which underlie some of your conclusions, are simply not verifiable. Among these is the thinking of the women of Our Lady of Sorrows parish, who preferred you not speak at a meeting of the Women's Guild of the parish. Another is the attribution to Monsignor Telthorst, by the writer of the correspondence of May 3 last, of reasoning which is reported secondhand."

Archbishop Burke's letter proves his commitment is to protect the church's image, assets, and clergy.

I received a very nice letter on June 7, 2005, from Monsignor Telthorst, thanking us for talking with him (entire letter in appendix). He was quite gracious in mentioning what he had learned from us and said he was sorry for what my brother's behavior caused me to suffer over the years. It appeared that he understood what we had told him. Monsignor mentioned he was praying for sexual-abuse victims in the petitions at Mass and would look for other ways to bring up the topic, such as in his homilies.

After reading his letter, I felt some hope, but I think he may have been telling me what I wanted to hear. We have yet to receive an invitation to speak to the parishioners of that or any parish.

Around the middle of June 2005, Tim called to say another man had contacted SNAP about having been molested by my brother. He called from Washington, DC, and said Norman had molested him at St. Peter's parish in Kirkwood, Missouri, in the early 1960s.

That was Norman's first parish assignment after being ordained a priest in 1961. I find it especially disturbing that he, as a newly ordained priest, began his criminal acts on children at the very first parish he was assigned. Question after question went through my head. What happened during all those years he spent in the seminary? What was involved in the church's preparing him for the priesthood? How could they have not noticed something was wrong with him during all the "formation" he went through? How could he have received the Sacrament of Ordination and then immediately rape children? What was instilled in him throughout the seminary years that allowed him to behave in such evil ways and still believe he was a chosen man of God?

It sickened me even more to realize my brother was acting out his evil desires during the time he performed my and Joe's wedding ceremony in 1962. The brother I had held in such high esteem for becoming a priest was not at all the special, holy man I thought him to be. I wondered what he honestly thought of himself.

I received an e-mail from Tim in the early part of September 2005, along with a file containing parts of his personal journal that he wanted to share with me. I was once again moved to tears. Tim's personal writings revealed how badly the church had hurt him and his family. If I'd had any doubts about whether I was doing the right thing in speaking out, they were wiped away as I read his journal notes. I was gratified when I read a comment he made about Pete, Sue, and me: "They have restored my faith in mankind. In my wildest dreams I would have never guessed this would have gone down like this. Their kindness has gone farther than they'll ever know. It has given hope to all of us in SNAP."

Among other comments, Tim also said that Pete's relaying his exact message to Norman was "the biggest blessing, that [Father Christian's] own family is helping me through this."

I thanked him for sharing his personal thoughts with me. "It makes me feel good to know we were of some help to you," I said. I have the greatest respect for Tim for courageously reporting his abuse by a priest. Thanks to his speaking out, many others are now finding the courage to report their own childhood abuse.

On July 2, Joe and I received a letter from the archbishop regarding the 2005 Annual Catholic Appeal. The letter stated the church's goal was within reach but was behind last year's pace, and our help was needed more than ever. We had not participated in this collection for many years, preferring to make our donations privately to various charities. We had signed the pledge card at church and marked it "unwilling to participate." I wrote a letter to the archbishop, explaining what it would take for us to participate in that collection again, but I did not receive a response (entire 07-06-05 letter in appendix).

Joe and I attended Mass one Sunday at our daughter's parish, and I noticed a little prayer in the parish bulletin that could be said for the protection of our troops in active service. There was also a section explaining the importance of the parish's being in compliance with the archdiocese's new rules pertaining to protecting God's children. I looked a little further, thinking possibly I would find a prayer for those sexually abused by clergy but found nothing.

I decided to write the pastor with my suggestion (entire 07-06-05 letter in appendix). Once again, I was simply ignored. It should not have been difficult for the pastor to have at least acknowledged my letter and maybe say he was giving the matter some thought, but he did not. Sadly, I had become accustomed to not getting a response to my correspondences with the church. It seemed when I mentioned anything the clergy didn't want to discuss, they just ignored me.

CHAPTER 29

Press Conference

It was July 19, 2005—a very hot summer afternoon—when members of SNAP gathered once again to hold a press conference, this time outside the Boy Scouts headquarters in the Central West End of Saint Louis. I had been invited to join them, as another of my brother's victims had filed a lawsuit against a Cub Scout leader, along with a priest, Father Norman Christian. The boy was a member of Sacred Heart parish in Crystal City and had been sexually abused by the two predators, who shared him as their victim—two adults in powerful positions sharing a child in sexual abuse. I was appalled, and my heart went out to him as I listened to his story.

These unspeakable crimes happened in the early 1970s, when the victim was about twelve years old. The sexual-abuse report stated both adults often "skinny-dipped" in a creek, "after which the scout leader allegedly sexually molested the plaintiff in a pickup truck. Christian then came along and molested the boy as well." The victim told his father what happened but wasn't believed.

Lawsuits were filed against Norman, stating he sexually abused two other boys in the 1970s. Those lawsuits claimed the scout leader had witnessed Norman's abusing the boys but did nothing to stop it—a disgusting pair! Those poor children must have felt completely alone and so very frightened.

The *St. Louis Post-Dispatch* ran an article by Elizabeth Holland on Wednesday, July 20, 2005, about the Jefferson County man suing the

Archdiocese of Saint Louis and an ex-scout leader. I sent her a thank-you for helping the victim get his story told. Both the archdiocese and the Boy Scouts organization had handled things badly and needed to acknowledge that fact to the victim, along with making a sincere apology for what he and his family had endured for so long. Her article publicized how terribly this victim had been being treated by the church and the Boy Scouts organization. I hoped it would make people think and begin asking questions. I hoped too that it led parents to have serious conversations with their children about any possibility of their having been abused, as well as discussing ways to help them stay safe now.

On July 26 I sent a request to the pastor of our parish, asking that he add a prayer for sexual-abuse victims to the petitions prayed during Mass. I even gave him a suggestion for one: "For all the victims of sexual abuse, may our compassion help them to heal. May they find comfort in God's love and in knowing we care. We pray to the Lord." This prayer had been said at another parish during Mass, and I hoped our parishioners could do the same.

At Mass on August 7, 2005, a very watered-down version of that prayer was said—but at least something was said. At the very end of the petitions during Mass, I heard, "For those suffering from acts of terrorism, war, and sexual abuse, we pray to the Lord." That was it. This prayer was said for three Sundays, but I haven't heard it since. Prayers are said for the troops in war and the sick of the parish on a regular basis. The sexually abused are ignored, even in prayer, and I hadn't even specified clergy sexual-abuse victims. I had made a request at the same time through the parish prayer chain and to them, I did specify to pray for those sexually abused by clergy. I can only hope they followed through on my request.

The *Post-Dispatch* ran an article August 9, 2005, about a lawsuit alleging that a priest had sexually abused a man when he was a teenager in All Saints Parish in St. Peters, Missouri, in 1981. The priest's name caught my eye, as I remembered his being assigned at Our Lady of Sorrows when I was a child. It was obvious back then, even to me, that this priest liked spending time with boys. He, like my brother, ignored the girls.

After Norman told me of being molested at our parish when he was a kid, I wondered if that same priest might have molested him.

Since they're both deceased, I'll never know, but it's possible he was one of my brother's molesters. Whatever happened, it was Norman's decision to molest children. The only ones to blame for the harm he's done are Norman and the church for allowing him to remain in active ministry.

Sadly, the lawsuit filed against this priest was dismissed by the Appeals Court on the grounds of the statute of limitations. Again, the molesting priest and the church won. Thanks to that unfair law, the victim was never given justice.

An article by Barbara Watkins in the *St. Louis Review*, a Catholic newspaper, proudly announced that on August 12, 2005, the Archdiocese of St. Louis had implemented a new Safe Touch program in its elementary and parish schools of religion, beginning that fall. The program was meant to teach students about child sexual abuse. Children would be taught to set boundaries for how their body was touched or dealt with and to let an adult know if anything happened that made them feel uncomfortable, to make sure anything inappropriate would stop.

It is a very good principle for children to know, but I fear it may not work in a couple of instances. Because of the overall Catholic attitude of "blame the victim" that has not been appropriately addressed among the congregation, this may not fare well for the child who tells an uninformed or very devout teacher or adult. The adult may not want to hear what the child has to say and could be dismissive. The child could also innocently confide in another predator priest. Also, was the staff trained properly to listen and really hear what a child is saying? Do all things that a child says get followed up? Or do some get dismissed as "probably nothing"? Do they consider the feelings of a child who speaks up to a teacher and yet nothing is done?

Chapter 30
And Another

On August 20, 2005, the *Post-Dispatch* reported a new lawsuit filed against my brother.

"A Virginia man sued the Roman Catholic Archdiocese of Saint Louis Friday, claiming a priest sexually abused him in 1962 and 1963 under the guise of talking to him about joining the priesthood. The suit says Rev. Norman H. Christian took the then youth into the basement of Saint Peter's Church in Kirkwood in the fall of 1962, showed him pornography, then fondled him. The abuse continued through the spring of 1963, the suit says."

Members of SNAP held a press conference on August 19 to discuss this lawsuit.

The August 24, 2005, *Post-Dispatch* ran an article, by Tim Townsend, about a Texas man who filed a lawsuit against another priest, who also grew up in my childhood parish. Norman was ordained a priest just a few years ahead of him. The Texas man accused this priest of sexually abusing him when he was a child at St. John Nepomuk Church in Saint Louis. The priest was pastor of that parish but was removed from active ministry for credible allegations of abuse after thirty-seven years in parishes. He has lived in supervised residential settings since November 2000 but is free to come and go as he pleases and is not confined in any way.

I attended grade school with his sister and at times, we played together. As with my parents and brother, her parents too, being very religious people and active in the church, were overjoyed to have their son become a priest. Having a child enter the religious life was a parent's greatest blessing, at least when I was a young.

Chapter 31
Twist of Faith Controversy

Don Corrigan of the *South County Times* reported the showing of an award-winning documentary that exposed clergy sexual abuse in a Toledo, Ohio, diocese. Kirby Dick's *Twist of Faith* was shown on August 31, 2005, at Webster University's Moore Auditorium, which was filled to capacity. Following the film's viewing, there was a forty-minute panel discussion of the shameful crime of clergy sexual-abuse against minors, in which St. Louis prosecuting attorney, Jennifer Joyce, participated.

The documentary gives a clear understanding of the pain and betrayal caused by the church's own actions (or lack of them) toward abuse victims. As I watched the movie, I found myself agreeing with all of the victims' comments about the church. Tony Comes was thirty-four years old and feeling lost because everything he believed about the church was gone; I was sixty-four and felt the same. The church, as I had known it, was no more. Catholics would have their eyes opened if they watched this movie but sadly, most of them likely will refuse to do so.

It was very disappointing that the archdiocese chose not to be represented at the movie viewing or on the discussion panel that followed. Their absence indicated the church was not interested in reaching out to clergy-abuse victims. It was the response the victims had come to expect from the church; few were surprised. Many years ago, there were bumper stickers that read "Proud to be Catholic." I can't remember when I last saw one of those on a car.

Our pastor's October 9 column in the parish Sunday bulletin cried out for a response. I questioned if it was just a coincidence that the Philadelphia archdiocese grand jury's report on the priests' sexual-abuse scandal was the big news of the week with the media.

I wrote him that I noticed he had kept the topic of sex in his column but had put the spotlight on something other than the scandal within the church. He never responded to my letter.

Excerpts of our pastor's Sunday bulletin column (Mitas, 10-09-05, Immaculate Conception Church):

> Alfred Kinsey (1894–1956)
> The sexual revolution is still upon us. Unlike the Republican Revolution of the '90s ... it actually changed society by changing peoples' hearts and minds and, as a result, our laws and even our culture. ....
> Free love ... is the hallmark of the sexual revolution. ... its fruits ... a large population of illegitimate children, a skyrocketing divorce rate, the decline of the European and American birthrate to way below replacement levels, an epidemic of old venereal diseases and the advent of ... AIDS, the 'normalization' of ... gay marriage, the legalization of baby killing, the proliferation of pornography, etc. ...
> Science produced 'the pill'. ... The courts cut down the laws which prohibited the sale of contraceptives and ... the laws which prohibited abortion. They also made it very easy for a man to dump his wife, and vice versa, through 'no fault divorce.' ... The sexual revolution found its 'prime mover' in Alfred Kinsey.
> Kinsey, subject (and title) of a recent motion picture, was born into a strict Methodist family in 1894. Earning a doctorate in zoology (specializing in

wasps), he began a career at the University of Indiana, where he would make his reputation in 1948 with his classic tome, *Sexual Behavior in the Human Male*.

He boldly went ... studying the true, intimate sex lives of real people. ... He concluded:

Homosexuality is normal (and extremely common).

Children, even small children, are sexual and sexually engaged.

Masturbation is good (and so is the pornography that leads to it).

Extramarital affairs help to strengthen the marriage bond.

Well, this was all quite new to a "puritanical" nation that was very "uptight" about sex. It turned out to be a stick of dynamite at the base of the levee. Soon Hugh Hefner, citing the work of Kinsey, began his own career as America's chief mammographer, and the whole idea took off that sex is purely recreational. God forbid that it should also be procreational! Kinsey was hard to refute. After all, he was a scientist (even if his scientific training was in bugs)!

A lot of people smelled a rat with Kinsey and now all the evidence is in. Frankly, the case against him is a slam dunk. In books by James H Jones (*Alfred C Kinsey: A Life*, 1997), Jonathan Gathorne-Hardy (*Sex and the Measure of All Things*, 2000), and most of all, Judith Reisman (*Kinsey: Crimes and Consequences*, 2001), a new picture of the father of the sexual revolution has emerged. It turns out that this strict Methodist was a bisexual pedophile who constantly cheated on his wife with partners of all ages and sexes, while forcing her also to partake in orgies. Worst of all, all his research is absolutely, irrefutably bogus. His surveys, through which he tried to establish what the normal mainstream sexual practice in America was, were conducted exclusively with prison populations and homosexual groups.

His conclusions on the sexual behavior of children were based mostly on his own personal "research" with them, for which he should have been arrested, convicted and executed. On top of that, when even the data from his biased samples didn't produce the result he was looking for, he just made up new ones. A case in point: Kinsey had a huge collection of pornography (for research, of course), he kept on open display in his office and which was so big everyone who came to visit him was shocked at its enormity. When they asked him about it, he would very casually comment that his was only the second largest photo library in the world; the first, he told them, was in the Vatican. ...

It's a preposterous, incredible lie ... it was accepted as fact without any serious examination by the academic community. In fact, to this day the Kinsey Institute perpetuates that lie with absolutely no other source to verify it than Kinsey himself. ...

My grandfather always said people will believe what they want to believe and the truth be damned. ...

Father Mitas

I sent his article to my niece, and she found it to be "unbelievable." She couldn't understand how our pastor could write such things about Kinsey and not show the same rage about the pedophile clergy who, by having harmed so many innocent children for many decades, were destroying Catholics' faith in their church. She said she was so incensed by reading his column that her stomach was tied up in a knot.

Excerpts from my response to our pastor's bulletin article on Kinsey (Kuhnert, 10-11-05, letter):

Dear Father Mitas,
After reading your October 9 column in the Sunday bulletin re: Kinsey, my first thought was that you found a good way to distract your parishioners

from the priests sexual-abuse scandal, especially since the Philadelphia archdiocese grand jury report ran in the news. You kept the topic of sex but put the spotlight on someone else. ...

Now, when can I expect to see such a column of yours on the subject of the pedophile priests and the bishops who still shamefully deny their crimes and/or responsibility for the mismanagement of this disgraceful behavior all these years? Surely you feel the same about them!

It sickens me that I have personally known many of these pedophile priests. ... I ask you to try to understand the difficulty my family is having with all of this. The church fails miserably in reaching out to its members on this subject.

I would like to see you dig into the priests' sex-abuse problem, something that's really on most Catholics' minds, but I ask you don't blame the sex-abuse victims and their families for wanting to be heard, believed, understood, and given apologies. Until priests of integrity like you stand up and speak out in support of the victims, the silent faithful of the church will continue to wonder just whom they can trust, and the church will continue to lose members.

Sincerely,
Carol Kuhnert

Chapter 32
Destroyed Clergy Records

The *Post-Dispatch* carried Robert Patrick's article on October 17, 2005, stating that all the patients' records on abusive priests and religious brothers had been destroyed by the treatment center in Jemez Springs, New Mexico. The program at that location was closed in 1995. It was run for decades by the Servants of Paraclete, treating any clergy battling addiction, depression, and sexual problems.

"In a 1995 deposition, the former servant general of the Paracletes order, told lawyers that until 1989 or 1990, copies of progress reports and evaluations were sent out from New Mexico with language instructing religious leaders to destroy their copies of treatment and evaluation records or return them to the Servants facility for destruction."

Destroying all those patient records unquestionably erased enormous amounts of evidence, making it all the more difficult for clergy sexual-abuse victims to prove their cases. Not having these records available for those who are struggling to prove they are telling the truth about their abuser is of utmost significance. Whoever ordered them to be destroyed was again covering up for predator clergy, protecting the church's reputation and assets. It's difficult to believe this outrageous behavior could happen in the Catholic Church.

A friend e-mailed me a website article written by Professor Marci A. Hamilton from the School of Law at Yeshiva University, titled "Has the Catholic Church Put the Clergy-Abuse Problem behind It? Not by a Long Shot: What We Have to Do to Truly Get Past the Issue." Professor Hamilton felt that at the 2005 Catholic Conference of Bishops, they were looking at the clergy sexual-abuse issue as history and that now, somehow, the church itself was a helpless victim of its own crimes. I believed she was right on target.

She had stated the church needed to identify clergy abusers. If need be, "Congress should exert financial pressure on the states to make it happen." She felt the first step was to make all abusers' names public. I couldn't agree more.

She stated, "Abusive priests may escalate their behaviors, and laws may need to be changed, as even murder was possible when abusers walked free. In a perfect world, one where bishops reported all abusers to the authorities before the statutes of limitations lapsed, the abusers would be publicly fired, prosecuted, and sent to jail. Moreover, their names would be published on Megan's List [neighborhood listings of registered sexual offenders] in the states so parents, and their children, and other potential victims could steer clear" (Marci Hamilton, 11-17-05, School of Law Yeshiva University).

Wouldn't that be superb!

I was extremely happy to know that someone of Professor Hamilton's status was supportive of the victims. I e-mailed her that I fully agreed with her article and thanked her for what she had been doing to help bring about change in how the church handles its clergy sexual abuse. She was kind enough to respond with a supportive e-mail (entire 11-18-05 e-mail in appendix). I truly appreciated that as busy as she most likely was, she didn't ignore me.

As Thanksgiving Day drew near, I decided to write a note to Monsignor Telthorst, thanking him again for talking with us back in June. But I mainly wanted to inquire if he noticed any changes in his parishioners' attitudes. Some time had passed since he told us he would pray for and discuss the difficulties of the victims periodically during Mass.

The response I received from him was really no surprise, and in some way, it made me feel bad for him (entire 11-28-05 letter in appendix). He admitted his own parishioners were not comfortable coming to discuss their concerns with him, and strangely, that didn't seem to bother him. I didn't hear any more from Monsignor after that. I guess my work didn't fit into whatever events he was planning for his parish's Lenten sessions.

This holiday season was enjoyable, as our family was able to gather together for a few days without focusing on the sex-abuse scandal.

On December 16, 2005, a letter I wrote defending David Clohessy and SNAP appeared in the Letters to the Editor section of the *St. Louis Post-Dispatch*. Other letters that had appeared recently in that column seemed to indicate there were many people who couldn't believe a priest would lie. They would not even entertain the thought that a priest could commit such horrible crimes against children. I wrote, in part:

"We must stop giving clergy our trust and respect just because they are priests. The safety of our children and ourselves may depend on it. Even vulnerable adults fell victim to my brother, the Reverend Norman Christian, while counseling them as a priest. Some priests lie, even to themselves. My brother did. He told me he never forced any of the kids to do anything. ... What ten-year-old boy ... wants to be molested and raped by a priest? ... It is painful to accept that this happened, but denial allows the crime to go on. ... Love our church enough to encourage change. ... Show compassion to the victims."

We must all demand the removal of known molesters from ministry and help all their victims in every way possible.

Contrary to what the archdiocese promotes, the Survivors Network of those Abused by Priests is a great blessing to the Catholic Church, for all they do in trying to get known clergy molesters removed from active ministry. Their vigilance may make molesters still in active ministry wary. My brother made nervous comments to me, once he knew his name appeared as number thirty on SNAP's website list of clergy abusers. He had tried to convince himself it wasn't that bad, but he was very worried.

After having read the latest update of Tim's website on February 11, 2006, I e-mailed my niece that he had changed a lot since we'd first met him. He was now more expressive and a help to so many people by telling his personal story of abuse on his website. Many readers contacted him about their own molesters; some found the courage to go to the authorities. Tim had taken control of his situation by reporting his abuser. He had been guarded when first we met; now it was good to see his fears were gone.

Tim e-mailed me in the middle of February 2006, asking if I would write a summary of what I had experienced with Norman and the church since learning he was a child molester; he wanted to put it on his website. I was surprised by his request and wondered if I'd be able to do it, but I agreed. I gathered the material—eighteen years' worth—as quickly as I could and immediately went to work. Many different emotions surfaced as I typed. I knew I was doing the right thing in supporting my brother's victim; actually, all clergy-abuse victims. I hoped those who read of my experiences would begin questioning the hierarchy themselves and start holding them accountable for keeping molesters in ministry.

By March 15, 2006, Tim had my notes and entered the first segment of "Spinning My Wheels for Eighteen Years" posted on his website. On March 16, he added more. The final segment, "My Wheels Are Starting to Grip," was added March 18. In all, I had sent ten pages of my summarized experiences from the previous eighteen years, using those titles because that's how I felt about my situation with Norman and the church. I had gotten absolutely nowhere with them in all that time, and it was frustrating, to say the least.

I received another e-mail from Tim in the middle of March with a copy of a letter he'd seen that was written anonymously to the *St. Louis Post-Dispatch* newspaper. He also sent me a copy of his response letter to the editor.

An anonymous writer had written:

"Put them under a microscope. I think it would be a good idea to investigate that David Clohessy and his bunch. I don't think they're worried about any victims of sexual abuse. I think they want to take down the Catholic Church. Every time someone makes an allegation, then all of a sudden here come all these other ones out of the woodwork. My suggestion would be to have lie detector tests for the whole bunch, from that David Clohessy and his bunch to the priest to the victims making the accusations. I think a good thorough investigation is in order."

Tim's response to this person was superb. I hope that writer read it and gave the matter a lot more thought.

Tim responded with:

> I would love to go under the microscope for you, as long as we could get Archbishops Burke, Rigali, Law, and Jamie Allman to come with me. As a proud member of "his bunch," I'm tired of petty criticism from your kind, those who have tried to keep this ugly truth hidden. This is not about attacking the Catholic Church; it's about getting pedophiles out of it. It's about making the world a bit safer for our kids. Any time you would like to see the over 600 pages of evidence compiled on my rapist, Father Norman Christian, let me know, and we'll see if the Saint Louis County Police Department will give us access to their two-year investigation on him, up until his death. I would have never come forward, never gone to therapy, never started healing, never stopped having suicidal thoughts, and maybe never survived, if it would not have been for this kind and caring organization (SNAP, www.snapmidwest.org [now www.snapnetwork.org]) that is totally about caring for victims of sexual abuse. Bring on your lie detector, truth serum, or maybe some Spanish inquisition technique that you and your bunch would like to see me go through so you'll believe. Happy to help out. ...

Sadly, the trauma of remembering the abuse, day in and day out, took its toll. For personal reasons, Tim took down his blog and website, and for now, it is not available. For years, anyone reading it found it to be a real eye-opener. It helped many to come forward to report their own abuse.

That anonymous letter-writer gave a perfect example of the attitude I have seen for years—one that victims and their families face on a daily basis. The fact that this attitude comes from members of their own church makes it all the more painful. It's so much easier to blame the victims and the group who is trying to get perpetrators removed from active ministry than to accept that something is terribly wrong within the church itself. I think this might be because Catholics are instructed what to believe and what to do and to just follow the rules of the church. Catholics are taught from infancy to trust, respect, and obey the church and clergy and never to question them.

I'm not sure what hurts more: learning my brother was a pedophile priest or knowing the church does not truly care about its flock. It cares only about protecting its reputation, its assets, and covering up what my brother and other predator clergy have done. This is definitely not the church I knew and loved from my childhood. On second thought, sadly, I guess it is. I just hadn't had my eyes opened to its methods of operation.

I continue to pray for the church I thought I knew, that they will make the appropriate changes to be more Christlike so all Catholics can regain their trust and respect for its leadership.

Unfortunately, the church seems to have a long way to go in understanding how to express real compassion. Tim was so pleased when he unexpectedly received a letter from the Office for Child and Youth Protection of the Archdiocese on March 13, 2006. His first thought was that the church actually cared about him after all. But when he excitedly called his dad to tell him what he had received in the mail, he learned that his dad had received a letter too—a letter identical to the one Tim received, word for word. Only the name to whom it was addressed had been changed. When he checked with his mom, he learned that she, too, had received the same form letter, simply addressed to her. Identical mimeographed letters sent to a victim, his mother, and his father lacks a real sense of sincerity.

Tim's feelings of excitement at having received another letter from the archdiocese were gone once he realized they were only going through the motions with a form letter, most likely a public-relations effort on their part. It was obvious to him that after he told the church about Father Christian's raping him when he was eleven years old, their biggest concern seemed to be that he was going to bring it to the attention of the public—and they wouldn't be able to cover up this priest any longer.

Tim never experienced the church reaching out to him with

compassion or understanding at any time. Any contact they had with him was brought about by his lawyer. That's why he was so pleased to receive that last letter. He thought they actually cared about him by sending the follow-up letter, but he soon learned there was nothing personal or caring about it. It was just another let-down, but this time, Tim had somewhere to turn for real support.

Chapter 33
My Supportive Family

After thinking about it for quite some time and receiving some gentle encouragement from Tim, Pete, and Sue, I made up my mind to write this book, telling of my experiences and observations with my brother and the church. I knew I had years of material accumulated for references. After making my decision, along with my husband, I e-mailed our four children on March 27, 2006, and told them my plans. Pete and Tim were also informed. I asked all of them to keep me in their prayers, and my work of compiling information began. I believed that writing what I knew would benefit others, and this encouraged me to accomplish this emotionally difficult task.

I had trusted the church when I was told the church was taking care of everything. My questions were always answered that it wasn't mine to worry about. I watched as decades went by but saw little if any change in how they dealt with clergy sexual abuse. Still a faithful Catholic, I continued to trust them, wanting to believe what the priests and bishops were telling me. Yet I never saw anything that indicated they were doing the right thing. No one ever told me what actions the church was taking, and it would have seemed like I didn't trust them, had I asked. They lost all credibility with me when my brother died, and the archbishop himself celebrated Norman's funeral. Giving a self-admitted pedophile priest, who took his last breath without ever apologizing to his victims, a funeral as a priest in good standing seemed disgraceful. I knew then and there, I had been deceived all those years.

Once my contributions to Tim's website were read, family and friends began contacting me, expressing their sorrow for what our family and others had endured. After all those years of keeping Norman's shameful secret while trusting the church, it was an enormous blessing that many of our relatives and friends now reached out to us with comforting words and understanding. It was such a relief to finally be free of the disgraceful secret I had been keeping for Norman and the church for so long.

If ever there was a time I would like to have had a "do over," it would have been that night my daughter first told me about "Uncle Norman" being a pedophile. I should have immediately taken her to the police department and reported what my brother was doing. Why didn't I? His being my brother didn't matter. Most likely, it was the fact he was a priest and at that time, I foolishly expected and trusted the church to make things right.

I know now I didn't fully understand the magnitude of the situation. I was a fully programmed, brainwashed-from-infancy Catholic. I firmly believed the church could do no wrong. My daughter had sobbed while telling me that my brother was a child molester. That evening was like a monstrous nightmare. Troubled by what I heard, I couldn't think of anything to do other than listen, hold her, and let her cry—and me along with her. With all I've discovered since then, however, I deeply regret that we didn't go directly to the police.

Joe and I did receive a response from Archbishop Burke when we declined participation in the Annual Catholic Appeal until the church dealt with the clergy sexual-abuse issues openly and honestly. As we expected, however, his response gave us no reason to expect changes anytime soon. He assured us he was doing everything he could to ensure all credible allegations of abuse of minors by priests were handled swiftly and appropriately. This included removing priests with credible allegations from active ministry. He deplored sexual abuse of minors and encouraged anyone harmed by clergy to come forward. It seemed he knew what needed to be done, but in all the years we've watched, the church took action only when threatened with lawsuits. We wrote him again June 10, but never received another response (entire 06-10-06 letter in appendix).

The archbishop had sent members of his archdiocese a letter on August 31, 2006, asking for their participation in the Returning God's Gifts campaign. He was extremely pleased to state that since the campaign had begun in 1996, "none of the sacrificial offerings made by the faithful of the archdiocese have been spent. Only the earnings from the principal amount, more than eight million, to date, have been distributed to support our people, schools, and parishes."

Still, he was pressing families already struggling to meet their own financial obligations—Catholic school tuitions among them—to pledge even more for this very wealthy church.

I wondered when we could expect to see an equally enthusiastic letter sent out, stating the archbishop's shame and outrage over the sexual-abuse crimes that have been perpetrated against children by priests and other religious for so many years.

An article by Cindy Wooden, which appeared in the December 22, 2006, issue of the *St. Louis Review* ("Convert sex-abuse shame to repentance, papal preacher says"), left me feeling even more disappointed with the church. It seemed Vatican City was still encouraging clergy to cover up its sexual-abuse problems. The article reported that a papal priest had said the guilty priests must be given assistance so that they recognize their sins and reconcile themselves with God. However, he was quoted as saying, among other things, "But there is one thing these brothers absolutely must avoid, something unfortunately some are trying to do: profit from the uproar to lessen their own guilt, giving interviews or writing memoirs in an attempt to place the blame on their superiors and the church community. This reveals a truly dangerous hardness of heart."

It's outrageous that anyone would think guilty priests, who have found the courage to tell of their pedophile behavior and how it was permitted to go on, are revealing "hardness of heart." Disclosing all the information, accepting responsibility for what they've done, and apologizing for the pain they've caused the victims and the church is the honorable thing to do. Every pedophile priest needs to tell the truth, as does every innocent cleric who is aware of any abuse.

I read an article by Steve Givens in the February 2, 2007, *St. Louis Review*, stating: "Too many have given up on the church because it has not proved to be perfect enough for them. Our church ... will never be perfect because its pews and rectories are filled with imperfect people ... many people have been hurt and confused by the imperfect people who make up our church. And so many of them have left or stopped practicing their faith."

After reading that, I sent the *Review* a letter, stating that most adults look past imperfections, as everyone has them. I gave them my thoughts for why people were leaving—and I wasn't surprised that my letter never appeared in their paper (entire February 2007 letter in appendix).

Monsignor Shamleffer wrote a wonderful apology to victims of clergy ("Monsignor John Shamleffer, Church Strives for Healing after Scandal"), but I wondered how many of them would ever see it, as it was placed in the March 9, 2007, issue of the *St. Louis Review*, the Catholic newspaper. After reading his article, it became clear that Monsignor's apology was mostly a public-relations move meant to make him and the church look good in the eyes of all members of the church. It appeared he was trying to make the members think the scandal was over, and the church had been doing all the right things.

"The voices of courageous survivors and those who have stood by them have been heard, and healing has taken place," he wrote. "We have listened to many survivors tell their painful stories. We have provided assistance for healing. Clergy abusers have been removed from ministry."

Catholics want to believe what he said. They'd like nothing more than for all of this clergy sexual-abuse talk to go away. Most don't want to deal with it.

It seems to be extremely difficult, especially for the older generation, to stand up to the hierarchy and to think and speak for themselves in regards to the clergy-abuse problem. The younger generations are another matter, which is possibly why the pews are emptying and churches have been closing. Young people aren't blindly following and trusting, just because someone is clergy. They're doing some thinking for themselves, but it seems the church doesn't realize it. Times have changed, eyes are being opened, and people aren't as easily controlled anymore.

I sent Monsignor Shamleffer a letter on March 16, 2007, suggesting that many victims' families had left the church out of disgust and probably don't read Catholic papers. If his apology was serious, he'd do better to reach the victims through neighborhood papers (entire letter in appendix).

I stated, "Your comments about the church having listened to survivors tell their stories and claiming to have removed clergy abusers also made me wonder, as I'm only aware of the church doing those things when forced to do so through mediation hearings and court orders, not willingly on their own. ... Nowhere did I get a feeling that you were calling upon the parishioners to reach out to these victims themselves with compassion and understanding, to stop blaming them for what had happened. ... Making all clergy mandatory reporters of any abuse they have knowledge of would be the right thing to do."

What troubles me most is the fact that these are the individuals we have turned to all our lives for guidance. I expect them to hold themselves to the highest of standards and lead by example. For bishops to have knowingly said or done little to nothing, over and over, when told of children being sexually abused by clergy is outrageous. Wrong is wrong, no matter who does it. They must be accountable and accept the consequences. Our church leaders need wisdom and courage to repair the damage that's been done. Turning known molesters over to the authorities immediately and reaching out to those they've harmed may help disheartened Catholics regain their trust and respect for the church.

Chapter 34
Father Tom Doyle

My husband and children have remained very supportive of me, never preventing my advocating for clergy-abuse victims.

Joe and I, along with a friend from our parish, were eager to attend a gathering in Webster Groves, Missouri, on March 3, 2007, to hear guest speaker Father Tom Doyle talk in regards to the Catholic Church and accountability. I had been waiting a long time for the chance to hear this heroic man speak. Father Doyle is someone who truly exemplifies Christ. He is one of the few clergy known for putting the victim first, without regard for his own vocation. There were well over two hundred people listening intently as Father Doyle told how his life in the priesthood significantly changed in 1985, when he was in the presence of the parents of an eleven-year-old boy who had been raped by a priest. He had not known how to respond to them. He said, "Once I started speaking out for clergy sexual-abuse victims, the church began demoting me. The church acts like a corporation instead of a church ministering to its people."

I've had the same thoughts myself.

Father Doyle stated, "I've seen no effort or request, from the Vatican on down, to help victims and their families, but I have seen dioceses fight victims." Hearing that statement brought to mind the eighteen years I had been watching the church, and I realized we had both witnessed the same behavior; only Father Doyle had a much better view of it than I.

Father Doyle said, "All clergy need to be made mandatory reporters of any sexual abuse of which they have knowledge. They should report what they know, not just pray, pay, and obey." He suggested that a "hotline for reporting such abuse would be ideal, but it would be most successful if manned by someone other than the archdiocese."

During discussions following Father Doyle's speech, a young woman painfully told how one of her brothers had taken his own life after being abused by a priest. She asked how all the information presented to everyone that day could be brought to the people in all parishes. "So far, there has been no way to reach any of the parishes with this kind of information," she said, "because the hierarchy refuses to allow it." No one had an answer for her.

I offered a little of what I had experienced with the church over the years and agreed that the young woman was exactly right about needing to reach the parishioners with these truths. "I've been trying to get information to them for years with no luck," I said. "Pastors won't allow such speakers on parish property, and parishioners seem afraid to meet elsewhere to hear them. It's as though they fear something horrific will happen to them, should they ever listen to a victim tell of being sexually abused by a priest."

Father Doyle presented his speech at the Eden Theological Seminary, a non-Catholic organization, which was evidence of the church's trying to keep its members ignorant of the facts. He managed to joke about not being allowed to speak on Catholic properties anymore, but it's actually very sad to realize what happens to clergy who are courageous enough to stop the silence and cover-ups. I wonder what the church would do if all religious who are aware of abuse came forward to report it.

Monsignor Telthorst represented the archdiocese on the panel during discussions following Father Doyle's talk. I spotted Monsignor talking with a few people after the discussions had concluded and approached him, saying, "I'm happy to see you here today, Monsignor. Thanks for coming. I hope after all you heard here, you have a better understanding of what the church needs to do."

He just nodded his head and smiled. With others still standing there, I asked, "Monsignor, have you given more thought to inviting a few clergy-abuse victims to speak at your parish? Surely after all Father Doyle revealed and the panel discussion that followed, you realize the importance of helping your parishioners understand the victims' plight. You'd be helping the victims in their healing as well, by allowing them to share their stories of abuse."

He seemed flustered, maybe because I had made my request in the presence of others. His quick response was, "I have ten other things I need to get my parishioners to understand. I really don't know how to do what you are asking."

His answer surprised me, but I replied, "Monsignor, an intelligent man like yourself can figure a way to make it happen. Keep in mind, many older parishioners will remember Norman and me—our whole family. With your encouragement, they may be willing to hear what victims and their supporters would have to say."

At that point, Monsignor abruptly turned his back on me and began talking to someone else. I realized then that he had never seriously considered inviting clergy-abuse victims to speak at his parish. His kind words to Mary Ellen, Joe, and me earlier that year when we met at my house were meant only to placate us. It was very disheartening but a good example of how victims and those supporting them are treated by the church. I walked away, convinced that he had been insincere all along.

I sent Monsignor Telthorst a letter, reiterating my thanks for his being on the panel the day Father Doyle spoke. I wanted to urge him to give more thought to my suggestion of inviting survivors of abuse and their supporters to speak at his parish. I asked that he lead by example in helping his parishioners change their attitudes toward them. I pointed out something he had said—that his parishioners had made it clear to him that they were not interested in hearing from any of the victims of clergy sexual abuse—but that in itself was proof of the attitude they have toward them. I said that he seemed to be intentionally looking the other way.

I respect Monsignor for being on the discussion panel that day. He was alone in trying to defend the church when questions came at him. He appeared to listen to all that was said that morning, and I hope he reported back to the archbishop about all that took place.

Chapter 35
Disagreements

It's a fact Father Norman H. Christian was a sexual predator who used his position as a respected Catholic priest as a means to befriend vulnerable children for his own evil intentions. However, it's as important to know that it was the church that allowed him to continue those heinous crimes against children for so long by moving him from parish to parish. Norman admitted he had abused children, yet he was kept in active ministry. He should have been removed the first time his actions became known; other clergy who rape and molest children *must* be removed the first time they are caught. No one can think that being raped once, as a child or as an adult, is something to shrug off and say, "It was just one time."

As I've mentioned, Archbishop Raymond Burke gave the final slap in the face to all of Father Christian's victims by celebrating his funeral and burying him as a priest in good standing. Someone who attended said the "beautiful funeral was a great tribute" to Norman, something he clearly did not deserve.

I will never understand Norman's refusal to apologize to his victims, especially when he realized he would face God in a very short time. Again, I question the therapy he received through the archdiocese's treatment facilities. I wonder how differently my brother's life might have turned out if he hadn't chosen to enter the seminary.

Halfway through 2011, I was enlightened as to why Norman was given the funeral he had. The Archdiocese of Saint Louis actually has a document called "Funeral Arrangements for Priests Removed from Active Ministry but Not Laicized." They e-mailed it to Tim Fischer upon his request on June 3, 2011, and Tim was kind enough to share it with me (entire document at end of appendix 2). However, one rule that I doubt was followed after Norman's death was the following: "Where applicable, the Diocesan Assistance Coordinator will contact as many victim survivors as possible after the funeral and give them notice of the priest/deacon and offer them any appropriate support." I wonder if that's ever been done. After all the unanswered questions in letters and e-mails I sent to the various bishops and clergy, my question is, "Why didn't they send this document to me?" I had to learn this through one of my brother's victims, seven years after Norman died.

The March 30, 2007, issue of the *St. Louis Review* had arrived in our mail. Browsing through it, one article especially caught my eye, though I had serious doubts about what I read. Nothing the church says or does should surprise me after all these years, but smack on the front page was an article by Joseph Kenny ("Archdiocesan Review Board Reaches Out to Victims"), singing the praises of the board for the fine job it had been doing in reaching out to clergy sexual-abuse victims over the years. If my teeth weren't the ones God had given me, they'd surely have fallen out of my mouth. I thought it would be wise to put boots on, too, before reading any further.

"Many times the victims had left the church but came back after they were helped by the board," it read. This sounded more like wishful thinking to me. With the paper in hand, I grabbed the phone and called Barb Dorris, the outreach director at SNAP, asking if she'd read the article.

"I'm finding this very hard to believe," I told her, "and thought I'd check with you. Maybe I'm mistaken, and there have been victims helped by the board, as they're claiming in this article."

Chuckling, Barb told me, "Yes, I saw the article. I always enjoy reading fiction." She couldn't think of anyone the review board had helped. We could have asked, but we both agreed the board would most likely claim to be protecting victims' privacy if asked who they had helped. We also noticed nothing was said about removing these victims' molesters from active ministry. This just seemed to be the latest of the hierarchy's public-relations stunts.

Fortunately, it wasn't long before a happier event was able to distract us again. In mid-May 2007, Joe and I excitedly welcomed our fourth beautiful granddaughter. Huge smiles beamed from her siblings, and her parents were thrilled. All the family was anxious to get their first glimpse of her.

Joe and I are blessed with ten grandchildren. As each one has arrived, we have basked in the delight that accompanies the birth, temporarily forgetting the distressing things in life. However, it was never long before somehow, I'd be reminded of the church's failure to protect our children.

Another revealing article, written by Shawn Pogatchnik of the Associated Press, appeared in the March 21, 2010, *St. Louis Post-Dispatch*. Pope Benedict XVI had given an "unprecedented" letter of apology to the children of Ireland for the abuse they suffered within the church, but he didn't calm the anger of many victims. As one said, "I don't need the Pope to apologize for the child abusers. I and untold thousands of victims like me needed the Pope to apologize for the church hierarchy's role in choosing to protect the abusers at the expense of children."

The following year, a guest editorial in the *St. Louis Review*, February 25, 2011, "The Painful Process of Restoring Trust," addressed a 2005 Philadelphia grand jury report that had exploded with vile details of hundreds of cases of clergy sexual abuse against minors in that archdiocese back then. The article acknowledged that "trust in priests, trust in the hierarchy that governs the archdiocese had been shaken." It then stated, "For most people, the pain and bitterness eased over time. With the release of a new grand jury investigation last week and, for the first time, criminal indictments against alleged abusers, and a former archdiocesan official, Catholics have plunged again into the pain and disillusionment. Yet somehow it feels worse this time."

Could it be these Catholics now realized how dishonest their church leaders had been with them all along? Suddenly, the facts were right there for all to see. Of course they are upset and in pain; they've been duped, but they were really no match for the hierarchy's superb manipulative words and deceitful behaviors.

The article went on: "New measures featuring greater transparency must emerge." They expect that process to take time, saying, "The Catholic faithful are waiting with hope."

Yes, I'm sure they are, but Catholics would be wise to keep their eyes, ears, and minds open and hold those who govern their church accountable. They are not deserving of anyone's blind trust. (That editorial originally appeared in the February 17, 2011, issue of the *Catholic Standard and Times*, the Archdiocese of Philadelphia's newspaper.)

Still today, as I write this in 2014, many staunch Catholics hold firm, refusing to accept that priests have sexually abused children. I'm hopeful that now, with greater worldwide awareness of these appalling crimes, more will respond supportively toward victims and demand accountability of the church.

It speaks volumes that the SNAP network has continued to grow across the nation, inspiring the confidence of abuse victims. As they find healing and empowerment in breaking free of the guilt, hopelessness, and need for secrecy, they join in, working tirelessly to help others heal. Thanks to their courage and perseverance, church leaders are beginning to be held accountable. I look forward to the day when the hierarchy freely publicizes all known clergy molesters' names, along with truthfully stating the reason for their removals. All parishioners, the general public, and everyone who trusted that priest around their family need to look into the possibility of a victim within their own home who possibly is afraid to tell anyone.

I'm filled with more hope with the installation of Pope Francis. Besides the molesters being removed from ministry, hierarchy found to have covered for them may find themselves dealt with severely as well. It's going to take time and consistency in taking appropriate actions before the church can earn back people's trust and respect. The church's public-relations skills, cultivating and selling their ideas to faithful donors, are tantamount to those of successful con artists. We must pay less attention to what they say; their actions will speak louder than any words.

I am sorry that Norman was sexually abused as a child. It's extremely sad he never asked for help or told anyone. However, his inflicting the same terror he experienced himself on other innocent children, especially while representing himself as a priest, is nothing short of deplorable.

After decades of observing the hierarchy's covering up for Norman and others like him, I was given the opportunity to read numerous documents that could eliminate everyone's doubts of his guilt and the church's concealment. Even now, some adamantly refuse to believe Father Christian sexually abused children. They simply reject the facts that he was removed from active ministry, with settlements made to many of his victims. I can only assume they find the truth too difficult to accept. Norman's church-sanctioned, archbishop-celebrated funeral encouraged those refusing to accept that Norman could do such things to remain firm in their denials of his guilt.

Clergy sexual-abuse survivors are long overdue in being heard, believed, and seeing some form of justice. They are certainly as important as the unborn and deserve every Catholic's and pro-life group's defense too.

I believe if the members of the Catholic Church think for themselves and recognize and fight for the truth, especially where children's safety is concerned, we can be the Christians we claim to be.

Author's Note

As I neared the completion of this book, I gained access to information from Norman's archdiocesan personnel file. At my request, a victim's lawyer provided me with copies of numerous documents that were not under court-protected order. Reading through all the material took many days, and the further I read, the more astonished I became of my brother's narcissistic, criminal behavior throughout his priesthood. The negligence of various cardinals, bishops, and priests, outlining the cover-ups of his deceptive life and abuse, became obvious.

He had told me about some of the things I read, but I learned much more about him from those documents, including the fact that there were more victims that the hierarchy had successfully covered up. I am certainly no psychologist, but Norman seems to have been self-centered throughout the entire destructive life he led. Those he answered to in the archdiocese were well aware of his self-absorbed, manipulative, sexually abusive behavior.

Norman's grades throughout his seminarian years were nothing to brag about (Seminary School Report Cards, 02-08-50 to 06-11-61). "Very poor. His poor work, we feel, is due more to a lack of ability then to any negligence" (Seminary Profile, 1960). They found him to be "pleasant and approachable, yet there is something enigmatic about him. Readily shows externally his lack of interest in things not to his liking. ... Speech: one of his interests. His extra work has made him better than average in both, matter and delivery. ... Special ability: Has done remarkable work in directing choirs for a number of years. His success in this work indicates also possible organizational abilities."

The seminary's recommendations: "We feel that this candidate will do work that is satisfactory in any parish. It would be well to give him to a pastor that will, at least in the beginning, see to it that his activities are dictated by the needs of the parish rather than by his own inclinations."

Cardinal Joseph Ritter appointed Father Christian as a part-time religion teacher at Bishop DuBourg High School as of April 5, 1961, to teach for "a period of at least two years."

The following was documented in a lawsuit case for John Doe Case No. 052-01647: "Sometime during the early 1960s, Christian informed his supervising pastor that he had a sexual relationship with an 18-year-old male. 'After acting out and falling in love with an 18-year-old male (a mutual experience), I sought referral help through my pastor.' Christian stated that after his 'lover' went away to a seminary college, Christian began weekly sessions with a psychiatrist for 1½ years. In the same document, Christian said that his treatment by the doctor was during his first assignment, which, according to defendant's records, was from 1961–67."

Also, document in the Missouri docket, John Doe, Case 052-01647: "After becoming a priest, Christian reported to his 'big brother' and spiritual director at the seminary about his sexual acting out."

Norman wrote a request to Cardinal Carberry on Palm Sunday March 30, 1969, while assigned to Ascension parish in Normandy, Missouri. "I am requesting an interview with you and hope that it might be completely private. I need your help and Episcopal counsel in order to determine whether I should seek to be transferred out of Ascension parish or not. ... There is a definite problem, and I ask humbly for your advice." In lawsuit document Case No. 052-01647: At that time while at Ascension, Norman said, "I was acting out by cruising parks to pick up boys."

On May 13, 1969. Norman wrote to the Personnel Committee, Priests' Council of Saint Louis, stating, "Having considered many factors surrounding my ministry at Ascension parish, I have concluded that said parish would be better served by someone other than myself. ... I am not happy at Ascension parish, and when I am unhappy, I find myself committing many blunders, both in my ministry and my personal life; blunders that could retard the spiritual growth of the parish and myself. ... Please, honor my request as my continued stay at Ascension could become troublesome for the diocese as well as the parish."

On June 12, 1969, Cardinal Carberry informed Father Christian that "he was being appointed associate pastor of Sacred Heart Parish in Festus, MO."

Again, in lawsuit document Case No. 052-01647: "He reported that in his third assignment, he began the pursuit of victims. He said at first he didn't recognize what was happening; he just wanted someone to connect with sexually because his 'addict' had done that in fantasy. He said in fantasy, he was an adolescent, because that was when he most enjoyed himself, and he wanted to get back there. Consequently, this age group was the focus of his fantasy. He said he had liked children, in general, and taught the servers their lessons and knew them through that. He said he would do something with the servers during the summer. Some of the boys led him to their swimming hole, and Norm both watched them and played water games, and eventually ended up molesting them. He also invited certain boys to a private viewing room at the movie theater. He did not realize that what he was doing was a felony until he asked someone about it. He said that he was transferred and not given treatment because no one knew to give treatment at that time."

In August 1971, Norman was sarcastic in filling out an archdiocesan personnel form update. Asked for his personal preference with regard to parish work appointments, he wrote, "What difference would it make!?" His final comment at the bottom of the page was, "Why bother with such marvelous updating of personal files—nobody on the committee bothers to read them!"

On September 3, 1971, now assigned at Saint George Parish in Saint Louis, he was angry with his new pastor for telling him to "get a substitute priest who would say Mass in my place on Labor Day if I intended to be absent from the parish that day. I object to the penalty of being forced to hire a replacement out of my personal expenses. ... Having achieved the age of thirty-five and ten years of priestly ministry, I hold myself adult enough to recognize my responsibilities with regard to the celebration of Mass. ... Weekday Mass attendance rarely exceeds a total of fifty people for all three Masses." The other two priests in residence "would more than provide for the needs of Saint George parishioners" on that "weekday holiday of no obligation. ... I submit that you, Monsignor ... are demanding more than canon law demands of a bishop where his priests are concerned" (Christian, 09-03-71, letter).

The Chancery Office of the Saint Louis Archdiocese received a document dated February 20, 1974, from the diocese of Belleville, Illinois's vice chancellor advising, "The officials of this chancery office are very upset with Father Christian and this couple trying to circumvent our diocesan procedures. ... All couples in these circumstances should be interviewed by qualified people from our Catholic Social Service Office. This report is then submitted to the Chancery Office for judgment." He further asked that Father Christian be informed "of our feelings."

An October 27, 1975, letter from Norman to Cardinal Carberry revealed, "Very good fortune has come my way. ... I will be making a pilgrimage to Rome." He'd be leaving with a priest friend "from New York City on November 19 on a nine-day tour, with five days in Rome, two in Florence and two in Venice. ... returning to Saint Louis on November 29."

Two years later, October 19, 1977, Norman wrote the Commission for the Life and Ministry of Priests, advising that "I would like to be assigned to a parish in the country somewhere. That is my secret and selfish wish." He stated he was also open "to accept an assignment to the inner city" to work with the poor. Norman mentioned he had just begun "a house-to-house visitation" with parish families, and "I am uncovering a lot of need for reconciliation with our parish due to misunderstandings during the previous pastor's thirty-one year's stay here (all these families really deserve the opportunity to be reconciled and to return to active life in the parish)."

Norman believed the parishioners needed healing from the previous pastor's behavior. What about his own? How many families of Saint George parish are still in pain today because of his raping young boys in the parish and from around the neighborhood?

Within two months, Norman received Cardinal Carberry's December 27, 1977, letter, advising that he was being assigned as parish priest at Nativity of Our Lord parish in Saint Louis, Missouri, effective January 11, 1978.

He quickly responded on December 30, thanking Cardinal Carberry for "the beautiful Christmas present—a Nativity of our own!" (meaning God's poor and himself). "Three years ago, I might have been close to quitting the ministry of priesthood." Norman had been "pushed" by a married couple to make a Marriage Encounter Weekend. He "disliked the weekend but learned a lot that would help married couples. ... I discovered that the Lord really loves me even though a big sinner. I had a very poor image of myself.

"From this I became involved with TEC (Teens Encounter Christ), the retreat program for sixteen- to twenty-one-year-olds. ... Your Eminence, I was quite aware of how much God was using me for His work in helping people, and I was very envious of the people who came to me. ... I was God's tool and quite effective indeed as they would so lovingly thank me for being such a man of God, while I was on the outside of the kingdom looking in with a despairing attitude. ... three months later, I was a director for a TEC retreat. ... a sinful summer followed, and I was getting depressed once more." After seeking help through a spiritual director and making "an eight-day one-on-one retreat with no speaker other than the Lord Himself," he became "convinced now of the power of God to save me and anyone else He might choose to send to me.

"I directed another TEC ... about this time the Lord started putting the poor in my path ... so I finally gave in. ... I would accept an assignment to the inner city. How lucky for the people of Nativity to have the Lord spend three years getting one man ready for them!"

His arrogance was unbelievable.

Three and a half years later, April 26, 1981, Norman wrote Archbishop John May regarding some concerns at Nativity parish. He was "distressed within myself over my behavior toward you ... you may now believe I am more afraid than I am faithful. ... I pray that I will never say no to anything you ask of me again. ... Jesus has forgiven me many times during my priesthood, for I have made many mistakes (rather, blunders, is the better word). I promise that I will keep trying to be a good priest."

Archbishop John May wrote Norman on October 9, 1984, stating, "The new Code of Canon Law (Canon 1742) prescribes that there should be a number of pastors available for consultation by the diocesan bishop when he thinks it best to remove a pastor. ... I am happy to appoint you to this consultative group of pastors and I look forward to your counsel in the above mentioned situation."

On February 25, 1986, Archbishop May wrote the director of Foundation House in Jemez Springs, New Mexico, after reading their first report on Norman, stating, "In accordance with Father Christian's wishes, I have destroyed the report immediately after reading it very carefully."

On October 12, 1986, Norman wrote Archbishop May while still assigned to Saint Adalbert's parish. "You have meant a great deal to me during 1986, my 25th anniversary as a priest in this archdiocese. I love you with a very real desire to give you my life. After all is said and done, you have been very instrumental in giving me mine! It is four months since the completion of the wellness program with the Paracletes."

Norman updated the archbishop on how he was doing. He told of an aftercare visit with the psychotherapist from Jemez Springs. "She pointed out to me that I was still retaining a 'blind spot' in my attitude about one young man I was involved with previously. What she had to say really touched me, and I believe has helped me to 'slam the door' at last on that potential danger. At least I feel that I will be able to turn him away from me if he comes around, (because he did when I first returned and it upset me terribly). ... I found out how strong old feelings can be. ... I will try to be the 'good priest' you said I can and should be, and I am humbled by the tremendous trust you are placing in me."

Norman wrote Archbishop May again January 29, 1987, "to indicate my desire for a change of assignment away from the inner city apostolate. This inclination began shortly before Christmas, and I have been working it through with my therapist, who concurs ... I am ready for a transfer. I continue to hold you so very close in my personal affection for you because of your total kindness and dedication to helping me in crisis."

Norman then described the kind of parish he'd like to be assigned to—"a parish where there is at least one more priest in residence. I prefer to remain a pastor ... in a balanced (senior citizens and young marrieds) community. ... Because I value good liturgy, I would enjoy having a nice church to celebrate in, and ... prefer to be in striking distance of the Saint Louis metro area."

Norman had enclosed a ministry profile he had made of himself. Under "experiences," he stated, "Finally, after twenty-five years in priesthood, I benefited from a Renewal Program by the Paracletes ... a holistic wellness program. This was extremely important help; my personal identity is now catching up with my role identity as a priest." Norman of course did not state on this profile that he had been ordered to participate in that program because of his pattern of raping little boys.

On June 18, 1987, Norman was appointed pastor of Saint William's parish in Woodson Terrace, Missouri.

Eight years later, a case file report states an initial sexual-abuse report was made against him in October 1995, by another abuse survivor who had called the Saint Louis archdiocese, telling Monsignor Naumann that he had been "molested in a rectory ten or eleven times, he was ten to thirteen years old, says Father did to him what happens in prison." The man had stated that Father Christian "ruined my entire life!" (Case File Summary Initial Report, 10-1995, "Victims Call to Fr. Naumann"). A committee recommendation form (Consultation Center, 09-19-96, Archdiocese of St. Louis) states that "Father Christian admitted [to this incident], but no further details furnished. Regarding other incidents: He admits as a total number of cases—twelve."

The committee had recommended that Father Christian "communicate to the parishioners of Saint William that he will not be returning to the parish. We ask that he is honest with the parishioners, but he not disclose more than he judges necessary about the reasons for the leave. He could handle this by stating that he has asked for an extended medical/administrative leave in order to address problems related to depression. He is permitted to celebrate a Farewell Mass and have a Farewell Reception, if he so desires."

Norman had certainly demonstrated his shrewd, manipulative way with words in his December 5, 1995, emotional sell to the unsuspecting parishioners of Saint William's (entire letter in appendix 2). "The mini-sabbatical [from which he had just returned] included a thorough examination of my health; a professional evaluation of my physical, mental, emotional and spiritual life. It became apparent that I would need to deal *now* with depression and its diabetic impact. To put things off might impair my present and future ministry in the church."

He further stated that Archbishop Rigali "affirmed my request for a leave-of-absence from all ministry to take whatever steps are needed to heal the brokenness. ... I will not be returning to Saint William after all. Unfortunately, the human machine is quite fallible." He craftily omitted the real reason he was leaving—that he was being removed because of his history of sexually abusing minors. A document listing Father Christian's "Parish or Chaplaincy Appointments" notes his last assignment as being pastor, Saint William parish, Woodson Terrace, 1987, June 18, followed by 1995, May, sick leave. The truth had again been concealed.

A January 24, 1996, memo from Father Joe Naumann stipulated, "Father Norman Christian should receive his total compensation ... begin with Father Christian's salary for this month ..." Norman's current address was given. "It is my understanding that Father Christian's PMBS, car insurance, and Continuing Formation assessments have already been paid for this fiscal year by Saint William's parish. Any future assessments, until further instructions, should also be paid by the Clergy in Transition account. Please ask your staff to treat this information and all related transactions with the utmost confidentiality." Norman had told me he was still receiving his salary and priest benefits; it was just surprising to see such transactions documented that the staff was to conceal it.

The archdiocese had helped prepare a promissory note for Norman's responsibility in paying one of his victims a remaining nine thousand dollars of a settlement over successive ninety-day periods, following the execution date, February 15, 1996. Each payment was $450. Twelve percent interest was to be added, should his payment be late. Norman had recorded the dates as he sent payments.

I had hoped Norman added an apology to the last payment he made, but was not surprised to find in his file that he had not. Norman had written his bishop in 2001 regarding the last quarterly payment he had made to that victim, stating, "I have never sent any comment to him throughout this period, only the money order. This feels like closure to part of my work in recovery." How shameful—he didn't have the common decency to say he was sorry for what he had done. Again, it was just about him.

Another document was a copy of a woman's two-page typed

letter to Archbishop Justin Rigali, praising Father Christian (Former Parishioner, 05-96, letter). She and her husband had known Father for about twenty years, it read; "a wonderful man who became a wonderful priest until his illness." She told of the many ways he had been helpful to them over the years. "I wish so very much that you let him have a parish again. ... To us there will never be another priest like him; be good to him, Bishop Rigali, and give Father Christian a parish of his own again please."

On May 24, 1996, Archbishop Rigali responded to this sweet, unsuspecting woman by writing the following: "I have received your letter concerning the efforts of one of the priests of the Archdiocese of Saint Louis. Please know that I am grateful for your letter as well as for the kind sentiments expressed. With best wishes, I remain, sincerely in Christ, Most Reverend Justin Rigali, Archbishop of Saint Louis" He didn't even mention Norman's name.

Archbishop Rigali had received a memo regarding the Advisory Committee's recommendations regarding Norman (Consultation Center, 09-19-1996, Archdiocese of St. Louis). They stated that he should "not be returned to ministry. ... [He should] remain at Wounded Brothers, and seek some kind of secular employment for his support. Father Christian is seen as too great a risk for acting out, [*and if he were to minister in any capacity as a priest in good standing*], we are afraid that you could not really give him your full confidence."

Norman received a letter dated September 25, 1996, from Archbishop Rigali (entire letter in appendix 2) informing him, "Based on this judgment of the professionals at the Consultation Center and upon your history of acting out sexually, the Advisory Committee does not think it will be advisable to assign you to any kind of priestly ministry in the archdiocese in the foreseeable future. ... For the immediate future, you would remain in residence at Wounded Brothers and follow the recommendations of the Saint Louis Consultation Center for your ongoing recovery, including the follow-up session in January, 1997. ... It also seems advisable ... you seek some kind of secular employment for your support. ... Monsignor John Gaydos and I stand ready to be of assistance in any way possible."

Norman was angry and extremely disappointed. Still trying to get them to reconsider his removal, he sent a typed two-page letter to Monsignor Gaydos on October 17, pleading with him to "bring before them [Advisory Committee] my personal point of view about my history." He listed many things "in support of my changed behavior now," noting, "I have a deep love for the church, and have always known great joy in giving priestly ministry to the People of God. While my secret life's addictive behavior was destructive of my personal life and the lives of my victims, my other life in ministry was very effective for the many parishioners I served. I really want another chance. ... I will always hope for a return to some priestly ministry." Norman's arrogance overflowed, but finally, the hierarchy refused.

By the middle of November, Norman wrote Monsignor Gaydos again, requesting he be allowed to accept a ministry at "a very private retreat location in Pevely, Missouri." He had been told "the priest who had been with them for many years" was leaving; they needed a replacement. He had already spoken with the nun director of the retreat program, "disclosing the reality of my priesthood at this time due to my sexual addiction history. ... She even used the phrase that I 'might be the answer to her prayers.' ... Almost all [those making a retreat there] are woman religious, with a low percentage being lay women. ... I feel good about taking the initiative in exploring this opportunity."

I wonder how honest Norman had been in his interview. I could not understand how any woman would feel safe with a sexual predator living on the premises.

A memo (Gaydos, 12-12-96) in Norman's file stated that it was believed Norman would have "no problem exercising" that particular work. "The difficulty with Father Christian is his sexual predations on the larger community." His request had been turned down.

In a January 6, 1997, letter, Norman notified Monsignor Gaydos of accepting part-time employment taking phone orders for a major theatrical theater in Saint Louis. He also mentioned he was considering moving closer to his workplace, as he was presently driving about sixty miles one way.

An August 14, 1998, Sheridan memo revealed another sexual-abuse survivor had called the archdiocese, "very upset as he recounted being sexually molested by a priest in 1974. [He] reported 'walking in south Saint Louis,' springtime as he recalls, 'he was picked up by a priest in his car and taken to a rectory,' which he recalls being located at Heege and Gravois, although [he] did not know the name of the parish. This is the location of Saint George church. The priest lured him with promises of 'showing him something interesting and fun.' The priest took [him] to a second floor room in the rectory where he was made to engage in oral sex with the priest. This was the only encounter with this priest.

"[He] says that he needs 'help.' He identified the help he needs as counseling. I asked that he call [recommended doctor] to discuss this with her. He said that he would get back to me after speaking with [the doctor]."

An added note stated, "Although [he] did not know the name of the priest he accuses of molesting him, Father Norman Christian was assigned to Saint George at that time. He fits [the man's] description of the priest as being a man in his late thirties or early forties."

It was lastly noted, "August 17, 1998: I spoke by phone today with Father Norm Christian. While he does not remember precisely this incident, he said that it fits his modus operandi of that period."

I found this absolutely disgusting. There's no way to know how many more children Norman sexually abused and casually forgot about after heaping such devastation on their young lives. I have no idea if or how the archdiocese helped any of these other victims, once made aware of them. If they didn't file lawsuits, they probably received little satisfaction for reporting their abuse.

A March 6, 2002, memo to Bishop Dolan at his archdiocesan office revealed a woman had called on behalf of her husband, stating, "He has a problem with a priest and was told to call you. He was told to call before 4:00 p.m., which is impossible for him. ... He's not home from work before 4:30 or 4:45 p.m." The woman asked "that you please call her husband ... after 4:30." Notations were made on the memo in pen that indicated he'd called the woman's husband and had submitted a report.

After Tim's lawsuit against Norman and the church became public knowledge in March 2004, the archdiocese continued to provide for Norman. He lived comfortably in the priests' retirement home. In early April, he wrote them (Christian, 04-05-04, letter) requesting "reimbursement of fees or related expenses for these seminar events. I am in a financial bind and may have to be absent due to lack of funds." He planned to attend an annual Focolare convention, July 23–27, in Indiana; a family reunion/retreat in Wichita, Kansas, April 23–25 ("this is a twelve-step program to help sexually addicted persons work on their sobriety and recovery"); and a national convention for SA in Oklahoma City, for three or four days in July. Though granting his request on April 12, the vicar general stressed, "You may not represent yourself as a priest and do not represent the Archdiocese of Saint Louis in any capacity. Given your understanding of this ... let me know the costs. ... I would be willing to give my approval for reimbursement" (Stika, 04-12-04, letter).

Norman had quickly written Archbishop Raymond Burke on March 26, 2004, after the lawsuit was filed against him: "I am a 68-year-old cleric of the archdiocese (class of 1961) in retirement status, living at Regina Cleri. ... My ministry is inactive. I am recently named in a sexual misconduct civil lawsuit by a John Doe plaintiff, and have as my defense attorney, Mr. J Martin Hadican, in Clayton, Missouri (entire letter in appendix 2).

"My current income is about $700 per month ($386 from Priests Mutual Archdiocese Retirement stipend, and $309 Social Security monthly payment). I am able to pay my attorney very little of the retainer fee he is seeking. ... I have learned ... there are no canonical rights to a civil attorney. ... There are some dioceses that do provide coverage for all or part of the attorney's fees ... Thanking you for considering this serious personal financial crisis, I am

Sincerely yours, Norman H. Christian."

Within weeks, Norman was informed, "We agreed to assist Father Christian with his legal fees" (Stika, 04-15-04, memo). The Vicar for Priests, Archdiocese of Saint Louis, received the following from Norman's defense attorney (Hadican, 04-16-04, memo).

"Re: John Doe TF vs. Father Norman H. Christian, et al.
Dear Monsignor ...,
Thank you for your call relative to the above. In a matter of this nature, our normal agreement is a $7,500 deposit, which we then bill against at the rate of $250 per hour. Please return the same retainer

to me, less 10%, or $6,750. Thank you, very truly yours, J. Martin Hadican."

Based on this information, one can only imagine the millions of dollars spent by the church for predator clergys' defense alone.

An archdiocesan memo dated June 10, 2004, stated: "Norm Christian called this afternoon to inform us that he is going with Father [friend] to his condo in Florida. ... leaving Sunday, June 13, and returning Friday, June 18."

Norman provided them with the phone and room numbers at the condo. It appears that after the lawsuit against him and the archdiocese became public, he spent a good deal of time and the archdiocese's money in traveling.

October 2004 memos (Vogel & Curtis, 10-06-04 & 10-07-04) gave a bit of information as to what happened to Norman that led to his demise. "Not feeling well for days, Norman thought he had eaten something that didn't agree with him. A visit to the doctor sent him to the hospital for tests, which led to his being admitted. As of 7:30 that evening, he was still waiting for test results. A specialist was consulted, and he told Norman his liver was not functioning at all; 'prognosis is not good.'"

A cousin told me this same information when she learned it from her son, who had been visiting Norman at the hospital when it happened. Norman's full medical records remain under court-ordered protection; they could not be released to me.

The case against Norman had to be closed after his death on October 29, 2004. The Missouri Circuit Court (Saint Louis City) sent a Trial Docket Notice to Archbishop Justin Rigali stating:

"By order of COURT, Plaintiff shall notify all Defendants of trial settings and file certificate of service with the court. Cases not deemed ready under Local Rule 31 will NOT be assigned out to trial. Application for continuance of cases deemed ready must be presented in person to the Presiding Judge in Division 1. Cases CANNOT be continued by consent. These cases are assigned to Division 01 on 9-07-04. Rollover for cases not reached 11-01-04: 042-00721 John Doe Tf vs. Father Norman H.

(Another John Doe case versus a priest was listed above Norman's.)

It is mind-numbing and insulting to all of us that the hierarchy thinks so highly of itself and clergy that they allow molesters to minister to the unsuspecting faithful. Just as Jesus cleansed His temple of the money changers, He may become angry again and cleanse His church by driving out all the clergy molesters and the hierarchy who continue to protect them.

For my daughter and me, the decades-long emotional roller-coaster ride with Norman and the church is like a terrible nightmare, but we did endure all that happened, facing challenges as they occurred. Though unable to completely forget the painful memories from her past, Sue has wisely chosen to continue to make a difference. She strives to prevent abuse by empowering children through education and awareness.

Her compassion for others is admirable. Remembering the hurtful, disapproving comments made to her long ago compels her to encourage others who are trying to get their lives back on track while under that same harsh scrutiny of righteous, judgmental people. Sue continues to find the good in people and in life. She's an amazing woman, and the bond between us has only grown stronger.

I deeply regret that I was not able to protect Sue from my brother. I marvel at her loving, protective, communicative ways with her own children. Having learned from what she experienced, she is unwavering in her attempt to protect them from harm.

Joe and I are blessed with close relationships among all four of our grown children and their families. Their love and concern for each other and us is the best gift a parent can receive.

As for Norman, I never turned my back on him. I just continuously encouraged him to follow the church's treatment programs and, during that last year of his life, pleaded with him to apologize to all the people he had hurt. It was then that Norman stopped communicating with me.

I have not missed him since his death in 2004. There's only relief in no longer needing to be concerned about him. I've searched my memory for good times to remember him by, but those I might consider such are shattered by the realization that he already was molesting children during those times. Norman had managed, with the help of the church, to keep it all concealed. Thoughts of him now only bring me sadness for all the lives he destroyed in seeking evil desires.

The continuous cover-ups were apparent throughout the many documents I read. As long as the archdiocese's needs were met, it seemed they were comfortable being deceitful about Norman. Whenever Norman shared his personal struggles at a parish with various members of the archdiocese, their remedy was simply to move him around to different parishes, some at his own request. The reality is that the church leaders covered for him until they no longer could. These documents strengthened my belief in the necessity of writing my book, holding these people accountable for allowing the lifetime of anguish Norman inflicted upon his victims and their families.

I wonder how much thought or concern the hierarchy has given to all the souls dishonored by Father Christian—children, vulnerable adults, and their families— whose lives and faith were destroyed by this evil priest's vile actions.

I saw no indication in the documents of any form of compassion for his victims, not from Norman or the hierarchy. Just the opposite; those who had come forward were dealt with coldly. Pay them a settlement if they must, refer them to a doctor, but avoid accepting responsibility or expressing sincere apologies that it happened to them. Nor was there any mention of Norman's or the archdiocese's concerns for his parents or sisters and their families. Nothing indicated the archdiocese ever cared about at least protecting his own nieces and nephews or helping us cope in the aftermath.

The church must publicly acknowledge that the abused are the innocent ones. From the Pope down, demonstrating compassion and understanding for survivors of clergy abuse would help bring about change in the hurtful attitudes that many of the faithful give them.

The Archdiocese of Saint Louis did have a Healing Prayer Service in December 2012 at Saint Luke the Evangelist Church in Richmond Heights, Missouri, followed by another a year later in January 2013, at Queen of All Saints Church in Oakville, Missouri. A third healing prayer service was held March 6, 2014, at Our Lady of Lourdes church in Washington, Missouri. "They are open to all who are victims/survivors of physical, sexual, emotional or verbal abuse by anyone; clergy, family, friends, coworkers or strangers. ... Family members and friends of survivors are encouraged to participate, as well as those who are involved in helping abused people."

Archbishop Carlson said, "On behalf of the Archdiocese of Saint Louis, I apologize to anyone who has been abused by a priest, deacon, religious, employee or volunteer associated with our parishes, schools or other ministries" (*Missourian* newspaper, 03-05-14, Union, MO).

The archbishop's reaching out to all abuse survivors is a step in the right direction. However, I would like to see these services held monthly or quarterly at every church in the archdiocese, not just one, annually. Hearing one's own pastor's compassion for all victims and their families could help Catholics accept the reality of clergy sexual abuse and soften their harsh attitudes toward survivors speaking out about what they've endured.

Clergy are no longer on pedestals; they never should have been. All abusers and those who covered for them must apologize for the appalling abuse of their powers. The church's actions now will determine if Catholics' faith and trust will be restored.

I encourage everyone to stop their silence. Write letters to your priests, bishops, and archbishops, letting them know you hold the church accountable for the harm that's been done to so many innocent children and their families. Advise them to acknowledge their responsibility and stop covering up these shameful crimes. Tell them to remove molesters from ministry immediately. Point out that not only the victims and their families need help but all members of the church as well, in understanding and coping with it all. Express your concerns at every opportunity. If we give editors bundles of mail from which to choose, they may cover the clergy sexual-abuse topic even more, giving abuse victims the support they need and deserve.

Crimes are crimes, no matter who commits them. Those responsible must be accountable and suffer the consequences for what they do. Clergy are no exception.

Appendix

Following are correspondence I wrote or received over the past three decades. They are included here in entirety for those who choose to read them.

The following are listed by dates written. (Those mentioned in Author's notes are listed in Appendix 2.)

My January 19, 1986, letter of response to my brother while he was in New Mexico:

Dear Norm,

I was really glad to get your letter letting us know where you were. To be honest, I was feeling hurt that you hadn't felt you could trust Jeanne or I with at least a phone number where we could reach you in an emergency. But then, after reading your letter, I felt disappointed with myself for not having recognized the fact that perhaps you might have been having serious problems. You just always put up such a good front, and I was always so involved with my own problems, I just never thought you might be struggling with something yourself. I'm really sorry! I wish I could have been of some help to you. But I'm glad you're taking action on whatever it is that's troubling you. If there's one good thing that came out of Sue's problems, it's that I've learned how important it is to talk about my feelings, especially with people who are experiencing similar things. The support groups have been my biggest source of strength, along with prayer and trust in God. Talking with and listening to other people and their families who are suffering with the same problems has given me the strength to get through some very difficult times with Sue. I came to realize when I felt like hating her was when she needed my love and understanding most. I truly feel that I've become a much stronger person over the past year and a half that I've been going to all the support group meetings for eating and mood disorders. It's not only helped me with Sue's problems but it opened my eyes to the fact that I cannot control anyone's lives but my own. I've got to accept whatever comes along and deal with each day and problem, one day at a time, as things happen, trusting God will give me the strength to get through it. I've quit asking why things happen and realize that by worrying about a problem, I'm only putting obstacles in the way of clear thinking. It's okay to make mistakes; I learn by them.

What I'm mainly trying to say is I'm glad you're working on your problem. Everyone has something to deal with, and it takes a very strong person to face up to whatever it is and seek professional help. The weak person says I can handle it myself and does nothing about it. There's no shame in having a problem, only in ignoring it.

Recently, I've been wondering if I could have handled all the stress we've had with Joan's brain tumor if I hadn't been strengthened over the past year and a half dealing with Sue's problems. I can't imagine why our family is being blessed or punished with so many hardships. Then, when I think about them, I can see we are becoming a closer family because of them, and I can see lots of other people who are in much worse situations that I wouldn't want to trade places with. Then I feel lucky.

It took me almost a year, I guess, to realize that talking and listening in the support groups was a real help to me. I can see how much it helps Joe, too, when he goes. But he himself hasn't realized it completely enough to make him want to reach out to them on a regular basis. They're such a marvelous way to unload all the things we keep bottled up inside and we really get a lot of good feedback, suggestions.

So, while I don't know what type of help you're getting, I'm just suggesting you pour everything out to whoever's helping you. You've made the biggest step in just going for help. Now completely trust God and unload everything. You'll be able to work out a solution. It will probably be quite difficult, but you'll be able to do it. And, if I can help in any way, even if it's just to be a sounding board to bounce your thoughts off, feel free to write or call.

Joan's been pretty sick this past week. She was vomiting for two full days and I ended up taking her to Cardinal Glennon's emergency room Friday. They ran different tests and said that surgery wise, all was okay. Possibly she picked up a flu bug. She had been on a capsule for nausea since coming home from the hospital, but it hadn't helped at all. So the doctor gave me a suppository to try. Good news! It seems to be working. She felt nausea coming on but the medicine worked and she kept her food down all day Saturday. She had been doing well with her physical therapy. Walking with a walker and just before getting so sick, trying to walk with a cane. The therapist is pleased with her progress. She still has double vision and wears an eye patch to correct that. We're hoping with time that'll improve, too. At times she feels angry with God for letting this happen to her. It's hard for an 11-year-old to understand. I don't understand myself. Don't try! Just say this is how it is and go on from there. We're in the process of getting a tutor for Joan and some of her classmates are also going to help her keep up with the class.

Sue's been doing better. But I know she's been struggling, especially since she's now worrying about Joan. And we just learned her insurance coverage for emotional problems is about to run out. Joe's pretty uptight right now after hearing that. But there are plenty of free self-help groups for her to make use of in the program. I've got to trust God will see that she does.

I hope I haven't depressed you with all this, but I feel you are interested in what's going on. If you think writing Sue would help her, go ahead. Her low self-esteem is still a big problem. You might even know of a way to write Joan about accepting what God's sent to her. For the most part she is in good spirits, but at times she really shows her anger. She's been such a good kid all her life, why would He let an awful thing happen to her. She can't walk or write or do any of the things she used to take for granted. It's hard to explain to an 11-year-old that God sends suffering to those He loves. But before you worry about them, take care of yourself!

I love you and care an awful lot about your happiness. We weren't raised much on being allowed to express our feelings or even be entitled to having them. I know Mom and Dad did what they thought was best, that's what we all do at the time. But expression of love by hugs or spoken words just wasn't there.

Just know that you're loved and cared about very much. Just because you chose the priesthood as a vocation doesn't mean we expect you to be perfect or have answers to everything. No matter what your problem may be, I'll love you and support you. You're certainly in my prayers, more than ever. I just hope you'll let me know if there's anything I can do to be of help.

As someone recently told me in regards to Joan, God sends troubles to families in order to bring them closer together, to strengthen them and make them realize how much they really love one another. I really can see that now.

God bless *all* of us! And give us all the strength we need to keep on going. Thanks again for writing. I'll be praying for you and will be glad to see you when you return.

Love,
Carol

P.S. I gave your address to Jeanne and read her your letter. Joe also read it but no one else will be told anything unless you say differently. Good luck!

My brother's January 23, 1986, letter from Foundation House, Jemez Springs, New Mexico:

Dear Carol,

What a joy to get a letter from home! What you had to say meant more to me than I might have expected. It was very supportive indeed; and I needed it a lot today. I am attending a total wellness module offered by the Paracletes. There are 23 other priests (from monsignors to monastics, from the 60s to the 20s) who suffer from everything that human life will allow ... Things as simple as stress through a variety of relational problems, with many of us dealing with sexuality in our lives. Last October I had myself evaluated by professionals and as I already knew, I would be prime material for their module. Perhaps someday I will sit down one-on-one with you and tell you my whole story. But for right now I am where I need to be with the right professional persons to guide us through 5 months of exercises designed to take us apart and put us back together. To give you some idea of the extent of this experience, there are 20 professional people involved in our programs: Psychodrama, Peer Evaluation, a class on Literature & Christian Themes, Peer Consultation, keeping a Journal, Sexuality class, Cinema Therapy, Art Therapy, Movement Therapy, class on Stress, class on Life (how each deals life to others under favorable conditions or under stress). Personal interviews with spiritual director, psychiatrist, psychologist; and this happens every week. There will be two major interruptions in the form of workshops: a 5-day one on Liturgy and another 5-day one on Religion and Psychology. Later, during early May there is to be an 8-day Wilderness Experience here in the NM mountains. As a hobby class, I am learning about computer technology, and I forgot to mention that we have a Saturday morning schedule of Cardiovascular Maintenance. The time will pass swiftly enough with a schedule loaded like this. I already value the 23 other men who are here; we have bonded into community and will share one another's suffering as we go day by day through the experience. *I guess I should thank you for supporting the Archdiocesan Development Appeal, because that is part of the resource that is helping pay this huge bill (the program with professional teachers plus room and board is listed as $3,000 per month per person; that does not count the many extra medical costs that are normal procedure for every participant. I figure this "sabbatical" will end up costing over $20,000* [emphasis mine]. Archbishop May is fantastic! When I visited him he was so very supportive, too. Today I read the total "book" on me (which we may do at any time here), and the Archbishop had all this information on his desk before I came to visit him about leaving for a while. It was shocking to me to read about myself so many things that I didn't know he knew when I was there. Carol, for the first time in my life, I am trusting my secret life to these many others without fear of getting hurt in return. I have practiced hiding my secret life that goes back almost 40 years even to my childhood, and I guess with so much practice I became quite good at it (hiding my secrets). I am at the same time totally convinced of my vocation to the priesthood. I am a quality priest (better than many), effective in my ministry, and happy in doing it. So, I look forward to a great burden of guilt being lifted from my shoulders in the months I spend here. It should make me an even better priest for the next 25 years. I am with two other men from St. Louis, and I knew both of them well before coming here; that was sure a big surprise. We are sure a surprising and interesting lot! I wouldn't trade my life for your problems or anyone else's, but I hope I can get on with the project of growing up and becoming holy in the Life and Unity of the church. My faith has always been better than good, even in moment of depression years past when I seriously thought of leaving the ranks of the clergy. That won't happen now, and I am grateful to God for his love and patience.

Notice that the address is a little different from the previous one; this one is correct. The phone numbers are our personal phones (2 for the 24 of us). They said that if outsiders ask for us at the business phone, they will be told that we are not here (due to the need for privacy regarding our renewal). So if you ever call, do it about 9 to 10 p.m. St. Louis time because someone will be in our TV room and surely answer a ringing phone to take a message or call me to the phone.

Please keep me posted on family news. I am praying constantly for Joan, and I will write to her under separate cover. Likewise, I have felt very close to Sue from the time she entered her treatment and was so trusting in sharing her life with me. I will write to her now with even greater understanding as I strive for a healing in my own life. I'll be writing to her too, very soon.

You are right about tragic difficulties being a catalyst for bringing families closer together. I have never felt as close to you as I do right now, having received and enjoyed your beautiful letter. Thank you for taking the trouble to reach out still further (even to New Mexico) with your love.

Let us love one another,
Norman
P.S. Share what you think you should of this letter's content. Know that I am still pretty fearful and sensitive about my problem.

Following is page two of Norman's February 23, 1986, letter to me:

Things here are involved to the extreme. According to the first report (5 pages) sent to the archbishop, in the opinion of the staff here I am off to a very good start and they believe the module will be of much value for me. It really is embarrassing to see my problem described in clinical terminology. I look at it and say 'is that what I am; that's terrible!' and run to the other guys and find out that they are having the same feelings. This is certainly the most important thing I have ever done with my life, and the program is fascinating most of all because it is dealing with *me*. You should see me getting into aerobic dancing; I'll be able to swing with the best of my neighbors when I get back to Walnut Park. We had a Valentine's Day party, a real blast of food and booze; and when the movie didn't arrive, we ended up dancing with each other if you can believe that! For me that was the ultimate of letting go and I must admit it took a few drinks first, but it was a lot of fun. We laughed 'til we cried.

Last weekend we had an extra day off from programs, so five of us drove to El Paso, Texas (a 7-hour drive) and went across into Juarez, Mexico. That was interesting (they all talk funny there!). We stayed in a motel and caught Sunday Mass at a neighborhood church. It was the 10 a.m. children's Sunday mass. The priest was fantastic with the 150 little ones he brought to the front for his homily. I was surprised that I understood everything he said; I guess I could figure it out from my knowledge of Latin roots and his body language. He asked one of the 4-year-olds if he ever sinned and the kid answered "no, but my sister does a lot!" which brought the house down. Mexico is very conservative in liturgical changes; no special communion ministers (no cup to share), Communion on the tongue (only the celebrant gave communion) and only about 30% of the church congregation went up for communion. I was stunned! Driving back we enjoyed the White Sands National Monument, and some of the most beautiful desert mountain scenery all along the Rio Grande river valley. After a perfect dinner in Albuquerque topped off the outing, we were ready for a return to very intense programs once again. Up to this time I still haven't bought any souvenirs. I've had fun in Santa Fe visiting all the shops and art studios that abound there. That was fun too, but I still haven't been trapped into being the tourist victim.

I'm so busy that it doesn't seem like Lent. But I guess that my dying and rising is going on daily in the module. Thanks again for writing, and if I can help you think through your many worries, let me know. Hope things get better for everybody at your house and especially you! Take a day off, and go fishing!

I love you,
Norm

P.S. Tell Lynn I said hello and am looking forward to a fender-crunching hug when I come home!

The last letter Norman wrote me from his sabbatical, dated May 6, 1986:

Dear Carol,

First, thanks for writing as often as you do. It means a lot to me to feel included in the family; because before I came here I was actually excluding myself from the family. Anyway, your letters and love are certainly helping me to get ready to rejoin myself with the family. I am looking forward to the experience. Again, let me note that it was not your behavior in any way that created my problem; it was my own interpretation of my life and role. So thanks for reaching out to me. I am excited about the graduations and wish I could be present at the commencement exercises; however, there is a card I would ask you to convey to Jeff in my absence. It was mailed the same time as this letter. I have one for Sue also but will send it closer to her graduation date because she will be home to receive it. Glad to hear that Joan is enjoying fishing again. Also it is important that she receive the summer school program.

One of the current tasks I am dealing with in the program is identifying my feelings (like, any kind of feelings). I don't know how to stay with them once I have discovered them present. My practice was to always suppress my feelings. But that always led to stress in my daily life and all kinds of other problems as a result. So, it is extremely important that I work on this feeling problem. I cannot describe with words hardly any of my feelings, and yet if I am going to have an intimate friendship with anyone, I will have to share feelings without denying them because they are negative or inappropriate. God only knows what kind of impression I will make on you when I get home. I ought to appear different to you I suppose, but that will be your problem to deal with (just what you needed, another problem!) But it could be for the better, too, right?

I have enjoyed my 5 months in this program very much. I am also glad I have had the chance to tour the neighborhood while I am here. I've seen sights in Arizona, Utah, and Colorado, in addition to New Mexico and El Paso, Texas (where we spent an overnight in Juarez, Mexico, across the border). Last weekend I went with a companion across the Navajo Indian reservation, driving country roads with wild horses roaming the fields and even the highway. The Navajos are beautiful people, and very friendly (or maybe they just gave up when they reviewed the return they'd get on my scalp). A beautiful Navajo guide drove us into the secret places of Canyon de Chelly, where I visited cliff-dwelling ruins dating from the 6th century AD, which were inhabited by the Anasasi (ancient ones), who disappeared before 1200 AD. I dig historic sites like that. I am now an authority on Mexican food, and even understand what I am ordering from the menu in a good Mexican restaurant. My education is broadening (but my stomach seems to be keeping pace). Well, the page is full, so I will stop. If you write me, be sure I will receive any mail before June 6, my last day at Foundation House.

Blessings on you all!
Norm

My June 16, 1989, letter to my brother:

Dear Norm,

First of all, I hope you don't mind my letter is typed. It's easier to read and I can express myself better when I put it in writing. But I'll be glad to talk, or just listen, anytime you'd like. I could see at Jeanne's how you are really hurting and struggling, and I want to remind you that you are a good person and not to give up. I was just jotting down some of my thoughts to you again when I received your card today. I was glad to get it.

As I've said to my kids many times over the years, I feel there's no shame in having problems, only in ignoring them, refusing to do something about them. Well, you've certainly been getting help for yourself. I feel so sorry that you've felt so alone through it all.

I hope that you can start feeling less alone now that you've shared your fears with me.

It seems to me that your self-esteem is badly drooping. What makes you any less a good person now that some family members know your secret? You're still you, the same person; just another of God's imperfect human beings, like the rest of the family. I don't feel you chose to be gay. God just made you that way. I can relate to your feelings of shame, though. I felt that way when everyone learned of Sue's [*eating disorder*] and again with her pregnancy. I looked at her behaviors as a reflection of me as a mother. What a lousy mom I must have been in the eyes of my family and everyone who knew me. How embarrassed I was at first to be seen with her. I wondered how she could hold her head up. Guess her self-esteem was better than mine. Of course, Sue felt a shame closer to your own since it was she herself being stared at and wondered about. But with much help from her program, we all learned that she was still a very good person who had just happened to make some bad choices. I eventually realized that I was not responsible for the bad choices Sue had made. I learned to accept that I cannot control another person, I must let go and let them make mistakes and learn by them.

It was a big risk for me to send you that letter telling you Sue had confided in me. But it was eating me up alive the short time I was trying to figure out how to tell you. After I mailed my letter to you, I told Joe and he reacted by telling me all the "what if's" you might do when you read it. At first I was worried but I quickly reminded myself that I'm not responsible for how another person reacts to what I say or do. You would react how you would react. I'm glad you reacted as you did.

You can count on me doing whatever I can to help you feel more at ease at family gatherings. Even though it will be difficult for you, I feel it is necessary you don't run from them. You need to take risks in order to change things. I know that's scary and very hard. Trying to read other people's minds will drive you crazy. Keep in mind that anyone who is going to judge you or treat you differently is not worth worrying about having for a friend.

I certainly want you at the family gatherings, and I feel safe in saying Joe and the kids do, too. None of us are so perfect we should judge you. The past is over, can't change it. We need to accept the fact that this is the way it is now. What can we do to make it better? Don't look for trouble by worrying about the future. Deal with each day as it comes; take it one day at a time.

I wonder if you could get Archbishop May to help you get a support group for religious started here in St. Louis. The need is probably a large one. People feel alone until they can share similar feelings with others. Sharing feelings is uncomfortable and painful, but very helpful to both the person sharing and to those listening.

You seem to be carrying a lot of guilt and fear in regard to the people you've encountered. I feel like by disciplining yourself by saying "acting out" is no longer an option, you'll find it easier to develop healthier coping skills. It'll be like losing a friend; you'll feel the pain and mourn the loss.

I want to encourage you to continue to reach out for help and support and build your self-esteem good enough that you can put certain options aside as unacceptable. It's possible! You've got my unconditional love and support, brother! Hang in there.

Love and prayers,

Carol

P.S. Sue asked me to tell you she will get with you later. Right now she is working 9-hour days, has just started a college algebra course which runs for 8 weeks, has lots of homework, and wants time to spend with her son. She's afraid of messing up this algebra class if she doesn't give it full attention; she's not avoiding you on purpose.

Norman's letter of response to Jeanne and Carol on December 23, 1995:

Hello, Jeanne and Carol,

Of course you both expect a response from me. Jeanne suggesting that I meet her (or both of you) sometime after Christmas Day. I have prepared a copy of Jeanne's letter to me [12-13-1995, Jeanne Meyer letter] for Carol, because I do not believe that Carol saw the letter prior to it's [sic] mailing to me. There are several issues that I want to get into. I will use quotes from the letter to focus my response, but if I stray from an immediate answer to the quote you can chalk it up to whatever you like.

1. "We felt the need to talk to someone etc… Msgr. Naumann."

I am deeply hurt, outraged might better describe it, that you went behind my back to talk to Msgr. Naumann about me. Jeanne had to depend on Carol's friendship with Joe Naumann to act on this decision. I am furious that you care so little about me, and that you are trying to cover your own ass because you have a 'brother-pervert priest', which I do not believe myself to be. I have no difficulty talking with you about any aspect of my sexual compulsion/addiction and the program I am assigned to, a program that I welcome as a Grace. Why did you bypass me!? I should have been the first one you approached. Actually, the history details of my compulsive sex addiction are none of your business. Aren't some things private for obvious reasons? And the danger of public disclosure is increased every time you approach some 'trustworthy' person. Had you done this in a confessional situation, you would have been safe (i.e., the seal of Confession). Anyone else is free to pass on the news.

The Archdiocese of St. Louis could be sued many times over for civil damages. If this one allegation becomes public, it could awaken others to a possibility of 'winning the lottery' (some giant settlement in or out of court) for professional malpractice by one of its priests.

2. "We have had guilty feelings for 6 years for not saying anything."

I don't think you are concerned about being sued out of house and home because you have sibling ties to me. I suppose that you are feeling 'guilty' for not calling the child abuse hotline to report child abuse and have me removed from ministry (i.e., you 'broke the law' etc.) If your conscience is bothering you, you too might benefit from the help of a counselor (but then they are obliged by law to report child abuse however it comes before them). You never told me anything about your "guilty feelings." Msgr. Naumann said 'not to worry', but that was not what you wanted to hear. I suppose if the Archbishop himself told you the same 'not to worry', you would have stuck with your prejudice toward me. I say that Jeanne needs to be 'in control' of all details before the affair is being handled correctly.

3. Of course you "love me" too

It sure doesn't feel like love! What it feels like is, that you want to keep a safe emotional distance. I do not feel any compassion toward me, any affirming love in your letter. What I do feel is your fear of embarrassment. What I do not feel is any empathy whatsoever. You have permission to stop loving me, if that is the best you can come up with.

4. "A sexaholic, like an alcoholic, is 'incurable'.

There are a lot of 'incurables': paranoids, scrupulous people, all the forms of phobia victims, compulsive shoplifters, compulsive liars, compulsive gamblers, compulsive BINGO players, etc.... Do they get cured? ....no. But can they be brought to function in a healthy way? ...YES!! If they learn what it takes to control their behavior and commit to using the means available to escape the dangerous flashpoint (trigger) that sets them off, they can live a life of 'sobriety' relative to their addiction. That is what a 12-step group is for. "Keep coming back; it works, if you work it!", is said by the group as each meeting is closed. 'Sobriety' in any dependency implies using the means at hand (other AA members, a sponsor, etc.) to be at the ready to help me be safe at moments when in the past I acted out the compulsion.

You speak as though you know about this, but I believe that your understanding is quite shallow. So I fear that you will intervene in my situation, giving your uninformed opinions to some official, thus getting me thrown out. I would then no longer be a problem for you. You will be back in the driver's seat, shaking your head that I turned out to be such a failure.

5. The issue of our "Relatives": [names withheld] ----"Do they know?"

Being a chip-off-the-old-Mom, I project that you would probably want to tell them what you know, and then they could say "Oh yes, I was told about that." On the other hand, if they did not know anything, they surely will after you disclose it. You give yourself too much credit for thinking you know what the other person knows or is thinking. (Mom did that with dad all the time, remember?) You never knew my secrets in a lifetime of being my sister; you learned it when Carol brought it to you, right?

My private sins are no more the business of any relative than they are any business of yours. You don't have to confess my sins to anyone. Why do you want to make this your business? If you choose to make yourself uncomfortable about something over which you had no control, I guess that is your choice. Mom was a classic gossip. She always needed to be "the first to know", and then she became the "first to tell." She could burn up the telephone for hours, passing on the latest story to relatives (especially if it was bad news, be it sickness or sins).

Why should my secret affect your interaction with family kin? Of course Joe and Helen would be crushed! So you interpret their voice and face as in-the-know, without them saying or asking anything. Why would you protect them before you would protect me?! If you want to know why [name withheld] left the seminary, then you better ask [him]! If he told you everything, would you then go back to Joe & Helen with your new-found information?

Mom never know [sic] who I was, and your approach to me tells me that you know very little about who I am. You know one small part (by comparison with the rest of my life); you know my age and my sexual compulsion. The latter appears to prevent you from wanting to know who the rest of me is. If you could just "get rid of me" that would take care of your self esteem in the face of our relatives.

6. What's with this "it's left bad feelings with the kids as well.

Have you told your children and grandchildren all about me already? (Small wonder Ron never responded in any way to my outreach to him, following his family breakup.) If you have told them, you seriously violated my privacy, and I hold you accountable for it. How would you feel if I decided you are a compulsive gossip, and then went to every relative to tell them what I know. You don't know that I am a pervert any more than I can show that you are a gossip. People will find such things out without help from either of us.

If your kid or anyone else's would need to come forward with and [sic] allegation of abuse, I am sure you would help them do it, just as I would if one of our school's students came to me to say that someone was abusing them.

7. Fr. Joe offered that we might have a meeting in the presence of my Therapist [sic] to vent your concerns and get some answers.

The professionals in any program like mine are not permitted to disclose what is learned during treatment. You would be refused such a meeting even if I personally asked them to meet with us. They are careful to put in writing/notes only broad characteristics, in case a subpoena required them to submit something to a court procedure. Details are kept off-the-record.

SUMMARY OBSERVATION: Jeanne, I am your family, YES. But, you are not responsible for my behavior (not my crimes, not my sins, not the way I dress, not how I deal with my diabetes, not how I drink or smoke, etc.). It appears that it is your own choice to be upset by things that should upset me (and they do). I am embarrassed, ashamed, self-convicting to the point of obsession about it. I certainly will not assume responsibility for you making my problem your problem.

This I know: the more people you disclose my sins to, the greater the risk of me becoming a public spectacle in the media. I am not going to help you deal with my problem. I believe you have manufactured a problem for yourself by wanting to be in control in advance (like Mom always needed to be in control of all possible outcomes). I am trusting myself to a program for recovery, and I hope you allow me to have the chance to complete it before you have me out of possible future ministry in the Church. That remains my God-given Vocation, just as yours is to remain married to grow in holiness and grace. If God has other plans, I wish you would let Him take care of that in His own way.

I am less trusting of you in the light of your going behind my back. It will be more difficult for me to share what is going on in my life. However if prayer, my group, my therapists, etc... tell me that I should share with you, you will be included. Meanwhile, let me work the program. Curious that you never asked for details about this program of Recovery, [sic] isn't it? All I hear is something like "What are you doing to us, horrible person?"

My March 17, 2002, letter to Bishop Naumann:

Hi, Bishop Naumann,

I'm attaching a copy of a letter I am sending to Archbishop Rigali. You must know the news of the past weeks is very disturbing to me. I feel so let down by the church, like I've been kicked in the gut over and over.

I believed you a while back when you told my sister and me not to worry about priest abuse cases. It was the archdiocese's problem, not ours, and it was being handled. I didn't see any signs of things changing since then, but I kept telling myself to believe what you had said. Please, do something. Priests do not deserve special treatment. Trust in the Catholic Church cannot be regained unless there is proof positive the disgusting covering up is over. Covering up is as bad, if not worse, than the abuse itself.

My heart goes out to all the innocent priests in our archdiocese. All the covering up is as damaging to them as it is to the victims of the abuse. I'm praying very hard for God to give strength to everyone to get this horrible problem corrected. This has got to be an awful time for you, Bishop Joe. Hang in there. God help us all!

Sincerely,
Carol Kuhnert

My March 17, 2002, letter to Archbishop Rigali:

Dear Archbishop Rigali,

It saddens me to write this letter, but the Catholic Church's reaction to the evils of clergy abuse of minors has been heavy on my mind for better than 14 years. It was about then that I learned my own brother, a priest, was an abuser and had himself, been abused in his youth by priests.

My then 19-year-old daughter, his niece, came to me in tears saying how her uncle was taking her to homosexual movies and saying sexual things to her. He was also telling her about his own disgusting behaviors, which I knew nothing about. I was shocked! My husband and I had been feeling comforted by the fact that my brother was trying to help our daughter at a time when she was very vulnerable and under a doctor's care herself. It makes me physically sick just to think of how he deceived all of us. We trusted him. All the while, the archdiocese knew what he was about; shameful. We, his own family, didn't even have a clue to watch out for him. To make matters worse, to this day, I don't think he feels he did anything wrong with her. He was angry she told me about him.

I can't understand the church's criminal way of intentionally covering up the damaging behaviors directed toward unsuspecting parents and their children all these years. People, who in their faith had trustingly turned to clergy for guidance, were left unprotected. Priests have been moved around when the men in charge were told there was a problem with a priest's behavior. The betrayal and damage done to so many for so long is inexcusable. I am waiting to hear an apology for allowing this cover-up to go on for so long. This is as serious as the abuse itself, if not worse.

How can victims, priests, or any of their families ever recover when they must bear such a heavy, dirty secret for the rest of their lives? My trust and respect for our archdiocese is gone. It will be extremely difficult to regain. Why should anyone believe what the Archdiocese says at this point? Our religious leaders sound more like politicians finding ways to avoid telling the truth.

I hope the church will take a hard look at what kind of therapy has been given to clergy who abuse. What message was given to them and how do they view their guilt in these matters. It seems there is more concern about getting found out, paying off the victims, being in the news and losing their jobs than about being concerned and remorseful for having ruined so many young lives.

I wonder if seminarians truly realize the position of trust they will have as a priest. What message has the seminary given men all these years for them to feel so free to act out over and over, feel forgiven by God but not remove themselves from their own occasion of sin. I can't think of anyone I had more trust in than the religious. I trusted that abuse matters were being handled properly when I was told years ago that I didn't need to worry; the archdiocese would handle it.

I can tell you I feel dirty for hiding my brother's secret, and I have found it difficult to make excuses for him when people have asked me how he is, what's he doing, etc. He doesn't seem to see how it is difficult for his sisters to respond to people's questions about him since he had left his parish. Has anyone with the archdiocese thought about the abusive priest's family? I suppose most of them don't even know the truth. I only learned of my brother's behavior because my daughter was courageous enough to tell me what he was doing to her. I was angry with him and frightened that he may have done something to my other children or to my nieces and nephews. I confided in my sister and we talked with our children about him. Then we confronted him and asked him to explain. He became angry and felt my daughter had betrayed him! I can't find the words to say how I felt at that point. I began praying for my brother in ways I had never done before. I prayed for all the young people he's harmed. I pray he has stopped those behaviors and encourage him to continue with all his support systems and therapy. Yet, I wonder just what is being told to him in that therapy. Is it made clear that the victim is the innocent one? He tells me he never forced anyone. They were willing participants. It disturbs me that he chooses to blame the victims; children/teens who were taught to trust and respect priests. His attitude makes me question the therapy he's received.

Also, he doesn't seem to understand how any of what he's done affects his own family. When asked what should be told anyone asking about him, he became upset and said we shouldn't talk about him. Did he think no one would notice he was gone? I seriously question his way of thinking. If it weren't for the fact that I know by his own admission my brother actually abused young people, and I have seen how his follow-up was being managed, I'd be right in there with all the other old-time Catholics who are willing to blindly believe what our clergy is telling us now. I'd be trying to believe the victims must be lying about the ugly clergy behaviors being reported. I have found myself keeping the dirty secret all these years while trying to convince myself that I could trust that the Archdiocese was truly making things right. I have not been able to convince myself. I feel ashamed for keeping it to myself, yet I do; after all, a priest told me it wasn't for me to worry about.

Now today, I read Joe Lessard's disgusting interview. I can't bring myself to call him Reverend. I could hardly believe reading his comment to Carberry. 'I was going to get help for the asthma, arthritis, and this sexual situation.' The most horrible was referred to as a 'situation' and ranked third in his comment. I believe he had been given therapy at some point in time. I can't help but think all of our church leaders must look at sexual abuse of minors as not being that harmful. It horrifies me to think that!

Talk is cheap; the Catholic Church needs to do something other than cover up its ugly mess. Anyone else guilty of similar crimes would end up with prison time along with therapy. I do not think clergy deserve any special treatment. If anything, the position of trust they have makes their crimes even worse. My heart goes out to all the innocent priests in our Archdiocese. All the covering-up is as damaging to them as it is to the victims of the abuse.

I have faith and trust in God and will continue praying for all members of the church. I pray our church leaders will do the right thing and get rid of any other of the clergy that are not trustworthy. It's time to stop covering-up so the trust that has been lost can start to be regained. May God give all of us the strength and patience to get through this extremely difficult time.

Sincerely,
Mrs. Carol Kuhnert
Copy sent to Bishop Naumann

My April 21, 2002, letter to Norman:

Hi, Norm,

I find myself becoming more and more upset and angry with our church leaders and somewhat with your attitude. It bothers me that I've never heard you say you were sorry about causing the emotional damage you did to the kids you've harmed over the years. You were a deeply trusted priest; kids even 18-, 19-, 20-year-olds, had been taught and usually do look up to priests and obey them. Please don't take comfort in thinking they joined in willingly.

You chose to tell Sue your truths at a time she was extremely vulnerable and under a doctor's care herself for emotional problems. All you told her continues to trouble her to this day. She has been getting therapy for herself at considerable expense. I feel angry when I think of how you took Sue places and told her things, all of which she should never have been exposed to. Joe and I were feeling relieved when she was out with you. We foolishly thought you were helping her with her problems. If one can't trust a priest, my brother yet, who can a parent trust?

Bishop Naumann told me years ago not to worry about you; that it wasn't my problem. Clergy abuse would be taken care of by the archdiocese. I reminded myself of that over the years, but have felt very uncomfortable keeping your secret. I've met up with many people who knew and cared about you and they'd ask me how and where you were. I'd make up some excuse for your absence. I don't want to tell your secret to anyone. I do wonder, though, how you, the victims, or anyone who knows is supposed to be able to heal and get on with their lives while keeping such a secret.

My faith in God remains strong but my trust in the Catholic Church and its leaders is gone. I no longer respect clergy; I am ashamed of the way they do business.

Your recent e-mail is probably what prompted me to tell you my feelings. When you said you had to act quickly or lose by default, it made me wonder how you feel about all the victims who lost by not coming forward in time with their accusations and the accused clergy who were able to go on with their lives as though nothing had happened; kind of different when the shoe is on the other foot. Your comments about your addiction have always been about how it affects you. I don't remember hearing you say anything about how it affects anyone else.

I'm sure you've noticed I've not been inviting you for family get-togethers for a while. I must put my daughter's needs before yours, and I know how uncomfortable Sue is around you. I felt it was the right thing to do; I think you should be able to understand.

I still care about what happens to you; I pray you are continuing with all your therapy and doing whatever is needed to stay sober. I've been praying for God to give you direction ever since you were removed from active ministry.

I suppose the media is stirring up various feelings in a lot of people lately. I don't think that's a bad thing. It's time for the Catholic Church to act responsibly. I wonder how long it's going to take to earn back the trust from its members, if ever.

You are still welcome at our home. Take care Norm; you'll be in my prayers.

Love,
Carol

My April 26, 2002, letter to Archbishop Rigali and copy to Bishop Naumann:

Dear Archbishop Rigali,

I am so disappointed and angry with the men who have just talked with the Pope after hearing comments they made upon their return. I think the wonderful institution of our Catholic Church is being destroyed. Statements about such sinful and criminal behavior being a problem in all of society sounds like some kid telling Mom and Dad everyone else is doing it. That's beside the point! The Catholic Church is supposed to be setting the highest example of moral standards for its members. What is it going to do about this cancer in its own ranks? After hearing what the Pope told them, how can they even think of allowing a first-time, caught anyway, offender remain in service? One time is too much; the crime needs to be reported to the police! Then at least, the good priests' reputations can be saved.

I am so ashamed of the immoral and unacceptable statements our church leaders have made as to what may be done with the sex offenders. Either it is a crime, or it's not. It is, and it needs to be dealt with, not overlooked and covered up.

I do realize sex offenders are in all religions and walks of life. Let's at least see it dealt with properly in the Catholic Church. Let God forgive the offenders, if they are sorry, but *please*, make them accept responsibility for their sinful/criminal choices. Remove them from their positions of trust in our church.

Sincerely,
Mrs. Carol Kuhnert

My May 15, 2002, note to Bishop Naumann:

Hi, Bishop Joe,

I guess Norman has deleted me from his life. On April 16 he told me he was trying to find a canon law advocate as he needed to act quickly in a canonical timeline in the procedure or he'd lose by default, be laicized, and lose priest benefits. I guess that was the straw that broke the camel's back. On April 21, I let him know my feelings and concerns about him. I haven't heard from him since. His attitude is that what he does is none of my business; it doesn't concern me. Unless I agree with him, he's not open to hearing anything I say. Could I ask you to keep me informed on what is happening to him as far as the archdiocese is concerned? Or is it not any of my business? He is my brother, and I am worried about him. Am I supposed to just forget about him? As things stand now, I really don't know what to do.

Love and prayers,
Carol Kuhnert

August 5, 2002, letter of response from our pastor:

Dear Carol,
Thank you for your thoughtful and well-written letter of July 26 responding to my recent column about the clergy sex-abuse scandal.

I can't disagree with anything you wrote. I hope you understand that it was not my purpose to take up and defend any point contrary to what you expressed. I am on the record, both in public and private conversations, saying how horrible the conduct of these priests was and how ridiculous the response of the bishops. I, in the words of Mr. Jefferson of Virginia, hold that truth to be self-evident.

My only purpose in writing that column was to point out what I thought was equally self-evident, namely, that the various media, in their coverage of the scandal, were not fueled by the milk of human kindness for the victims, but by the most poisonous kind of venom for the Catholic Church.

There's no doubt that our current difficulties are self-inflicted wounds, but the coverage of them by the media was vastly disproportionate to how the exact same thing is covered when done by non-Catholics and non-religious. I'm not asking the media to be silent about this situation; no one is served by that. I'm not accusing them of causing this situation; we did it to ourselves. I'm in no way trying to minimize the evil or excuse the damage done. I don't mind a clean hit; I strenuously object to the media's piling on.

Sincerely,
Reverend Matthew M. Mitas

My January 3, 2003, letter to Bishop Naumann:

Hi, Bishop Naumann,
I've turned to you in the past for help in dealing with some of

life's difficulties, and I thank you for being there. I've been feeling rather frustrated and figure you won't mind my unloading in your direction. I believe 2002 must have been the most difficult year of your priesthood. I wouldn't want to be in your shoes. Likewise, 2002 ranks way up there in difficulty, disappointment, anger, and fear in my life as a Catholic. I pray daily for God's guidance. My loss of trust and respect for our church leaders has left me feeling empty inside. I go to church but the feeling I once had for the church and my believing what our clergy say just isn't there. I'm unable to convince myself that the church leaders are being truthful. I think they put a spin on things, just as the politicians do, to try to manipulate people.

Channel 2 had a fairly long news segment on Friday, December 27, at 9 p.m., which has left me wondering. I find it odd that other TV stations didn't cover the situation nor did Channel 2 mention it again after the initial report. Nothing was mentioned in the *Post-Dispatch* newspaper either. It looks like someone in the church has connections to make bad press go away; another blow to all victims. Channel 2 showed a bunch of people picketing the [Catholic youth musician/choir] concert which was going on inside Seven Holy Founders parish. Among other things, Steve Pona told the reporter that Father [name withheld] had molested him when he was a member of the group many years ago. I believe him. I know he had done something to a girl in the group back then, and I had pulled Sue out of it because of what happened. I had talked with you about it at the time and you told me nothing could be done if the girl wouldn't press charges. What I cannot understand is how the church leaders can disregard reports made against this priest about his disgusting behavior, and allow him to remain working with children all these years. I realize the victims refused to press charges, but church leaders were at least made aware that this priest has serious problems! It angers me to see them willing to look the other way until they are forced to remove him. Any good he's accomplished is overshadowed by the damage he's done to kids who were too afraid and embarrassed to go public and press charges.

The church I have loved and respected all my life is going down the tubes. I hear many older Catholics making excuses for the offending clergy, refusing to believe they did it even after they admit guilt. Accepting such ugly truths is difficult. It's less painful to convince themselves that others are out to destroy the church by spreading lies about the priests. I keep waiting for all the innocent priests to stand up and do something to save their reputations and restore people's trust in the church.

I wonder if the universe is God's TV set; His entertainment. If so, it's full of violence and immorality, just like ours. I pray 2003 will bring justice and peace for victims, innocent clergy and the offending clergy. Something needs to happen, and soon, to restore people's trust and respect for the church. It's going to take a long time for the church to regain that. You are in my prayers; please pray for me and my family.

Carol Kuhnert

P.S. I know things do not happen to my timing but God's. I need to be patient and continue praying. I'm okay Bishop Joe; just needed to vent.

My February 7, 2003, letter to Bishop Naumann:

Bishop Naumann,

I'm sending the same attached letter to Archbishop Rigali, but I doubt that he'll pay much attention to it. I have greater hopes that you are trying to see things from the lowly church member's point of view. I don't want to annoy you, but when something smacks me as being so wrong, I must question it.

It doesn't surprise or bother me that Hess jumped at the lesser plea; look what he is. But for church leaders to see "accepting the lesser plea" thanks to a mistake being made as the right thing to do scares me.

Carol

My February 7, 2003, letter to Archbishop Rigali and Bishop Naumann:

Archbishop Rigali and Bishop Naumann,

I keep looking for things that will help me start to regain my trust in the church leadership; instead, yet another huge disappointment in our archdiocese. I read the article in the *Review* about John Hess's lawyer being able to get him a lesser plea because of a mistake made by law enforcement; never mind the fact that Hess had confessed to the crime. I think it's shameful that church leaders thought his accepting the lesser plea was the right thing to do.

There may not have been evidence that he had acted inappropriately with children, but all those children he got so much sick pleasure from in the pornography were someone's children, God's for sure. Somewhere they are in pain from what was done to them.

I don't think justice was served in Hess's sentence. I can understand that a lawyer is going to do everything he can to get his client off. I cannot understand the Catholic Church leaders backing Hess as he dodges the punishment he deserved for choosing to indulge in criminal activity!

I didn't think it was possible for the church leaders to drop any lower in my level of respect for them; I was wrong.

I pray that a hard look will be taken at what example is being set for all Catholics. Is running from the responsibility of our actions what God would want us to do?

I'll continue to pray for all Catholics. May God have mercy on us all.

Carol Kuhnert

Bishop Naumann's February 17, 2003, letter of response:

Dear Carol,

Archbishop Rigali asked me to thank you for your recent letter and to reply for both of us to your letters.

Perhaps, the article in the *St. Louis Review* and the statement released by the Archdiocesan Communication Office regarding the sentencing of Father Hess were not as clear as they could have been. The archbishop and everyone in leadership in the archdiocese, since we first became aware of the investigation of Father Hess, have encouraged him to be honest and to cooperate fully with law enforcement authorities. To my knowledge, he has done so.

While the church recognizes and respects the right and responsibility of civil authorities to punish criminal activities for the protection of individuals and the good order of society, we do not celebrate the necessity for anyone, clergy or lay person, Catholic or non-Catholic, to be incarcerated. It is my opinion that the priorities for our criminal justice system should be l) the protection of the innocent and promotion of the good of society, 2) assistance to victims to help them overcome the effects of the injustice done to them, 3) the rehabilitation of the perpetrators.

The rehabilitation of offenders is premised upon their recognition and acknowledgment of the evil that they have done and remorse for the hurt and pain that they have inflicted upon others. True rehabilitation evidences itself when perpetrators seek to do all that they can to make restitution to their victims and they manifest a determination to change their behavior by adopting a set of disciplines that will help them break destructive, unhealthy and immoral living patterns.

The church has consistently condemned all pornography not only because it is a violation of the sixth commandment but also because it degrades the human dignity of all those involved. Child pornography is considered an even more serious sin, because of the innocence and vulnerability of the victims. A person, who purchases child pornography, cooperates in the victimization of children by the pornography industry. It is objectively a serious sin, but it is not the same sin as personally sexually abusing a child.

I understand your frustration with the tragedy of abuse of children by some priests. I appreciate your profound disappointment with the mistakes made by some bishops. However, I think that you misjudge the intentions of the vast majority of bishops and even those few bishops who have made serious errors in judgment. In my experience, bishops have taken seriously their responsibility to protect children and the vulnerable. Based on the advice and counsel of professionals, they took steps that they felt would protect children.

Bishops have been very concerned for the victims of abuse and responsive in providing assistance for victims coping with the consequences of abuse. I know in St. Louis that we have offered counseling for some whose allegations seemed very doubtful. The rational for assistance was that, even if they were not abused as they claimed, they were obviously hurting and troubled. Part of the mission of the church is to try to bring the compassionate love of Jesus to those who are suffering.

At the same time, bishops have sought to protect innocent priests from the destruction of their reputation and their ministry by false accusations. Priests are entitled to the benefit of the foundational principle of American justice, namely that one is innocent until proven guilty.

Finally, the church by its nature is about the work of mercy, not inflicting punishment. What the media has declared a "cover-up" was never that. The church does not advocate for public humiliation and punishment of anyone who has sinned. Based on the advice of professionals in the areas of human behavior, bishops made decisions that they felt protected the innocent, responded with compassion to the needs of victims, and challenged perpetrators to repent and to change their lives.

Please give my regards to Joe and all your family. I remain grateful for all the kindness and support to me over so many years. I feel blessed by your friendship. Please be assured of my prayers for you and all your family. Know that I rely upon your prayers for me.

Sincerely yours in Jesus, the Lord of Life,
Most Reverend Joseph F. Naumann
Auxiliary Bishop
Archdiocese of St. Louis

My September 17, 2003, response to Bishop Naumann:

Hi, Bishop Joe,

I was surprised to hear from you. The 2-17-03 letter I received from you was so politically correct in your wording, I realized you were now completely one of them and wrote you off. I felt like the man I had known, respected, trusted and turned to all these years was no longer there. I can't speak for Joe, but my trust and respect of all of our church leaders is zero. It's a nightmare that won't go away.

The fact that completely uninvolved strangers sitting on a jury find it so difficult to judge and punish a man in the defendant's chair just because he is a priest is sad. I am referring to Brian Kuchar's case. For a jury to disregard overwhelming evidence presented to them, to struggle to find him guilty and then to give him a mere slap on the wrist, delivers a blow to the dignity of all victims! It shows anyone with their eyes, ears and mind open, how hard it is for the victims to come forward with their accusations against a priest. What chance do they have; how much must they suffer to get justice for themselves. Church leaders see the importance of priests getting justice (if found innocent), but they make it difficult for victims to get justice. I continue to feel ashamed of our church leaders. They don't practice what they've been preaching all my life. I don't celebrate anyone going to jail, but I do take comfort in seeing some form of earthly justice for the victims. My religious upbringing tells me everyone will answer to God for their actions or inactions here on earth. I pray daily for God to give me the patience, courage and wisdom to do the right thing. I pray the same for all clergy and all those victimized.

Errors in judgment made by bishops in the past could be forgiven if bishops today would clean house and start fresh. Innocent priests are still being painted with the same brush.

You may say there is no cover-up by the church but I strongly disagree. It seems to me the Catholic Church is just a business that is being run very badly. I think the church fears going bankrupt if it honestly admits all the horrors that have been allowed to go on. I cringe when I hear church leaders bending the truth, like ordinary people do, or allowing their lawyers to win on technicalities. One is innocent until proven guilty, but knowledgeable lawyers can use tactics to get clients off. It doesn't seem right for those I look to for an example on how to live to be okay with winning by finding some loophole. Then to make matters worse, church leaders continue to support the priest and keep him in service all the while saying that nothing was proved against him! Politicians and priests seem to follow the same playbook.

The church may be about works of mercy and not inflicting punishment, but it also needs to set good examples for its members. What I've been seeing goes against what I had learned growing up in Catholic school. It leaves me feeling empty. Church used to be a comfort for me. It isn't anymore. I find myself seriously questioning organized religions in general. Non-Catholics question why I still value Catholic education for my grandkids. I find myself wondering that myself. The church's "do as I say and not as I do" attitude makes me feel like a fool in the eyes of my non-Catholic friends. I want to stand up for my faith, but it's very hard to do these days. Please don't blame the media. We all need to live our lives in a manner that when bad things are said, no one will believe them.

Joe and I do appreciate your prayers for us. No doubt you can see I need them badly. We have been and will continue remembering you and all clergy in ours.

Sincerely,
Carol

My January 11, 2004, letter responding to our pastor's bulletin article:

Well, Father Mitas, since you've asked, when I was growing up back in good old 1955 (grade school years), all Catholics I know had 100% trust in anything any religious said or did. Religious were held in high esteem because we believed God had called them to their special vocation. Trust and respect were never an issue. With all that has come to light lately about how some of the religious took advantage of the trust given them over the years and how badly the church leaders dealt with complaints brought to their attention, the lack of people coming to church these days should come as no surprise to church leaders. The fact that it does tells me our church leaders still don't understand how big a hit trust in all religious took. Trust can't just be given back; it needs to be earned; that takes time.

Now in 2004, many Catholics I know still have their faith in God; it's their trust in church leadership that is gone. There are those people, of course, who refuse to believe the religious would do such horrible things and refuse to believe the accusations even when the religious has admitted to doing it. (I know several people like that.) If one accepts a religious did something horrible, one has to deal with it. A lot of people find that too painful and find it easier to tell themselves Catholic-haters are just spreading vicious lies about their beloved church.

I'm glad the church is taking steps to be more protective now in 2004. But, it really burns me to see our church leaders maintain the innocence of some because of loopholes of one kind or another and keep them in service. My heart goes out to all the victims and their families who for whatever reason haven't been able to go forward with prosecuting the guilty party. The only peace I can find in that respect is to believe all those religious and their lawyers will one day have to answer to God for what they've done.

Catholics, maybe not all but a large number, simply doesn't put much trust in what is coming out of our church leader's mouths. It's not like back in the good old days of 1955. I wish more people would voice their thoughts to our leaders, but I think the majority of them feel like it would be the old "you can't fight city hall" thing.

I look at how my brother feels so secure and loved at the priest retirement home, being cared for and protected by the church. He tells me he doesn't have a care in the world. It makes me sick when I think of all the kids' and their families' faith and lives he's ruined in his lifetime. My heart and prayers go out to all of them. I feel ashamed of how some of our church leaders and their well-paid lawyers treat them. I pray every day for God to give our church leaders the wisdom and courage to do whatever is needed to make things right.

It's no surprise to me the church attendance is down. Maybe our church leaders don't want to accept the fact that trust in them is gone, just as some Catholics can't accept that these ugly things have really happened. In both instances, the truth is extremely hard to accept.

Please pray for my family and I will continue to do so for you; and thank you for your homilies at mass. You usually get your point across nicely and in an interesting way. Thanks, too, for being there to listen. I don't feel my comments fall on deaf ears. God bless you in all you do.

Sincerely,
Carol Kuhnert

My March 4, 2004, response e-mail to my brother:

Hi, Norm,
We returned home late last night and heard your message. I called Jeanne as you suggested. Then I laid awake most of the night

praying over how I could be there for you. This may not be what you want to hear, but I have determined the only way I can be supportive of you is if you do what you should have done the first time this ever happened, accept responsibility for your behavior, express sincere remorse to the victim and his family, turn yourself in to the authorities and accept your punishment.

I regret your behavior wasn't dealt with properly by church leaders when it was first brought to their attention. Thanks to them, you have been free to continue abusing kids for years. I suppose at first therapist's conclusions gave those in charge hope that you were being cured, but somewhere over time, it must have become clear to them that the therapy wasn't working. At that point, the church leaders made the tragic decision to reassign you to unsuspecting, trusting parishes, leaving kids in harm's way. This became their policy with many fragile priests. It was a crime for which they need to accept responsibility.

My sympathy goes heavily to the families you've hurt. My anger is mostly with our church leaders for their horrible management of all sexual abuse. I question what men were taught in the seminary. Archbishop Burke's recent comment stating the most significant cause of sexual abuse was the hedonistic culture, not the bishops fault, causes me to lose faith in his leadership as well. We all grew up in that culture and the majority of people lived moral lives following God's commandments and avoiding occasions of sin. The hedonistic culture wasn't as controlling as Archbishop Burke would like everyone to believe.

It concerns me that with years of therapy you never expressed regret for hurting trusting children. I don't think you ever considered your behavior affected anyone but you. At one point you told Jeanne and I it was none of our business. We were left stunned to deal with it on our own. Remember how angry you were with us for turning to Naumann for help?

Put your own feelings aside for a moment and think of all the kids' and families' lives that have been devastated by you, the person they believed could be trusted deeply when turned to for guidance. I hate your behavior, Norman, but I do care about you. I believe you have in later years been trying to apply what you learned in therapy. I've always prayed for God to give you strength and direction to stay sober.

You had betrayed my family and me when we trusted you were helping Sue in her crises. It hurt terribly to discover how you had abused that trust. I don't think it even dawned on you that we experienced emotional and financial difficulties from the results of your behavior toward Sue.

The emotional turmoil you are experiencing right now is a taste of what your victims have been living with for most of their lives. I am praying you will dignify them with an apology for your behavior; for that you could be respected. I continue to pray that God will give you the courage to face up to what needs to be done and grant you peace after doing it. God bless you and keep you.

Love and prayers,
Carol

March 2004 Statement of the Archdiocese of Saint Louis Regarding Father Norman Christian:

The Archdiocese of Saint Louis has learned this afternoon of a civil lawsuit filed against Father Norman Christian and the Archdiocese of Saint Louis. We have not yet seen the lawsuit and it is the policy of the archdiocese not to comment on pending litigation.

Norman Christian was removed from active priestly ministry in the Archdiocese of Saint Louis in May of 1995 after an allegation of abuse of a minor over twenty years earlier was brought to the archdiocese. Norman Christian subsequently participated in an evaluation and treatment program. He lives in a monitored environment and is not permitted to exercise any form of public ministry. [*His faculties as a priest of the archdiocese have been removed.*]

A list of parishes where he served following his ordination in 1961 is attached. Contact Jim Orso (314) 792-7631.

My March 11, 2004, note to Archbishop Burke:

Dear Archbishop Burke,

I have one question. What are church officials encouraging my brother, Norman Christian, to do regarding the current sexual-abuse suit? I've wondered for a long time what he's been told all these years in therapy about taking responsibility for what he's done.

Enclosed is a copy of my response to him regarding his plea for my support.

Sincerely,
Carol Kuhnert

My March 11, 2004, note to Archbishop Joe Naumann:

Dear Archbishop Joe,

Thanks for your note and prayers. It is a painful time, but I also feel relief the ugly secret is out. I pray all his victims will draw strength from each other and find peace in their lives.

What are church officials encouraging Norman to do regarding the current sexual-abuse suit? I've always wondered what message he received throughout years of therapy about taking responsibility for his actions.

Enclosed is a copy of my response to him regarding his plea for my support.

Carol.

My March 18, 2004, note to Archbishop Naumann:

Dear Archbishop Naumann,

Thanks for your 3-13-04 note, but please address my question. What are the church leaders encouraging Norm to do in regard to the current abuse suit? Norm has admitted to Jeanne, Sue, and me that he's done these things throughout his life; I think he needs to own up to it and tell his victims how sorry he is for what he has done. That would be a big help in the recovery of his victims.

I don't blame you for what's happened in the past. I'll be praying for you and all the church leaders.

Carol

Father Mitas's May 2, 2004, bulletin article: "Sad but True"

Archbishop Burke faxed all the parishes with the sad news of the settlement in the case of the ex-Father Wolken, who was convicted of child abuse. He wanted to assure us all that the Archdiocese never has and never will use ADA money for such things. ADA money is dedicated (etched in stone, really) for well-specified purposes and cannot be redirected for anything else.

All I know about the case is what I heard via the various media, and since the charges were not contested I can only infer they are true. In my opinion, the man should have been flogged, drawn and quartered. Still, I have a hard time understanding why the Archdiocese has to pony up for his crimes. He was not a known, or even a suspected, abuser of children. He was not, as was the case in Boston, a serial abuser who was trundled about from one crime scene to another. He certainly was not under order from his superiors to commit those crimes. Just the opposite, it seems to me that his crimes are just that, his crimes. It used to be the case in this country that one was only liable for damages if it could be proven that he was somehow negligent, that he should have done something he didn't or did do something he shouldn't have. Before a man is ordained a priest, he undergoes twelve years of intensive formation and testing. This was the case with the man in question. How was the archdiocese negligent? What more could it have done? I think we all know the answer. The man I question didn't have any money, the archdiocese does. Plaintiffs know that. Their lawyers know that. It doesn't matter to them the archdiocese's money was given to support the merciful and spiritual works of the church. They're like Willie "the Actor" Sutton, the famous bank robber, who when asked why he robbed banks, answered "because that is where the money is." If the archdiocese can be proven negligent, that's different. But I disdain and deplore that it's obviously come to the point in this country that it's just taken for granted the diocese has to pay big bucks when one of its trusted priests, against its laws, without its consent and even without its knowledge, commits an actionable offense. Tort reform? Count me in!

Father Mitas

My June 17, 2004, e-mail to my brother:

Hi, Norm,

You are on my mind and in my prayers daily. I wonder if you have given any thought to what I had suggested months ago, that you do about the latest accusation. I imagine your canon lawyer and church leaders are encouraging you to admit nothing so as to protect the church's assets from more lawsuits. I know it upsets you greatly when the archdiocese has to pay a victim because of your behavior.

Norm, I am encouraging you to think about what has happened to your victims' lives. (That is what they were, victims, not willing participants as you would like to have me believe. If you can't see that, I seriously question the therapy you've received all these years.) Recognizing and accepting what you've done to them may make your conscience cause you to suffer physical and emotional pain. Apologizing and trying to make things right will help clear your conscience and ease those pains.

What I've drawn from my own Catholic upbringing is that whenever I sin, in order for God to forgive me, I need to make things right again for those I've wronged. Along with God's grace and forgiveness, I will regain my self-respect and integrity and have a clear conscience. My attitude and the choices I make in life determine how happy I am every day.

Please put aside your fears of what will happen to you by turning yourself in; while you may fear it, you have earned any punishment that's coming. Your victims didn't earn or deserve the misery they are living with; they were children, trusting someone they had been taught to respect and obey.

The archdiocese has made mistakes with many priests and has its own problems to correct. For a while they may not have known better, but at some point, they became enablers for you and others. It seems like they couldn't decide to lose these troubled priests after all the education and expenses invested in them, so they hoped and prayed and looked the other way. That's their doings to make right, not yours. I feel terribly angry with our church leadership. They still come across to me as trying to cover up what's happened over the years. They don't seem to understand how hurt many Catholics are and how there is no longer trust and respect for them. I pray for God to guide them to do the right thing now. Meanwhile, I'll continue praying God will bless you and guide you to do the right thing. May he bring peace in your life.

 Love and prayers,
 Carol

My September 1, 2004, letter to Norm:

Hi, Norm,
 I just read the 8-26-04 *Post* article stating, "The archdiocese has agreed to help people with their counseling expenses in response to their claims of sexual abuse," Archdiocesan lawyer Goldenhersh said, the accusers otherwise would receive nothing "because of the statute of limitations defense."

 How disgusting is that! The people I was taught to look to for spiritual and moral guidance are paying a lawyer to work the system in order to keep the Catholic church from going broke. God forbid the church leaders accept responsibility for past mistakes and poor judgment and cover-ups all these years.

 Norm, don't you find it strange that a priest who recently admitted to stealing money from his parish publically apologized for what he did, but you and others like you are told to admit nothing? What would Jesus do if He were here in person comforting the abuse victims? I can't believe He'd be pleased with the way our church leaders are treating them. Remember what He said about children in the bible.

 Please think about it, Norm. You know how expensive therapy is and the amounts being given won't go very far. Also, it's not just about the money. An "I'm sorry I did it. You trusted me and I let you down; I am so very sorry" would go a long way in helping your victims regain faith in their church, begin to forgive, and get on with their lives. It may even help you find peace.

 God love you and guide you.
 Carol

Father Christian's death notice placed in Catholic paper, *St. Louis Review*, 11-5-04:

Father Christian dies at age 69

A funeral Mass was celebrated Nov. 1 at St. Richard church in Creve Coeur for Father Norman H. Christian, a former pastor in the Archdiocese. Father Christian, 69, died Oct. 29.

He was ordained March 18, 1961 by Cardinal Joseph Ritter at the Cathedral Basilica of St. Louis. He served as an associate pastor at St. Peter Parish in Kirkwood, Ascension Parish in Normandy, Sacred Heart Parish in Florissant and St. George Parish in Affton. He was pastor of Nativity Parish in North St. Louis from 1978–81. St. Adalbert Parish in North St. Louis until 1986 and St. William Parish in Woodson Terrace until 1995.

The archdiocese had removed Father Christian from ministry in 1995 after allegations of child sexual abuse more than 20 years previously. Since then, Father Christian had lived in a monitored environment and was prohibited from exercising any form of ministry.

Survivors include two sisters, Carol Kuhnert and Jean Meyer.

My November 6, 2004, letter informing of Norman's death:

Most likely you've heard through the grapevine that my brother, Fr. Norman Christian, died October 29, 2004. The archdiocese did not run his death notice in the paper, and my sister and I had nothing to do with his funeral arrangements, so I'm letting you know of his death myself.

Maybe some of you saw Bill McClellan's October 27 column in the *Post*. A long story short, I learned about 16 years ago that Norman was a pedophile when Sue told me what he had told her and places he had been taking her years before. She had since been avoiding him, and I didn't understand why. I confronted him after that and he admitted his lifestyle to me. He was angry with Sue for breaking his confidence in telling me about him. I told him I was proud of her for having the courage to tell me, and it took her years to be able to do it. I have spent the last 16 years trying to get Norman and the church leaders to do the right thing for all sexual-abuse victims and to protect against there being any more victims. I have prayed for years for one of Norm's victims to have the courage to come forward and one finally did last year.

It's disgusting that the church leaders continue to cover-up their bad judgment and go on gambling with many more such priests that are still in service. It's outrageous. What they are doing is just plain wrong and they need to be held accountable. It goes against everything I ever learned growing up in a loving Catholic home and attending Catholic schools.

I am not mourning the loss of a brother, but I am mourning the loss of the church I loved, trusted, and looked to for comfort and guidance all my life. My faith in God is strong, but in the church leaders, it's completely gone. I have been and continue to pray that God will give us church leaders that will correct the way the sex abuse scandal has been dealt with up until now. Victims need to be treated with compassion, not as enemies. Church leaders need to stop using loopholes to keep problem priests from being prosecuted, and to stop risking innocent children by allowing these sick priests to go on in service for the various parishes, claiming they are innocent because of their tactics.

Sixteen years of phone calls, letters, and visits with Norman, bishops, etc., I've read and heard quite a few untruths from the archdiocese. Their #1 concern has always been to protect the church's money from future lawsuits. Norman went to his death never apologizing to our family or any of his victims for what he had done. Why? He said it would open the door for more lawsuits for the archdiocese. He couldn't do that to *them*! They programmed him well in therapy.

Those of you, who are still Catholic, pray for your church and its leaders. Talk to your kids and watch your grandchildren.

Norman was given a burial as a priest in good standing. To me, it was the ultimate slap in the face to my family and to all his victims. He *never* expressed remorse to me for the pain he caused to so many children and their families. Maybe the Archdiocese had second thoughts about it since they didn't run his death notice nor did they announce funeral arrangements at any church. They only mentioned at his home parish, Our Lady of Sorrows, that he had died. They didn't mention that he was laid out that same day with the funeral the next day and where. More cover-up; we didn't go.

Please keep us in your prayers.

My statement to the Mediation Board, December 14, 2004:

Good morning. I am Father Norman Christian's younger sister, Carol Kuhnert. I learned of his pedophilia in 1988 when my daughter told me he had victimized her. I met with him and he admitted it was true and he had the problem since before he entered the seminary. I've been in contact with Norman, various priests, bishops for the past 16 years regarding sexual-abuse cases. Mostly I've been told it's none of my business; they were taking care of it. I went to Monsignor Naumann once. We spoke on the phone and wrote letters. All I saw was cover-up, the church avoiding victims and their families. I saw no reaching out to victims, no apologies, no compassion and no change over all these years in how they deal with sexual abuse. It bothers me yet that the archdiocese didn't even warn my sister or me about our brother being a danger to our children. Had I known, my daughter wouldn't have become one of his victims.

I've forgiven Norman. He's answering to God now that he's dead. But until the church leaders start holding themselves accountable for the harm they've done and continue to do to sexual-abuse victims, I cannot trust or respect them. They continue to keep priests just like Father Christian in active ministry now. For example, Father X [name withheld—the director of a youth group]. He has had many accusations made against him. About 20 years ago, when he molested a friend of my daughter, I asked Father Naumann what he'd do about it. He told me it wasn't fair to dirty the priest's name if the victim wasn't willing to come forward and press charges. These kids are scared. Who will believe them? So Father X has remained in his position working with kids, parents unaware, molesting others over the years. Father Naumann did assure me Father X would get treatment and would be watched. So they knew the victim was telling the truth. They're just happy the kids are too scared to come forward and press charges. Of course, if they did, church lawyers would do a good job of victimizing them all over again.

My brother told all his victims no one would believe them if they told; they're just kids. They'll believe the priest and he was right! Do church leaders/lawyers count on that too? The really disgusting thing is that church leaders continued to support Norman, not his victim. Knowing after years of his being in and out of therapy, his continuing to act out on his addiction, and destroying more young lives, they still put the church assets and Norman's privacy before providing help and an apology to those that Norman had molested. The church's cover-up is so good if Norman hadn't victimized his own niece, and if she hadn't found the courage to tell me about him, I never would have known what he was!

Why does Tim have to convince the church leaders today to do the right thing? They are supposed to be the intelligent, moral ones teaching by example how God wants us to live our lives. There is no statute of limitations with God. I wonder how the church leaders justify in their own minds what they have been doing to victims and families all these years. How many people have left the church because of what they're doing? I was betrayed by my brother. His behavior was evil. Possibly he couldn't control himself. He went to his death never expressing remorse for all the pain he caused to so many. Why? Because the church had programmed him. As he told me, to apologize would open the door for more lawsuits for the archdiocese. He couldn't do that to them! I wonder how slanted the therapy was he received all those years.

I feel betrayed by the church leadership. It had to be obvious to them over the past 16 years I was in pain and having difficulty dealing with what my brother had done. Their answer to that was to ignore me. I'd like the church leaders to take a long hard look at themselves. Stop making the church the victim in all of this. The bad publicity is all your own doing. Put the people first, they are the church. What would Jesus do if He were with you in person today? The once most respected Catholic Church is mortally wounded. Religious vocations are almost nonexistent. Churches and schools are closing in large numbers. What's it going to take for the church leadership to accept the fact people no longer trust and respect them? Trust cannot just be given. It has to be earned, and that takes time. church leaders need to change how the sexual-abuse problem is being handled. Start putting the victims and their families first, make something available for all parishioners for dealing with their fears/concerns about these situations and priests, and remove the accused priest from ministry until things are proven one way or the other. It's not fair to keep a possible predator in active ministry either! Compassion needs to be shown all around. There are no winners in this, but for healing to begin, the truth must be told and acknowledged, an apology made, and appropriate action taken regarding the priest. If he admits guilt, turn him over to the police. His crime is worse because of his position of trust and respect in the church. He deserves no special treatment from anyone. We all must be held accountable for the choices we make.

I thank Tim and Mr. Chackes for allowing me to express my feelings on this very serious matter that weighs heavy on my mind. Since my brother died, not one person from the church has contacted me in any way to express any condolence. Doesn't seem very Christian-like. They seem to look upon me as the enemy. Why? My family was victimized by Father Christian. My faith in God is as strong as ever. I still attend the Catholic Church. It's the church leadership's way of doing business that needs mending. I pray God will give our leaders the wisdom, courage, integrity, and compassion to help the church heal and regain the trust and respect of its people, and especially, I hope they begin to understand the importance of showing compassion to all victims of abuse. They must make appropriate changes in how the church deals with sexual abuse from now on. They need to use their powers and voices to argue for justice for these victims, and they must stop being silent about one another. Their cover-ups are as bad, if not worse, than the sexual abuse itself.

My January 10, 2005, letter to Monsignor John Shamleffer:

Dear Reverend Shamleffer,

On December 14, 2004, I was given your business card and told to direct my concerns to your committee. I don't understand why I wasn't referred to you long before now; maybe I had not yet spoken publicly about it.

Over sixteen years ago, I learned my brother, Reverend Norman Christian, was a pedophile when my teenage daughter told me her uncle had victimized her several years before. I talked to Norman and he admitted it. From that time on, I stayed in contact with him, offering support and trying to encourage him to do everything required in his treatment. When I had concerns, I contacted Monsignor Naumann. He told me the archdiocese was taking care of things. It wasn't mine to worry about. As to any kind of action taken, I never saw anything but cover-ups. Norman refused to apologize, even to my daughter or me. As he put it, an apology would open the door to more lawsuits for the archdiocese, and he couldn't do that to them. I can't imagine what he was told to make him feel he was okay with God in going to his death, never once saying "I'm sorry for all the pain I caused you" to his victims. I was taught the priest's absolution was only part of being forgiven for sins; that you had to go and make things right, too. Do priests get to play with a different set of rules?

For the past 16 years I had been communicating with my brother, and various priests and bishops about the removal of pedophile priests. I was always told the archdiocese was taking care of things. Growing up Catholic, it was instilled in me to always trust the religious, so I hoped and prayed the church leaders were doing the right thing. It hurts terribly to realize the church I once turned to for comfort and guidance is no longer to be trusted. I told Norman that as a priest, he had let people down, and his victims needed to know he understood how badly he had hurt them. This applies to all the church leaders, too. By not removing the offending priests from ministry, they are enablers. They need to be held accountable. Catholics turn to clergy for guidance and moral support, and when pedophiles violate that trust, it is not only sinful but criminal. Victims' lives are destroyed. Entire families are in pain. The way the church has been treating sexual-abuse victims all these years is shameful. I grew up believing Catholics were to reach out to those in pain. So why is it when people speak out about being hurt by priests, or they question the church's handling of sexual-abuse cases, they are ignored or treated like the enemy?

I know I made it clear to the archdiocese I was not mourning the loss of a brother when Norman was dying in October, but I did say I was in pain over losing my trust and respect for the church I had always felt was so important to me. I can't understand the church leaders' and parish priest's un-Christian-like behavior toward me. Something is terribly wrong that they can't express some form of condolence for another human being's pain, especially considering their line of work.

I hold tight to my faith in God, and I pray for Him to guide me in ways to help bring about healing for our mortally wounded church. I pray God will give our church leaders the wisdom, courage, integrity and compassion to help the church begin to heal and regain the trust and respect of its people.

The church has always told us not to be concerned about acquiring material things; it's our spiritual lives we need to worry about. Surely that applies to the church as well. There must be justice for all sexual-abuse victims. Remember what Jesus said about those who hurt children. At times I get a sick feeling the bishops and priests don't believe sexual abuse of children is all that big a deal, and that's why it's just overlooked by the archdiocese leaders. God help us all if that is true.

I would appreciate receiving your committee's guidelines for the present handling of sexual-abuse cases and also a list of the changes being made to help the victims past, present and future. How do you intend to fix this shameful problem? I think I have been more than patient in waiting for over 16 years for some kind of answer. I am waiting for some action to be taken that will give me a glimmer of hope the church can start regaining its trust and respect. A good start would be to listen to the victims and put their needs first. Stop making the church out to be the victim. Stop protecting these pedophile priests! Their crimes are even worse because of the position of trust and respect they hold.

I pray your committee will make appropriate changes in how the church deals with sexual-abuse victims from now on.

Sincerely,
Mrs. Carol Kuhnert

My January 16, 2005, letter to Archbishop Naumann:

Dear Archbishop Naumann,
Congratulations, we are very happy for you and pray God will continue to bless and keep you in his care!

The man we came to know, love, and respect at OLS as Father Joe is the man we are now asking to use his powers as one of our church leaders to bring about healing for both, victims of clergy abuse and healing for the mortally wounded Catholic Church.

The church truly needs to reach out to its members, through weekly brief messages from the pulpit, in bulletins, flyers posted in churches and schools, messages run in Catholic publications, and neighborhood newspapers, stating how much it regrets the past handling of sexual-abuse cases, and ask that anyone who was sexually abused by a religious at any time in their life, please contact [state the name and number to contact]. Then give those who do contact the church a sincere apology and offer some form of help. This action would prove that church leaders care about their flock. It would do a whole lot to help the church start to earn back some of its trust and respect, and the weight that would be lifted from so many of the heavy hearts of those having been abused would be an immeasurable blessing!

I imagine you're thinking, if the church does that, it'd go bankrupt, as there could be a flood of lawsuits. Even so, why should that stop one from doing the right thing? We've been told not to hold on to material wealth, our spiritual wealth is what's important. That must apply to the church, too. God doesn't require fancy buildings, clothes, gold, etc., to praise and worship Him. He must be so sad watching religious acting in His name, harming children, then watching the church leaders covering up those crimes, protecting the pedophiles from prosecution and enabling them to harm more children by keeping them in ministry.

Churches and schools are closing in large numbers for lack of Catholics. That's due to trust and respect for the church being gone. You know that trust can only be earned back.

We feel God has put you in your present position as He knows you are a humble man, in touch with your flock. Please, reach out and listen to them. We pray God will give you the wisdom, courage and compassion to get the Catholic Church on the road to recovery.

God's blessings to you in Kansas City.

Joe and Carol Kuhnert

P.S. Norman died the end of October. Granted, I made it clear to the archdiocese I wasn't mourning his death, but I also made it clear I was mourning the loss of the church I had trusted and turned to for support all my life. So why, with people in the line of work, among other things, of comforting the sorrowful, have I heard nothing? That's not what I grew up expecting and believing about the church. It just strikes me as the religious behaving in an un-Christian-like manner.

It's because the church is important to me I have not left. Leaving won't fix the problem. Most Catholics I know are disgusted with the way the sexual-abuse scandal is being handled, but feel it's like fighting city hall. I've had four older-generation nuns call to offer condolence after Norman died and each strongly encouraged me to stay and fight to get changes made on how the church deals with this problem.

I pray daily for God's guidance in how I may be supportive of abuse victims and successful in encouraging church leaders to make appropriate changes for healing all around. The horrible management of sexual-abuse cases all of these years is as bad if not worse than the abuse itself. Please use your powers to bring about change. If anyone can do it, you can.

Monsignor John Shamleffer's January 25, 2005, letter of response:

Dear Mrs. Kuhnert,
I am writing in reply to your letter of January 10, 2005, concerning your trust and respect for the church and your desire to better understand how the church is presently handling sexual-abuse cases of minors. The sexual-abuse committee thought it might be helpful for you to personally meet with some of its members to get a better understanding of how the church is addressing this issue of sexual abuse. I would ask you to please contact Monsignor Richard Stika who is the Episcopal vicar for these matters. Monsignor Stika can be reached at [number]. Or his secretary, can be reached at [number]. Either one should be able to facilitate a time for you to meet with the committee.

Assuring you of our concern for all victims of sexual abuse, I remain
Sincerely,
Reverend Monsignor John B. Shamleffer, JCL
Judicial Vicar

My January 29, 2005, letter to Archbishop Raymond Burke:

Dear Archbishop Burke,

I've written you twice during the year that you've been in St. Louis, but I've never received a response of any kind. My sister told me the same thing happened with letters she had written to you last year. I wonder why a shepherd would treat some of his flock as if they didn't matter. Why wouldn't you, especially, have shown the example of a good shepherd by reaching out to those who are hurting? Instead, you chose to simply ignore us.

Recent news reported how you have launched proceedings that got three priests laicized (McGrath, Straub, and Yim) because of their sexual abuse of minors. That's good, but you didn't take it far enough. For those pedophiles not to be criminally charged is outrageous. It's like you've left a campsite after putting out a fire but letting it smolder. After you've gone, it reignites and burns down the forest. These pedophiles must not be left free to move about and prey on other innocent children, where their past criminal behaviors would be unknown. You must protect *all* God's children by doing everything you can to get these pedophiles locked up.

I don't understand why you refuse to meet with victims in your flock that have been abused by priests. When you had first arrived in St. Louis, I thought I had heard you say you intended to do just that. I had high hopes you would bring about the changes needed to help Catholics regain their trust and respect in the church and bring about healing for both the victims and the church. What happened? The Survivors Network of those Abused by Priests is nothing more than a group of people who through no fault of their own became victims of sexual abuse during their childhood because of the trust and respect they had for a priest. They were hurt terribly, and I can't imagine why you would turn your back on them. What parent or child could ever think a priest, of all people, would harm someone? It is so horrible a crime because of the position of trust and respect a priest holds. It gives him easy access to anyone's child. These priests are great counselors, wonderful personalities, etc. They are doing God's work; such behavior would be unthinkable, unbelievable for any Catholic! The victims have grown up carrying an unfair burden of guilt for something that was not their fault. Some did tell what happened, only to be severely punished for saying such a thing about a priest. They weren't believed. My brother, Father Norman Christian, told all his victims no one would believe them if they told. They'd believe the priest. Sadly, he was right. I've been trying to accept these ugly truths for 17 years. During this time I saw and heard admissions but never an expression of sorrow from my brother and have spoken to various church leaders. I've seen no changes with how the church is dealing with the priest or his victims in these situations. It's disgusting to say the least. The victims who have come together in SNAP are doing so to help each other. They receive no support or compassion from the church. Mostly, they want you to listen to what happened to them. They want to be believed. They want you to remove the offending priests from active ministry so they can't hurt anyone else. Why do you want to keep pedophiles in active ministry? If you say you don't, then please bring about changes that will require church staff to turn over any sexual abuse claims against a priest to the police. Help change the old statute of limitations laws that protect the pedophiles and cause more pain for victims by the unfairness of them. Please stop protecting pedophile priests and rejoicing when they win by such a technicality. It would be a wise decision to add a sexual-abuse victim to your sexual-abuse review board, too; work together to do the right thing for both the victims and the church.

As our shepherd, God urges you to reach out to all those who have been hurt. Please stop turning your back on the SNAP group. Church leaders do a lot of bad-mouthing SNAP as an organization out to destroy the church. Such statements are very untrue. Yet Catholics, trained from infancy to believe anything church leaders say, accept it must be so. The unfortunate victims are driven even deeper into depression as they are then looked upon as the villain who hurt the priest! I am so glad God doesn't have a statute of limitations when we answer to Him upon our deaths. He must be so sad watching some religious, acting in His name, molesting children, then watching church leaders covering up those crimes, protecting the pedophiles from prosecution and enabling them to harm more kids by keeping them in active ministry.

I understand you have recently urged anyone harmed by clergy to contact the archdiocese or authorities. I thank you for that. Please ask for ongoing weekly messages from the pulpit, in bulletins, flyers posted in churches and schools, messages run in Catholic publications and neighborhood newspapers, stating how much the church regrets the past handling of sexual-abuse cases and asking anyone who was abused by religious at any time in their life, to please contact [state name and number to call]. Then give those who do call a sincere apology and offer some form of help; this would show church leaders care about their flock. It would do a whole lot to help the church begin to earn back some of its trust and respect, and the weight lifted from so many heavy hearts of those having been abused would be an immeasurable blessing.

Are you thinking that might cause a flood of lawsuits, and the church could go bankrupt? Even if that were to happen, why should that stop one from doing the right thing? We've been told not to hold on to material wealth, our spiritual wealth is what is important. Surely that applies to the church, too. God doesn't require fancy buildings, elaborate garb, gold, etc., to praise and worship Him. Not to do the right thing because of financial gain or loss is wrong. Catholics look to their church leaders for guidance. The church leaders need to set good examples. Churches and schools are closing in large numbers because attendance is down. That trust and respect people once held for their priests and church is no longer there for the majority of Catholics. Most discuss their disappointment and complain to each other. Few feel it's possible to do anything about. It's like fighting city hall, so they just stop going to a church they no longer respect.

I pray daily for God's guidance in how I may be supportive of abuse victims and successful in encouraging church leaders to make the changes needed that will help Catholics begin to regain their trust and respect in the church. The horrible management of sexual-abuse cases for so long is as bad, maybe worse than the abuse itself. Please use your powers to bring about changes for healing for the church and victims.

Sincerely,
Carol Kuhnert

My March 3, 2005, note to our pastor:

Dear Father Mitas,

We strongly disagree with the editorial in the Feb. 25 *St. Louis Review*, "Healing Wounds and Preventing New Ones." We don't agree the church leaders are actually doing as it says. Actions speak louder than words. Therefore, from now on, we are sending half of our donation to ICC and the other half to SNAP to help the victims' support group in their efforts to hold our church leaders accountable for past wrongs and for continuing to protect abusive priests. We support the victims' efforts in getting molesters removed from active ministry and reported to authorities. Pedophiles belong in prison, not in church-run retreat-style facilities. All Catholics would do well to keep their eyes open, not just trust and follow blindly.

We don't understand why innocent priests are not addressing Archbishop Burke about this problem. The scandal is devastating to them as well. We continue to pray for him and all the church leaders that they will do the right thing to protect God's children and to regain the trust and respect of all Catholics.

Sincerely,
Joe and Carol Kuhnert

My March 8, 2005, letter to Archdiocesan Office of Laity & Family Life:

To Whom It May Concern,

In the March 4 *St. Louis Review*, your office kindly offered suggestions to people to help those grieving their parish being closed. Upon reading it, I couldn't help but wonder why it wouldn't be possible to offer a list of suggestions for people to know how to reach out and show authentic concern for those who are grieving the horrors of having been sexually abused as a child by a religious. Those people have grown up with an unfair burden of guilt. Through no fault of their own and because of the trust and respect children had for a religious, they were victimized. People tend to get angry with them when they as adults report what happened. There is an immediate need to educate people on how to help these grieving souls.

As in your list for those grieving parish closings, the following are ways to show authentic concern for sexual-abuse victims of religious and their families.

It's okay to share that it is hard for them to accept a religious could have done such a thing to them. Respect their pain and respect your own about it.

- Ask "What feels supportive?" to them.
- Say "I hurt to know you have been in pain for so long, carrying such an unfair burden of guilt."
- Use their names.
- Ask to hear their story and really listen patiently. They may have a hard time telling it.
- Reassure them that they were the innocent children, in the company of someone they were taught to love, trust, and respect. The religious were the adults and fully responsible for what they did to them.
- Your office cannot change what happened to them at the hands of a religious pedophile or take away their pain, but they can:
    o Experience your own losses because of the sexual-abuse scandal.
    o Convey caring and say how sorry you are this happened to them. Assure them the molester will be removed if still in active ministry.
    o Give permission to grieve.
    o Offer continuing support. A special prayer for healing for all sexual-abuse victims of religious could be said at every mass, etc.
    o Parishes could allow support groups for these victims and their families and friends to meet on a regular basis so they could share feelings and draw strength from each other. If a family is in the midst of reporting a sexual-abuse crime, they are in desperate need of support from the church. As things are now, the church treats them like the enemy.

I hope you will agree there is a real, immediate need for this type of ministry. Many are in pain, and there's no sign anyone from the church cares. Please reach out to them.

Sincerely,
Mrs. Carol Kuhnert

My April 2, 2005, letter to Monsignor John Shamleffer:

Dear Monsignor Shamleffer,

    Thanks for your letter of January 25. Finding you are unwilling to answer my questions in writing or send me copies of policies on handling sexual-abuse claims reinforces my belief church leadership feels it doesn't have to answer to anyone outside of canon law.

    Observing over the past 17 years how the church leaders have dealt with my brother's addiction and his victims alone, my faith and respect in the Catholic Church has been terribly shaken. After considering your request for some time, I do not feel comfortable meeting with any of your sexual-abuse committee members.

    I sent a letter to the Office of Laity and Family Life on March 8, asking they consider getting a ministry in the works to help sexual-abuse victims of religious, their families, friends, the offending priests' families, and all the parishioners as well. Every Catholic needs help in dealing with this tragedy when a loved and respected priest is suddenly removed for such a horrible crime. Everyone is suffering and wondering what is happening and why. Many are in pain, and there's no sign anyone from the church cares.

    This horror is not going away. Thank God, as today's victims speak out, others hearing find the courage to report what happened to them as trusting children at the hands of some religious. Many are finally finding relief from the unfair burden of guilt they've carried for so long. Please stop protecting the pedophile priests. The crimes they have committed are even worse because of the positions of reverence, trust and respect they hold. Pray for them, but encourage them to do the right thing as you turn them over to the authorities to investigate the reported crime.

I hope you will encourage and work with whoever would be responsible to start up a ministry to help everyone regarding the sexual-abuse crisis within the church. Thank you.

Sincerely,

Mrs. Carol Kuhnert

Monsignor Shamleffer's April 11, 2005, reply:

Dear Mrs. Kuhnert,

I received your letter dated April 2, 2005. As I mentioned to you in my letter this past January, I would encourage you to be in contact with Monsignor Richard Stika, who is the vicar for Child Protection and Welfare. He, along with the Diocesan Review Committee, is taking every conceivable step to make sure abuse of any kind, especially of children, does not occur.

Concerning policies, you can find copies of the policies for handling sexual-abuse claims on the archdiocesan website, or you can contact Monsignor Stika's office here at the archdiocese.

I agree with you that efforts have to be continually made to help any victims of sexual abuse, and it is an issue for the entire church. The archdiocese has undertaken a thorough examination of its practices and policies and has removed anyone who has any substantiated allegations of sexual abuse. The archdiocese is also in the process of seeking laicization or permanent suspension for anyone who abused a minor. As you well know this issue has many layers and many victims and will take a considerate effort by all members of the faithful and all their collective wisdom to make every effort that this never occurs again.

We must certainly forgive anyone who truly comes being contrite but there is still consequence in their action. For many of the priests accused of abuse, the consequences have been that they can no longer function in the priestly ministry. If the civil authorities believe that a crime occurred, these perpetrators could face criminal proceedings. Lastly, as a faithful member of the church, I ask you to continue to do all you can to support victims of abuse, to keep them and the church in your prayers, so that we as a church can again be faithful to the gospel message of Christ.

    Sincerely,
    Reverend Monsignor John B. Shamleffer, JCL
    Judicial Vicar

The following note dated May 3, 2005, received from the president of the Women's Guild:

Carol,
    I am finally responding to your plea to speak to the Women's Guild about the church and the sexual-abuse cases. I have to clear speakers with Monsignor, and he was gone, then busy; when I finally spoke to him, he was actually quite concerned when I told him just a few of the background info you told me. He asked for time to think on it, and I said okay. In the meantime I tried to feel out quite a few of the ladies and I was quite shocked when every single one I approached all told me that they did not want to listen to any speaker about this and would probably leave if I had one. When Monsignor finally got back to me he asked me what I thought and felt, and I had to say that after speaking to the ladies, I felt I would turn your request down. He agreed but mostly because we have so much stuff going on right now with losing our school name and all of the building stuff that he didn't think this was a good time.
    I feel like I'm letting you down, and I am really sorry. I hope you won't hold it against me, but there's no use getting the ladies any more riled up. I will continue to pray for you and for the cause you are fighting for; justice.
    Love,
    [name withheld]
    P.S. Congrats on the new baby, all okay?

My May 6, 2005, letter to Archbishop Burke, Monsignor Shamleffer, and Reverend Telthorst:

ATTN: Archbishop Burke, Reverend Monsignor Shamleffer, and Reverend Telthorst,

Attached is a copy of a note I received from the president of the Our Lady of Sorrows Women's Guild. The purpose of my letter is to draw attention to the attitude shown in the note and evident in most Catholics.

Do you, as men whose vocations have been involved with teaching Catholics how God wants us to live our lives, see anything wrong with Catholics displaying the attitude shown toward the sexual-abuse victims that is evident in the attached note? This extremely serious problem has been going on for years, and I don't understand how church leaders can condone it. Old-time Catholics would rather look the other way and deny these crimes have taken place than deal with the terrible pain of accepting that there are some pedophile priests who have been protected by the church. It's much less painful for Catholics to just say the victim must be lying than to accept the truth and deal with the loss of their faith, trust, and respect of the church. The victim and his or her family, of course, are victimized further.

I'd like you to think about this problem from what I've experienced. The shock of learning my own brother, a respected priest, being a pedophile, his victimizing my own daughter, the having to keep his ugly secret for 17 years while being told the church was handling it, having to make up things to tell people who asked me about Norman after he was removed from ministry. He was loved. People cared about him and didn't understand why he was removed. (The church didn't care about helping any of those people understand what was going on either.) Norman's answer to what I should tell people was "say nothing!" I shouldn't "gossip about him. It wasn't anybody's business." There too, he only thought about how it affected him. He didn't give a thought to the people who cared about him. Norman's betrayal to my family hurt us terribly. He did a lot of damage to my daughter, and I feel the church leaders were wrong in not warning my sister and me about the possibility of his being a danger to our children back in the early '70s when they sent him off for treatment after he had sexually abused boys then. (Read important note that follows this letter.) Had I known of his addiction, he would never have had the opportunity to victimize my own child. If you haven't already done so, you need to inform any family members of current priests with this problem.

Since I have spoken publicly about my brother's crimes and fully support his victims, I've noticed a majority of Catholic friends acting differently, and it's not very pretty. On the other hand, I've received a lot of support from others. Getting back to the attached note, if these women's attitudes are okay with you, an acceptable Catholic mentality, then I truly am ashamed to let anyone know I am a Catholic. My brother's criminal behaviors were shocking for me to learn of and difficult to believe, but he did at least admit to me he had done those horrible things to kids. I wish for all his victims' sakes he would have said he was sorry before he died. I've accepted that something must have been seriously wrong with him, and he's in God's hands now, but I am very frustrated with the same lack of concern for the victims by the church leadership that still goes on! I grew up expecting so much more of the religious. You can't begin to imagine my disappointment and my struggle to keep faith in the church.

I pray you will give permission to parish organizations at every parish to invite victims of sexual abuse by priests to come and share their stories with them. Parishioners need to support each other, but in order for that to happen, they must hear firsthand from the victims. They have to understand what the victims went through. Catholics need to learn what SNAP really is; a group of people who have come together to support one another after having been abused by a priest when they were kids. Right now, Catholics are being misled and told SNAP is an organization out to destroy the church. In reality it is only trying to get molesters removed from active ministry so as to make the church safer for all kids. That is something you should be working on with them, not fighting against them.

If you have a problem with SNAP that I am not aware of, please tell me. I was surprised to hear archdiocesan spokesman [name withheld] comment on TV last month that he had great respect for SNAP. It gives me hope as I believe only good things could happen for the church if it worked together with SNAP toward keeping all children safe.

The archdiocese in Orange County, CA, has done wonders for sexual-abuse victims by making public apologies. My cousin sent me a newspaper clipping showing pictures of the archbishop hugging victims as he apologized. It ran the sincerely worded apology along with the picture and expressions of gratitude made by the victims. That archdiocese seemed to be genuinely sorry for what happened to these people. Why isn't the Archdiocese of St. Louis doing the same? That acknowledgement of wrongdoing and a sincere apology is the most important thing of all to these victims, after the removal of the offending priest.

There is a tremendous need for a ministry to all Catholics in dealing with the sexual-abuse problem within the church. Everyone is touched by it in some way and would benefit from having somewhere to turn to be available at every parish. To say this is not a good time to deal with this situation makes as much sense as seeing a baby drowning in a neighbor's pool and saying it's not a good time for me to stop and help save this child. People need to do the right thing, even if it's not a good time. That's what I learned from my Catholic upbringing.

I pray you will give serious thought to my concerns and suggestions. The only thing I have ever asked of the archdiocese for its wrong doing in handling my brother's sex abuse problem is to do the right thing for all the sexual-abuse victims. There are the actual victims themselves, but the rippled effect makes every Catholic a victim. I look forward to your reply.

Sincerely,
Mrs. Carol Kuhnert

Disclaimer: It's important I mention that during the latter part of 2008, while I was talking with Tim's lawyer and my cousin regarding another of Norman's sexual-abuse cases, it occurred to me that I had misunderstood something she told me back when she became aware of my learning Norman's secret. It was regarding the time frame she said Norman had been sent for treatment for having molested boys in the Festus area during the early 1970s. I had understood her to say Norman told her about it then and was sent for treatment at that time, but actually he first told her about it in 1985 and was sent for treatment then. It wasn't until after the archdiocese subpoenaed me to give them a deposition in 2008 and afterward talking with the lawyer and my cousin that I learned my error. I asked the lawyer if I needed to contact the archdiocese to correct my deposition, but he told me it wasn't necessary, as he had already done so. Up until then, I believed Norman had been sent for treatment back in the 1970s.

My June 1, 2005, thank-you note to Reverend Telthorst:

Dear Reverend Telthorst,
    Thanks for coming out and listening to our concerns. I asked my friend, Mary Ellen, to join us as she could better answer any questions you may have had about SNAP. She, Joe, and I are very hopeful you will follow through with encouraging and praying with OLS parishioners in daily masses for all abuse victims and their families. You can lead by example in showing compassion and understanding for victims by inviting SNAP to speak of the abuse they suffered, to the people in your parish. Parishioners will follow your lead.
    Please ask Archbishop Burke to request all pastors to do the same at their parishes. This would be a good start toward healing for everyone. It's wrong to leave parishioners in the dark regarding these abuse cases. They deserve the truth and would most likely respect their church leaders, seeing them dealing with the horrific problem rather than hiding it.
    Let me know if I can be of help to you at OLS in opening the minds and hearts of the parishioners through communication with the victims.
    Sincerely,
    Carol Kuhnert

Archbishop Burke's June 2, 2005, letter to me:

Dear Mrs. Kuhnert,
    I acknowledge your letter of May 6 last, addressed to me, to the Reverend Monsignor John B. Shamleffer, and to the Reverend

Monsignor James Telthorst. I acknowledge, too, the copy of your transcription of correspondence dated May 3 last, received by you from Mrs. [name withheld].

I understand a number of circumstances related to the ministry of your late brother, the Reverend Norman Christian, are very troubling to you and have resulted in considerable pain for you and for others. I am aware of the various ways in which you have expressed this. In the name of the archdiocese, and of my predecessors, I express my heartfelt apology for the pain which you and others are suffering.

With respect to your letter of May 6 last, it is not possible for me to respond to it in detail. A number of the assumptions and assertions, which underlie some of your conclusions, are simply not verifiable. Among these is the thinking of the women of Our Lady of Sorrows parish, who preferred you not speak at a meeting of the Women's Guild of the parish. Another is the attribution to Monsignor Telthorst, by the writer of the correspondence of May 3 last, of reasoning which is reported secondhand.

What I can offer to you is the assurance that the manner of response to substantiated allegations of abuse of children or minors by clergy in the Archdiocese of Saint Louis has evolved in ways that are significant. Beginning in 2002, my predecessor, the then archbishop Justin F. Rigali, implemented a policy of public disclosure as soon as an allegation of abuse was substantiated. Priests with substantiated allegations were removed permanently from active ministry and instructed that they should not present themselves publicly as priests. Cardinal Rigali, or his designated representative, went to the parishes where these priests had been serving at the time of removal from ministry. A curriculum vitae of all parishes or institutions where they had served was made public. The cardinal, or his designated representative, went to each of the parishes to speak with the parishioners and to offer them support and encouragement. In some circumstances, designated representatives of the cardinal also spoke in the parishes where the substantiated abuse had occurred. Catholic Family Service counselors were made available at the parishes to speak individually with those who wished their assistance.

As did Cardinal Rigali, I have frequently offered a heartfelt apology to any and to all who have been victims of abuse by clergy.

As did Cardinal Rigali, I have publicly decried the crime of sexual abuse of children and minors, and have encouraged any alleged victims who have not done so to contact the archdiocese or the civil authorities. Since I became archbishop of Saint Louis in January of 2004, I have personally met with victims of clergy sexual abuse and with members of their families. I have made it known that I am most willing to meet with victims of substantiated allegations of abuse, or their families, and to do everything possible, for my part, to assist in their healing.

The archdiocese has offered and continues to offer assistance for the healing of victims of clergy abuse who have contacted the archdiocese. This has been amply reported in the media.

The commitment of the Archdiocese of Saint Louis to the protection of children and young people is strong and unwavering. To this end, since 2002, thousands of adults who are employed by or volunteer in our parishes or institutions, and who are, in those circumstances, in the presence of children or minors, have participated in a professionally developed and presented program entitled "Protecting God's Children." It equips them to recognize questionable behavior, to implement best practices with regard to the safety of our children, and to take the necessary steps when they have even a suspicion that a priest or church worker has done something inappropriate. Moreover all clergy, employees and volunteers working in the Archdiocese with children must agree to regular background checks conducted by the Missouri Department of Family Services. There is too, a Code of Conduct which has been implemented for the protection of our children and young people.

If you are not familiar with the details of the archdiocese's initiative to protect our children and to provide for them safe environments in all of our parishes and institutions, I encourage you to visit our archdiocesan website at www.archstl.org. There you will find, readily identifiable on the homepage, the link to our Protecting God's Children site.

Let me reiterate that, like you, I am committed to protecting children and youth. I am likewise committed to do everything possible so that no member of the clergy, or other church worker, who has harmed a child, will function in a church environment.

I hope that this information indicates that my commitment is unambiguous.

    Asking God's blessing upon you, I am
    Yours devotedly in Christ,
    (Most Reverend) Raymond L. Burke
    Archbishop of Saint Louis

Monsignor Jim Telthorst's June 7, 2005, thank-you letter:

Dear Carol,

    Thank you so much for your positive response to my offer to meet with you in your home. It was good to meet your husband and your friend, Mary Ellen. (I've enclosed a note for her since I did not have her address.) Thank you so much for the delicious lunch, still good after my delayed arrival!

    I learned much from you and Mary Ellen. I'm only sorry that you have had to suffer so much and for so long as you learned of your brother's behavior. I believe I gained a much better understanding of how the victims and families suffer long after the actual abuse. I learned as well how they suffer from others who simply view them as part of a picture that many simple don't want to see.

    You might be interested in knowing that not only have I mentioned the victims of abuse in the prayers I lead, but this past weekend the writer of the petitions had already included them in our general prayers. I will try to continue to do so, as well as to look for opportunities where the topic might be an apt example in my homilies.

    When our priests' council resumes meeting in the Fall I will try to look for opportunities that I might remind us all of how we need to better respond to the concerns of the victims.

    Again, Carol, I'm most grateful for your willingness to meet. I'm a strong believer that when the Lord used a table as a place to reveal the kingdom and to gather and feed us, he knew the power of a table and good food. Thank you for your patience with me as I tried to understand your own heart and your concerns.

    Sincerely,
    Monsignor Jim Telthorst

Our July 6, 2005, letter to Archbishop Burke:

Dear Archbishop Burke,

In regards to your letter of July 1, 2005, about the Annual Catholic Appeal Collection for 2005, we have been making our donations directly to various charities.

We continue to pray the church leaders will accept responsibility for the errors and bad judgment of the past in dealing with the church's pedophile religious. Sending them away for periods of treatment doesn't work. They need to be removed from active ministry, not given more opportunities to molest in new parishes. Removing them only when forced to by a victim finding the courage to face the archdiocese in court speaks poorly of the church leadership. When we begin hearing sincere public apologies being made to the sexual-abuse victims, offers of help in their recovery, and hear our church leaders explaining to all Catholics that it wasn't the victim's fault that they were abused but that some religious had shamefully betrayed the trust of a young child and his/her parents, we will begin to regain our trust and respect for the church. Church leaders need to start delivering this message to their flock in hopes of changing the un-Christian attitude many Catholics have toward the innocent victims. Until these things happen, we will not participate in the Annual Catholic Appeal.

Sincerely,
Mr. and Mrs. Joseph Kuhnert

My July 6, 2005, letter to my daughter's pastor:

Dear Reverend [name withheld],

My daughter's family is in your parish and I sometimes attend mass there. I noticed in your July 3rd bulletin the beautiful prayer for our troops. I read further hoping to see such a prayer for all those sexually abused by religious. All I found was a notice about Protecting God's Children and the importance of being in compliance with archdiocese directives. Where is the message to your parishioners to help them begin to understand how sexual-abuse victims and their families suffer long after the actual abuse happens. They had been hurt terribly when just young children by trusting, respecting, and obeying a religious. It was unthinkable that a religious would ever harm a child, and it made children easy prey for such pedophiles.

I ask you to start mentioning these victims of abuse in prayers you lead. Place a short prayer for them in every Sunday bulletin, and ask to have petitions that include them in the parish general prayers. Look for opportunities when this topic might be a fit example in one of your homilies. Encourage other priests to do the same.

My brother was Reverend Norman Christian. He died the end of October 2004 as a known pedophile, never saying I'm sorry to any of his victims. I first learned of his criminal behavior about 17 years ago when one of my then teen daughters told me what he had been doing and saying to her. (At the time my husband and I thought he was counseling her through some difficulties she was having.) I confronted him about what she had told me, and he admitted everything. He opened up to me about what he had been doing to children since his seminary years. I asked the archdiocese what they were doing about him and was told it was none of my business. I need not worry about it. They were taking care of things. No one asked if my daughter was okay. No one asked if I or any of my family needed help in dealing with Norman's betrayal. What I saw then was Norman being protected, church assets being protected, scandal being avoided at all costs and let the victims fend for themselves. I've seen no change yet. In 2005, unless a victim finds the courage to stand up to the church leaders, it's business as usual. It's shameful.

Monsignor, it would be helpful for your parishioners to hear these victims tell their stories of what happened to them as children. They might understand why the victims kept their ugly secret for so long. It would also be healing for the victims to be able to speak about what they're dealing with. The fear of not being believed is overwhelming, and my brother, for one, told every one of his victims no one would believe a kid; they'd believe the priest! Sadly, he was right. Even when the priest admits to the crimes, there are some Catholics who still refuse to believe it. It's less painful for them to condemn the victim for speaking out and giving the priest and church a bad name.

Will you please think about inviting some members of SNAP to come and speak to your parishioners? SNAP is nothing more than a large group, and growing larger, of people who have come together to support each other after having been abused by clergy and are working to get molesters removed from active ministry. I would be willing to join them. The church I loved and turned to for comfort and guidance all my life is gone. The Catholic Church no longer stands out as a good example; it's more of a horrible warning now. I'm praying for the church leadership to accept responsibility for what's happened, admit errors, make sincere apologies, and explain to all Catholics over and over that it wasn't the victims' fault this happened to them. The clergy betrayed the trust of innocent children. Catholics need to hear it from the church leaders. Right now, most of them blame the victims for reporting what the clergy did. That Catholic attitude toward the victims only adds more pain for them. Please do your part in helping change this un-Christian attitude toward victims.

Sincerely,
Mrs. Carol Kuhnert

Representative Mike Vogt's September 6, 2005, letter of response

Dear Mrs. Kuhnert:
Re: SB 17

My apologies for the delay in responding to your letter; it was originally delivered to a different representative.

As a Roman Catholic, I am also appalled by the denial of the hierarchy of the church in the decades-long problems we have been having with the pedophile priests. It has severely harmed our church, and nearly every single parish in my district has had incidents of this terrible abuse.

You can be assured I will support any legislation that will do what the church has failed to do. I am a firm believer in the separation clause of the First Amendment, but if the government needs to step in to solve the problem, then I will support such steps.

Thank you for contacting me and should you have any further concerns, please let me know.

Sincerely,
Mike Vogt

November 18, 2005, e-mail I received from Professor Marci Hamilton:

Thanks so much for your e-mail. I have represented victims on constitutional issues for several years now, and it is both depressing and rewarding work. We are making some progress, though it will take the whole culture to drop this childlike trust in priests before we really succeed. Good for you for turning in your own brother. I can't imagine how hard that must have been, but your moral compass is obviously in the right direction. Best regards, MAH

November 28, 2005, response from Monsignor Telthorst:

Dear Joe & Carol,
Thank you for your Thanksgiving card and letter. It was good to hear from you. I was just speaking with someone the other day about you. I'm sorry I don't remember the man's name but it was another contact from [name withheld] Electric.

Concerning your question about attitudes, I can't say I've heard anything either positive or negative. Actually, I'm amazed (sometimes saddened) about the news that's out and about in the parish that I never hear. When I do here it, I'm surprised either by its incorrect content or why no one brings the complaint or suggestion to me. Perhaps I'm not the best source of information.

We continue to use intentions periodically about those who have suffered abuse. We are presently planning an event for Lent, which may consist of three or more sessions on our parish's life, blessings, brokenness, and dreams for the future. It is still very much in the first draft stage, and you may be the only one to whom I've mentioned it. I will keep your work in mind as possibly playing some part in one of these sessions.

Sincerely,
Monsignor Jim Telthorst

Our June 10, 2006, letter to Archbishop Burke:

Thanks for responding to our recent letter to you. We hope you do deplore the evil of sexual abuse of minors by clergy. We wonder, though, how you can say "all credible allegations of abuse of a minor by priests are handled swiftly and appropriately. This includes removing priests with credible allegations from active ministry." We've only seen them removed from active ministry when the church was forced to do so by the courts. Why not, when there are red flags and one knows a religious could present a danger to children, remove that person on your own?

In my brother's case alone (Norman Christian), when he died in October 2004, having molested kids throughout his priesthood, you honored him with a funeral mass and burial as a priest in good standing. I was told you were the celebrant of the well-attended though not publicly announced mass. You had to know from reading the reports in his personnel files the accusations made against him were credible. Had the police not closed the current case due to his death, Norman would have gone to trial for abusing this victim, been found guilty, and been facing prison.

The church's Sexual Abuse Mediation Board believed Tim Fischer when he told them what Father Christian had done to him when he was a vulnerable child. For whatever reason, you made Mr. Fischer wait a long time before he received the letter of apology (what he wanted most of all) the Board had promised to him.

We can't understand how you can be so uncaring toward these victims. Why don't we see and hear you actually reaching out to them with compassion and understanding? You and all the church leaders need to lead by example in reaching out and helping these people. Many Catholics tend to blame the sexual-abuse victims for giving the priest and church a bad name by reporting the crimes that were committed against them as children. The church leaders' silence, in not speaking up for the victims, encourages their behavior. It's very sad and very wrong.

The religious don't deserve leniency because of who they are, but rather they deserve harsher punishment because of their betrayals of the reverent, trusted, and respected positions they hold. Many Catholics are in pain because they have lost their trust and respect in the Catholic Church leadership. Once that is regained, churches will

begin to fill again. We pray you will give thought to our concerns. You will be in our prayers.
Sincerely,
Joe and Carol Kuhnert

My letter to the editor of the *St. Louis Review*, February 2007:

Steve Givens' "Viewpoint" article in the February 2 *Review* stated people are leaving the church or have stopped practicing their faith because they were hurt or confused by the imperfect people who make up our church. I think most adults look past imperfections; everyone has them. It's the dishonesty and cover-ups of the church hierarchy and their refusal to hold themselves accountable for the harm that's been done over the years that's been driving people away from the church.

Many bishops have ignored victims of priest sexual abuse, gotten rid of evidence, put off prosecutors, been untruthful with parishioners and, showing no concern for children, transferred offending priests to parishes where they were welcomed by people completely unaware of the possible danger being placed in their midst.

Catholics feel betrayed and are simply disgusted. The empty pews are a consequence to the silence and cover-ups of the church hierarchy regarding the sexual-abuse scandal. People are waiting and watching for signs that the hierarchy is changing its ways and can thereby earn back that trust and respect. When that happens, imperfections will remain, but the church can begin to heal and pews will begin to fill again.
Sincerely,
Mrs. Carol Kuhnert

My March 16, 2007, letter to Monsignor John Shamleffer:

Dear Monsignor Shamleffer,
I've been asking myself why I've been uneasy with the wonderful apology you wrote to all the victims of clergy sexual abuse that

appeared in the March 9 *St. Louis Review* and then wondered if you had other motives for writing it.

My first thought was how it certainly made you and the church look good in the eyes of all those parishioners who are already angry with the sexual-abuse victims. Then I realized your apology wasn't going to even reach the main people meant to read it. The victims and their families mostly have left the church out of disgust and probably don't read the *St. Louis Review*. If your apology is sincere, you would better reach all the victims through the media via the *Post-Dispatch*, etc.

Your comments about the church having listened to survivors tell their stories and claiming to have removed clergy abusers also made me wonder, as I'm only aware of the church doing those things when forced to do so through mediation hearings and court orders, not willingly on their own.

One other important issue was not mentioned. Nowhere did I get a feeling that you were calling upon the parishioners to reach out to these victims themselves with compassion and understanding, to stop blaming them for what had happened.

You called on all clergy to "examine our priestly commitment, to reflect on the depth of our own relationship with God and to resolve to be as good and upright a priest as we can possibly be for the sake of our people, the church and our own salvation." Making all clergy mandatory reporters of any abuse they have knowledge of, would be the right thing to do! The silence and covering up that has gone on for so long must stop. I find myself questioning what a clergy's relationship with God actually is for so many of them to have been able to keep so silent for so long about such sinful crimes against children.

I pray you will use some of this Lenten season to turn to the Lord in prayer about my concerns. I will continue praying throughout Lent for everyone (victims, families, and clergy) who has been hurt over the years due to the sexual-abuse scandal. Please think about putting your apology in the news media where the victims will find it.

Thanks,
Carol Kuhnert

APPENDIX 2

Documents from Father Christian's Archdiocesan personnel file, mentioned in Author's Note:

Norman's December 5, 1995, letter to parishioners of Saint William's Church re: his leaving as pastor

Saint William Church
9322 Stansberry Avenue
Saint Louis, MO 63134

Dear Friends, My Sisters & Brothers in the Lord,

Advent calls us to wonder once again at the Divine Christmas gift; God-Love made human in Jesus His Son. I extend my greeting and wish for your happiness as you 'prepare the way of the Lord.'

Some weeks ago I announced to Saint William parish that I would be away for a mini-sabbatical. The sabbatical included a thorough examination of my health; a professional evaluation of my physical, mental, emotional and spiritual life. It became apparent that I would need to deal *now* with depression and its diabetic impact. To put things off might impair my present and future ministry in the church.

Today (December 5) I met with Archbishop Rigali. He has affirmed my request for a leave of absence from all ministry to take whatever steps are needed to heal the brokenness. So, you can see that I will not be returning to Saint William after all. Unfortunately, the human machine is quite fallible.

You, whom I have grown to love over the years, have been

particularly supportive of, and patient with, my service to you as pastor. I welcome your prayers for my physical and spiritual welfare during this time. Your kindness to me will be remembered with gratitude to God at the daily Eucharist I share with those with whom I am now living. Let's continue our holy journeys, in mutual support of one another, by living the gospel mandate to 'love one another' as Jesus loved us (even to death, death on a cross).

If you wish to contact me, please use the current address listed below. Meanwhile, be nice to Father Gene; human flesh is more fragile than we think.

Your brother in Christ,
[signed "Father Norm"]
Reverend Norman H. Christian
161-3-5 Vondera
Robertsville, MO 63072-2529

(He typed the letter on Saint William's parish stationery.)

Archbishop Rigali's September 25, 1996, letter to Norman:

Reverend Norman H. Christian
P.O. Box 220
Dittmer MO 63023

Dear Father Christian,

The Advisory Committee established by our new Policy on Allegations of Sexual Abuse, in their meeting of September 19, 1996, concluded the review and discussion of your case. You are aware of the opinion of the Consultation Center that you have a guarded prognosis for return of full-time ministry at this time and that some very limited ministry might be possible where there would be no contact with minors. Based upon this judgment of the professionals at the Consultation Center and upon your history of acting out sexually, the Advisory Committee does not think it will be advisable to assign you to any kind of priestly ministry in the Archdiocese in the foreseeable future. It is my understanding that they have come to this recommendation because it does not seem that a ministry that would be restrictive enough exists in the archdiocese. They point out that, as a practical matter, it is not really possible to restrict a priest's contact with young people, if they seek him out or he seeks them out. I know that the Advisory Committee has deliberated for several weeks on your case and I believe that I must accept their recommendation in this instance.

I would hope that, for the immediate future, you would remain in residence at Wounded Brothers and follow the recommendations of the Saint Louis Consultation Center for your ongoing recovery, including the follow-up session in January 1997. It also seems advisable that, if possible, with the assistance of the staff at Wounded Brothers, you seek some kind of secular employment for your support.

This letter was difficult to write, and I know it is much more difficult to read. We want to do whatever we can to assist you, a priest of our archdiocese, to continue on your path of recovery and to embrace the foreseeable future in a realistic manner. Monsignor John Gaydos and I stand ready to be of assistance in any way possible. I pray that God gives you the grace to bear this cross always seeking the peace and light of His Holy Spirit.

Fraternally in Christ,
Most Reverend Justin Rigali
Archbishop of Saint Louis

Norman's March 26, 2004, letter to Archbishop Raymond Burke:

March 26, 2004
Most Reverend Raymond Burke
Archbishop of St. Louis
4445 Lindell Blvd
Saint Louis, MO 63108

Dear Archbishop Burke,

I am a 68 year old cleric of the Archdiocese (Class of 1961) in retirement status living at Regina Cleri. This letter will acquaint you with my life situation. My ministry is inactive. I am recently named in a sexual misconduct civil lawsuit by a John Doe plaintiff, and have as my Defense Attorney, Mr. J. Martin Radican, in Clayton, MO.

My current income is about $700 per month ($386 from Priests Mutual Archd. Retirement stipend, and $309 Social Security monthly payment). I am able to pay my attorney very little of the retainer fee he is seeking for these services.

I have learned from Canon Lawyer, J. Michael Ritty, JCL of Saint Paul University of Canon Law, that there are no canonical rights to a civil attorney. He also said that there are some diocese that do provide coverage for all or part of the attorney's fees depending on the circumstances.

I would welcome meeting with you in person and will do so at your convenience. Thanking you for considering this serious personal financial crisis. I am,

Sincerely yours,

Norman H. Christian

Funeral Arrangements for Priests Removed from Active Priestly Ministry but Not Laicized

> In order to avoid any distress or confusion at the time of your death, it would be best to advise your family and the executor of your will of final arrangements upon your death. It is advised that you have all of your final plans on file with the Chancellor for Canonical Affairs and the Vicar for Priests Office.

1. The Vicar for Priests will be the contact for the immediate family and the Funeral Director. The Vicar for Priests will assist in choosing the time, date and place for the Mass of Christian Burial.
2. The Mass of Christian Burial may not be held in any parish church to which the deceased had been assigned or in which he was in residence during his years of priestly ministry.
3. In keeping with the restrictions for vesting at Mass, Mass Vestments may be worn if there is no public viewing of the deceased.

4. There should be no public visitation, at the church, prior to the Mass of Christian Burial.
5. The celebrant and homilist for the Mass of Christian Burial may be pre-designated by the deceased. A celebrant and homilist will be designated by the Archbishop should the above not be indicated.
6. All deacons and priests will be notified of the arrangements for the funeral and encouraged to participate.
7. There should be no indication of time, place and date for the Mass of Christian Burial or Interment in the obituary. The title of Reverend or Father may be used in the obituary. The obituary would read: Services and burial will be held at the convenience of the family. A notation that the deceased had served as a priest of the Archdiocese of St. Louis may be included in the obituary. There will be no publication of an obituary in the St Louis Review.
8. In accord with the policy of the Archdiocese of St. Louis a grave will be provided the deceased in the Priest Section at one of the Catholic Cemeteries. The title Reverend or Father may appear on the headstone.

*The above guidelines may be adjusted by the bishop according to particular circumstance.

*Where applicable, the Diocesan Assistance Coordinator will contact as many victim survivors as possible after the funeral and give them notice of the priest/deacon death and offer them any appropriate support.

Timeline and Works Cited – Part One

01-12-1986
Norm Christian
"Once I thought I would like to remain totally anonymous ..."
Personal correspondence to Carol and Joe Kuhnert, US mail

01-19-1986
Carol Kuhnert
"I was really glad to get your letter."
Personal correspondence to Norm Christian, US mail

01-23-1986
Norm Christian
"What a joy to get a letter from home!"
Personal correspondence to Carol Kuhnert, US mail

02-23-1986
Norm Christian
"Things here are involved to the extreme."
Personal correspondence (page two) to Carol Kuhnert, US mail

05-06-1986
Norm Christian
"First, thanks for writing as often as you do."
Personal correspondence to Carol Kuhnert

06-10-1989
Carol Kuhnert
"For reasons of her own, Sue recently decided to tell me about the 'secret' …"
Personal correspondence to Norm Christian, US mail

06-16-1989
Carol Kuhnert
"First of all, I hope you don't mind my letter is typed."
Personal correspondence to Norm Christian, US mail

06-18-1989
Norm Christian
"All that has taken place these last few weeks …"
Personal correspondence to niece Sue; included with a note to Carol on same date, US mail

12-23-1995
Norm Christian
"Of course you both expect a response from me …"
Personal correspondence to Jeanne and Carol, delivered to each one personally

09-25-1996
Archbishop Justin Rigali
"The Advisory Committee established by our new policy …"
Personal correspondence to Fr. Christian, US mail

12-15-1996
Father Joe Naumann
"Carol, you and your sister are in my prayers."
Personal correspondence handwritten on his annual Christmas letter to Carol and Joe Kuhnert, US mail

03-17-1999
Norman Christian
"It is now three and a half years … removed from active ministry"
Personal correspondence to Carol, US mail

03-13-2001
Norm Christian
"Durable Power of Attorney papers"
Delivered personally to Carol

03-03-2002
Patricia Rice and Norm Parish
"13-year-old incident involves the Reverend [prominent pastor]"
Saint Louis Post-Dispatch, A15

03-17-2002
Jeremy Kohler
"Retired priest who molested children says he likes 'to think they've forgotten.'"
Saint Louis Post-Dispatch, A9

03-17-2002
Carol Kuhnert
"I'm attaching a copy of a letter I am sending to Archbishop Rigali."
Personal correspondence to Bishop Naumann, US mail

03-17-2002
Carol Kuhnert
"It saddens me to write this letter."
Personal correspondence to Archbishop Justin Rigali, US mail

03-20-2002
Bishop Joe Naumann
"Bishop Joe Naumann called me 1:30 p.m., talked an hour. ..."
Notes from personal phone conversation between Bishop Naumann and Carol Kuhnert

04-02-2002
Bishop Timothy Dolan
"It is now imperative for us to state again your standing with the archdiocese ..."
Personal correspondence to Norman Christian, US mail

04-05-2002
Norm Christian
"Norm called Thurs., 10:30 p.m. He got a letter from Bishop Dolan ..."
Notes from personal phone conversation between Norm Christian and Carol Kuhnert

04-13-2002
Norman Christian
"This e-mail and attachment is being forwarded to you for your information." Contains Norman's background information, action taken, personal impact on his life and copy of letter he received from Bishop Dolan.
Group e-mail sent to Carol Kuhnert and many others

04-14-2002
Kevin Horrigan
"We were the good kids."
Saint Louis Post-Dispatch, B3

04-15-2002
Norman Christian
"Today I received good news ..."
Group e-mail to Carol Kuhnert and many others

04-21-2002
Carol Kuhnert
"I didn't want to send this over e-mail."
Personal correspondence to Norm, US mail

04-26-2002
Carol Kuhnert
"I am so disappointed and angry with the men who have just talked with the Pope ..."
Personal correspondence to Archbishop Rigali, US mail

05-15-2002
Carol Kuhnert
"This is sort of an update."
Personal correspondence to Bishop Joe Naumann, US mail

05-26-2002
Norm Christian
"What a beautiful day we had today!"
E-mail to Carol

06-01-2002
Archbishop Justin Rigali
"I received some time ago your letter concerning the present situation in the church."
Personal correspondence to Carol Kuhnert, US mail

07-21-2002
Father Matthew Mitas
"There's No Place Like Home."
Immaculate Conception Church, Union, MO, bulletin article

07-26-2002
Carol Kuhnert
"After reading your column in the July 21 bulletin …"
Personal correspondence to Father Mitas, US mail

08-05-2002
Reverend Matthew M. Mitas
"Thank you for your thoughtful and well-written letter …"
Personal correspondence to Carol, US mail

08-08-2002
Norm Parish
"Area Priest in Sex Case is Laicized by Pope"; re: Joseph D. Ross.
Saint Louis Post-Dispatch

08-16-2002
Joseph Kenny
"Laicization Not Considered a Penalty."
Saint Louis Review, p. 3

08-16-2002
Joseph Kenny
"J. Ross returns to lay state."
Saint Louis Review, p. 3

12-20-2002
Writer not listed
"Priest pleads guilty to charges" re: Father Gary P. Wolken
Saint Louis Review

01-03-2003
Carol Kuhnert
"I've turned to you in the past ..."
Personal correspondence to Bishop Naumann, US mail

02-07-2003
Joseph Kenny
"Father Hess sentenced for obscene materials."
Saint Louis Review

02-07-2003
Carol Kuhnert
"I'm sending the same attached letter to Archbishop Rigali ..."
Personal correspondence to Bishop Naumann, US mail

02-07-2003
Carol Kuhnert
"I keep looking for things that will help me start to regain my trust ..."
Personal correspondence to Archbishop Rigali and Bishop Naumann, US mail

02-17-2003
Auxiliary Bishop Joseph Naumann
"Archbishop Rigali asked me to thank you for your recent letter ..."
Personal correspondence to Carol Kuhnert, US mail

03-01-2003
William C. Lhotka,
"Priest gets fifteen years for molesting young boy."
Saint Louis Post-Dispatch, A2

03-12-2003
Norman Christian
"I am grateful for the emotional support."
E-mail to Carol and Joe

06-23-2003
Norman Christian
"On Monday, Wednesday, Friday I am doing physical therapy and occupational therapy ..."
E-mail to Carol and Joe

06-25-2003
Jeanne Meyer
"[Norman] told me a stress test indicated he had a heart problem; physical therapy stopped for now. He also mentioned a problem with his eyes."
Phone call to Carol

09-13-2003
Bishop Joe Naumann
"Each day of the year, I select [someone] for whom I offer the prayers."
Personal correspondence to Carol and Joe, US mail

09-17-2003
Carol Kuhnert
"I was surprised to hear from you."
Personal correspondence to Bishop Joe Naumann, US mail

09-20-2003
Norman Christian
"Your card arrived in Friday's mail."
E-mail to Carol and Joe

10-05-2003
"Rigali refuses to meet with abuse victims."
Saint Louis Post-Dispatch

12-03-2003
Norman Christian
"Your card arrived today while I am on retreat."
E-mail to Carol and Joe

12-05-2003
Norman Christian
"My name is number thirty on SNAP's website list of alleged clergy abusers."
Notes from phone conversation with Carol

12-05-2003
Kim Bell
"SNAP wants church to release names of alleged abusers."
Saint Louis Post-Dispatch, B6

12-18-2003
Norman Christian
"Nothing has come of public status."
E-mail to Carol and Joe

01-11-2004
Father Matthew Mitas
"Bits and Pieces"
Immaculate Conception Church bulletin article

01-11-2004
Carol Kuhnert
"Well, Father Mitas, since you've asked, …"
Personal correspondence to Father Mitas, US mail

02-12-2004
Carol Kuhnert
"The announcement of your promotion and upcoming move to Kansas City …"
Personal correspondence to Bishop Joe Naumann, US mail

03-03-2004
Cheryl Wittenauer
"Saint Louis man sues priest, archdiocese and archbishop in sexual abuse claim," Archdiocesan spokesman states. "It's only a matter of time," re: priest being "defrocked."
Associated Press

03-04-2004
Peter Shinkle
"Priest named in suit is under investigation."
Saint Louis Post-Dispatch, B2

03-04-2004
Carol Kuhnert
"We returned home late last night and heard your message."
E-mail to Norman

03-05-2004
Carol Kuhnert
"Wow! What an absolutely horrible time to remember such a blessed event."
Personal correspondence to Norman, US mail

03-05-2004
Sue (Carol's daughter)
"Wanted to let you know that the priest mentioned in ... *Post-Dispatch*, named in a sexual abuse suit, is my mom's brother."
E-mail to her in-laws

03-05-2004
Bishop Joe Naumann
"I imagine the publicity... lawsuit against Norman ..."
Personal correspondence to Carol, US mail

03-10-2004
Personal friends
"You are both in our thoughts and prayers."
Personal correspondence to Joe and Carol, US mail

03-11-2004
Carol Kuhnert
"I have one question."
Personal correspondence to Archbishop Raymond Burke, US mail

03-11-2004
Carol Kuhnert
"Thanks for your note and prayers ... what are church officials encouraging Norman to do."
Personal correspondence to Archbishop Joe Naumann, US mail

03-13-2004
Bishop Joe Naumann
"I have reviewed our files several times ..."
Personal correspondence to Carol, US mail

03-13-2004
Norman Christian
"I received your e-mail and ... your printout of same ... no reason to remember this anniversary in the future."
E-mail to Carol

03-18-2004
Carol Kuhnert
"Thanks for your ... note, but please address my question."
Personal correspondence to Archbishop Naumann, US mail

03-25-2004
William Lhotka
"From Jail, Priest Seeks Information on Victim."
Saint Louis [MO] *Post Dispatch*, A1

04-18-2004
Archbishop Joe Naumann
"The leaders of the archdiocese have to my knowledge always encouraged and counseled Norm to be honest."
Personal correspondence to Carol, US mail

04-19-2004
Archbishop Joseph Naumann
"Below are the addresses and phone numbers for my residence and office."
Personal correspondence to "friends and family," US mail

04-21-2004
William C. Lhotka
"Priest-abuse settlement may be record."
Saint Louis Post-Dispatch, B1

05-02-2004
Father Matthew Mitas
"Sad but True."
Immaculate Conception Church bulletin article

06-17-2004
Carol Kuhnert
"You are on my mind and in my prayers daily."
E-mail to Norman

06-25-2004
Norman Christian
"Do not e-mail me in the future."
E-mail to Carol

07-31-2004
Carol Kuhnert
"I think about you and pray daily for God to help us both."
Personal correspondence to Norman, US mail

08-26-2004
Tim Townsend
"Diocese Settles 18 Abuse Suits."
Saint Louis Post-Dispatch, A1

08-30-2004
Carol Kuhnert
"Again, I ask, please give serious thought to personally apologizing to those you've abused."
Personal correspondence to Norman, US mail

09-01-2004
Carol Kuhnert
"I just read the 8-26-04 *Post* article, stating, 'The archdiocese has agreed to help people with their counseling expenses …'"
Personal correspondence to Norman, US mail

09-03-2004
Joseph Kenny
"Mediation process touted in sex-abuse settlements." (Archdiocesan attorney states, "We don't feel the archdiocese has actual responsibility, but …")
Saint Louis Review—front page

10-17-04
Carol's cousin
"I hear that Norman is in ICU and very bad."
E-mail to Carol

10-21-2004
Friend of Norman Christian
"Norm asked me to use his e-mail list to let people, who care about him, know his health situation."
E-mail to "Dear Friend of Norm Christian"

10-21-2004
Carol Kuhnert
"My name is Carol; I'm Father Christian's sister."
Notes from phone conversation with Tim Fischer

10-27-2004
Bill McClellan
"Ex-priest's family comes to grip with his crimes."
Saint Louis Post-Dispatch, McClellan column

10-29-2004
Monsignor Richard F. Stika, VG
"It is my sad duty to inform you of the death of Reverend Norman H. Christian."
E-mail (archdiocese) to bishops and priests

10-29-2004
Carol Kuhnert
"Thank you so much for your caring and supportive phone call."
Personal correspondence to friend/Notre Dame nun, US mail

10-31-2004
Archdiocese of Saint Louis
"Funeral Liturgy Program and Prayer Card for Father Christian."
Available for attendees of funeral

11-03-2004
Saint William's Church parishioner
"Phone call from … eighty-year old woman …"
Re: phone conversation of woman's call to Carol after Father Christian's funeral

11-05-2004
"Father Christian Dies at age 69."
Saint Louis Review

11-06-2004
Carol Kuhnert
"Most likely you've heard through the grapevine that my brother ... died."
Personal correspondence to family and friends, US mail

11-08-2004
Carol's cousin
"I received a letter from Charles ... this weekend ... told me about Norman's funeral."
E-mail to Carol

11-11-2004
Fran Wood
"I am Frances Wood (Peterman), cousin to Carol Kuhnert in Saint Louis."
E-mail Fran sent David Clohessy, copy to Carol

11-11-2004
Carol Kuhnert,
"Here it is. If you have any questions, please call me." Re: story article obituary for Father Christian.
E-mail to Denise at *Saint Louis Post-Dispatch* (writer of story obituaries for newspaper)

11-12-2004
Carol Kuhnert
"I saw your e-mail address on e-mails I received from Norman over the years."
E-mail to Carol's cousin, a sister of Fran Wood

11-13-2004
"Norman Christian, Controversial Priest."
Saint Louis Post-Dispatch, story obituary for Father Christian

11-13-2004
Carol's cousin (sister of Fran Wood)
"Thank you for your letter. No, I was not aware …"
E-mail to Carol

11-14-2004
"Is this Carol?"
Another of Fr. Christian's victims
Phone call

11-16-2004
Carol Kuhnert
"Thanks for the apple pie. … Sadly, on another note …"
Personal correspondence to Jeanne Meyer, US mail

11-27-2004
Jeanne Meyer
"I'm truly sorry for any hurt I have caused you and your family."
Personal correspondence to Carol, US mail

12-06-2004
Barbara Dorris
"You are so right."
E-mail response to Carol

12-14-2004
Carol Kuhnert
"Good morning; I am Father Norman Christian's younger sister."
Comments read at Tim Fischer's mediation hearing with archdiocese

01-10-2005
Carol Kuhnert
"On December 14, 2004, I was given your business card …"
Personal correspondence to Monsignor John B. Shamleffer, JV, US mail

01-16-2005
Carol Kuhnert
"Congratulations, we are very happy for you ..."
Personal correspondence to Archbishop Naumann, US mail

01-25-2005
Monsignor John B. Shamleffer, JV
"I am writing in reply to your letter ..."
Personal correspondence to Carol Kuhnert, US mail

01-28-2005
Jim Suhr
"Saint Louis archbishop: Three priests defrocked for sexual abuse."
Associated Press

01-29-2005
Carol Kuhnert
"I've written you twice."
Personal correspondence to Archbishop Raymond Burke, U.S. Mail

02-01-2005
Tim Fischer
"Carol, if I haven't told you lately, thank you for all you have done to help heal my wounded soul."
E-mail to Carol Kuhnert

02-03-2005
Carol Kuhnert
"Today's objective is to make people aware of how badly the archdiocese treats clergy sexual abuse victims."
Notes from a phone interview with reporter for the Metro Networks news

02-03-2005
Kevin Lavery
"Archbishop Fails to Send Letter."
KWMU Public Broadcasting Network, article ID 735476

02-03-2005
Younger female cousin of Carol's
"My parents had Norman counsel me when they couldn't handle me."
Phone conversation notes from her call to Carol

02-12-2005
Tim Fischer
"I understand how you feel."
E-mail to Carol

02-18-2005
Archbishop Raymond Burke
"Through reports of members of the Gennesaret Committee …"
Personal correspondence to Tim Fischer, US mail

02-22-2005
Tim Townsend
"Abuse Victim Gets Apology from Burke."
Saint Louis Post-Dispatch, B1

02-25-2005
Editorial
"Healing wounds and preventing new ones."
Saint Louis Review

02-26-2005
Carol Kuhnert
"What I hear from … you are a real 'get the job done' president for the Women's Guild."
Personal correspondence to Women's Guild President of Our Lady of Sorrows Parish, US mail

03-03-2005
Carol Kuhnert
"We strongly disagree …"
Personal correspondence to Fr. Matthew Mitas, US mail

03-04-2005
"Some suggestions to help those grieving parish loss."
Saint Louis Review

03-07-2005
Tim Fischer
"I will be speaking at a forum on justice."
E-mail to Carol

03-08-2005
Carol Kuhnert
"Suggestions to help those abused by clergy"
Personal correspondence to Archdiocesan Office, US mail

03-20-2005
Tim Townsend
"Abusive US priests end up often at Saint Louis' back door."
Saint Louis Post-Dispatch, B1

04-02-2005
Mary Grant
"Many of our members are saddened by the death of Pope John Paul II, who was …"
E-mail from SNAP to Carol

04-02-2005
Carol Kuhnert
"Thanks for your letter of January 25."
Personal correspondence to Monsignor John B. Shamleffer, VG, US mail

04-11-2005
SNAP
News conference regarding new lawsuits against Fr. Christian.
E-mail

368

04-11-2005
Monsignor John B. Shamleffer, VG
"I received your letter dated April 2, 2005."
Personal correspondence to Carol, US mail

04-16-2005
Mrs. Fischer (Tim's wife)
"Carol, thanks for coming to the forum to hear Tim speak."
E-mail to Carol

04-19-2005
SNAP
"We need your help now."
E-mail

04-21-2005
Carol Kuhnert
"Re: Senate Bill 17, an extremely important legislation."
Personal correspondence to Michael Vogt, Missouri state representative, US mail

05-03-2005
Our Lady of Sorrows Women's Guild President
"I have to clear speakers with Monsignor …"
Personal correspondence to Carol Kuhnert, US mail

05-06-2005
Carol Kuhnert
"Attached is a copy of a note I received from the president of Our Lady of Sorrows Women's Guild."
Personal correspondence to Archbishop Raymond Burke, Monsignor John Shamleffer, and Reverend James Telthorst, US mail

05-07-2005
Ann Pepper and Andrew Galvin
"Ex-Orange County Catholic leader issues apology."
Orange County [California] *Register*, p. 1

05-13-2005
Survivors Network of those Abused by Priests
"New Sex Abuse Lawsuit Filed against Saint Louis Priest."
Press statement on website, re: Father Norman Christian

05-13-2005
Peggy Scott
"Three more accuse Reverend Norman Christian of sexual abuse."
For the *Leader*

06-01-2005
Carol Kuhnert
"Do you want to do something to rid the church of its pedophiles?"
Personal notes for referral and discussion with Monsignor Telthorst at her home

06-01-2005
Carol Kuhnert
"Thanks for coming out ..."
Personal correspondence to Msgr. Telthorst

06-02-2005
Archbishop Raymond Burke
"I acknowledge your letter of May 6 ..."
Personal correspondence to Carol, US mail

06-07-2005
Monsignor Jim Telthorst
"Thank you so much for your positive response to my offer to meet with you."
Personal correspondence to Carol

07-06-2005
Carol Kuhnert
"In regard to your letter of July 1, 2005 ..."
Personal correspondence to Archbishop Burke, US mail

07-06-2005
Carol Kuhnert
"My daughter's family is in your parish ..."
Personal correspondence to Pastor of Holy Infant Parish, US mail

07-19-2005
SNAP Press Conference
Boy Scout Headquarters
Central West End

07-20-2005
Elizabeth Holland
"Jefferson County man sues archdiocese, ex-scout leader."
Saint Louis Post-Dispatch

08-09-2005
"Saint Louis, Lawsuit Accuses Priest of Abuse." (Priest had been assigned to Our Lady of Sorrows Church during 1949–1953.)
Saint Louis Post-Dispatch

08-09-2005
No writer listed
"Archdiocese comments on lawsuit against ... [*another priest I knew*]."
Saint Louis Review

08-12-2005
Barbara Watkins
"New Safe Touch Program will 'empower students.'"
Saint Louis Review, p. 3

08-20-2005
"Man sues archdiocese claims sex abuse in 1960s." (Re: Father Christian)
Saint Louis Post-Dispatch, Law and Order

08-24-2005
Tim Townsend
"Priest, archdiocese are named in sex abuse suit." (Another priest raised in Our Lady of Sorrows Parish.)
Saint Louis Post-Dispatch

08-31-2005
Don Corrigan
Twist of Faith, Clergy abuse documentary
South Saint Louis County Times, August 26–September 1, 2005, p. 8

09-02-2005
Tim Fischer
"Did I ever send this to you?"
E-mail to Carol, attaching part of his personal journal notes

09-06-2005
Missouri State Representative Mike Vogt
"My apologies for the delay in responding to your letter."
Personal correspondence to Carol, US mail

10-09-2005
Father Matthew Mitas
"Alfred Kinsey (1894–1956)"
Immaculate Conception Church bulletin, pastor's column

10-11-2005
Carol Kuhnert,
"After reading your October 9 column in the Sunday bulletin ..."
Personal correspondence to Father Mitas, US mail

10-17-2005
Robert Patrick
"Records in priest sex cases were destroyed."
Saint Louis Post-Dispatch, A1

11-17-2005
Marcie Hamilton
"Has the Catholic Church put the Clergy Abuse Problem Behind it?"
http://writ.news.findlaw.com/hamilton/20051117.html

11-28-2005
Monsignor Jim Telthorst
"Thank you for your Thanksgiving card and letter."
Personal e-mail to Carol

02-17-2006
Tim Fischer
"Could you write a recap of your battle over the eighteen years …"
[to post on his website].
E-mail sent to Carol

03-06-2006
Tim Fischer
"When Fr. Christian … returned from … New Mexico … in the 1980's …"
Entry posted on Tim's website (no longer available online)

03-15-2006
Carol Kuhnert
"Spinning My Wheels for Eighteen Years." Tim posted it in three segments on his website: 03-15, 03-16, and 03-18-2006.
E-mail to Tim Fischer

06-10-2006
Joe and Carol Kuhnert
"Thanks for responding …"
Personal correspondence to Archbishop Burke, US mail

08-31-2006
Archbishop Raymond Burke
"When the Returning God's Gifts Campaign began …"
Personal correspondence to "Dear Friend in Christ," US mail

11-08-2006
Robert Patrick
"Priest's sodomy conviction is reversed."
Saint Louis Post-Dispatch, B3

12-22-2006
Cindy Wooden
"Convert sex-abuse shame to repentance, papal preacher says."
Saint Louis Review

02-02-2007
Steve Givens
"My imperfect faith is the air I breathe."
Saint Louis Review, p. 13

03-09-2007
Monsignor John B. Shamleffer
"Church strives for healing after scandal."
Saint Louis Review

03-16-2007
Carol Kuhnert
"I've been asking myself why I've been uneasy."
Personal correspondence to Monsignor Shamleffer, US mail

03-30-2007
Joseph Kenny
"Archdiocesan Review Board Reaches Out to Victims."
Saint Louis Review

03-21-2010
Shawn Pogatchnik
"Pope's apology doesn't appease Irish victims."
Saint Louis Post-Dispatch, A14

02-25-2011
"The painful process of restoring trust."
Saint Louis Review editorial, p. 18 (Editorial originally appeared in 02-17-2011 issue of the Catholic Standard & Times, Archdiocese of Philadelphia.)

07-15-2011
Tim Fischer
"Funeral policy for priests removed from active ministry but not laicized."
E-mail to Carol (Policy originally e-mailed to Tim from archdiocese)

03-05-2014
"Healing prayer service this Thursday at Lourdes."
Missourian newspaper, Union, MO

Timeline and Works Cited – Part Two

Father Norman Christian's Archdiocesan Personnel File

02-08-1950 to 06-11-1961
Seminary school report cards indicate grades average and below.

1960
Kenrick Seminary's Profile of Norman H. Christian

03-20-1961
Cardinal Joseph Ritter
"I am happy to appoint you herewith as a part-time teacher of religion at Bishop DuBourg High School."
Personal correspondence to Father Christian, US mail

03-30-1969 (Palm Sunday)
Reverend Norman H. Christian
"May I congratulate you …"
Personal correspondence to His Eminence John Cardinal Carberry, US mail

05-13-1969
Reverend Norman H. Christian
"Having considered many factors surrounding my ministry at Ascension Parish …"
Personal correspondence to Right Reverend Cornelius J. Flavin

(copy to His Eminence John Cardinal Carberry and Right Reverend William Drumm), US mail

08-1971
Norman H. Christian
Archdiocese personnel form update
Information completed by Father Christian to the Committee for the Ministry and Life of Priests.

09-03-1971
Norman H. Christian
"This letter is prepared with a view to the immediate and more distant future."
Personal correspondence to Right Reverend Mark S. Ebner, US mail

02-20-1974
Reverend James A. Blazine
"The officials of this chancery office are very upset with Father Christian."
Personal correspondence to Monsignor Drumm, US mail

10-27-1975
Reverend Norman H. Christian
"Very good fortune has come my way."
Personal correspondence to His Eminence John J. Carberry, US mail

10-19-1977
Reverend Norman H. Christian
"In previous recommendations to you and the Commission for the Life and Ministry of Priests ..."
Personal correspondence to Father Dietz, US mail

12-27-1977
John Joseph Cardinal Carberry
"I am pleased to appoint you ... parish priest of Nativity of Our Lord Parish, Saint Louis, Missouri."
Personal correspondence to Reverend Norman H. Christian, US mail

12-30-1977
Father Norman H. Christian
"In the name of God's poor and in my own name, I give thanks ... a nativity of our own."
Personal correspondence to John J. Cardinal Carberry, US mail

04-26-1981
Reverend Norman H. Christian
"I have enclosed a copy of our Sunday bulletin ... you will find relevant to our meeting tomorrow ..."
Personal correspondence to Archbishop John L. May, US mail

10-09-1984
Archbishop John L. May
"The new Code of Cannon Law ... Prescribes ... a number of pastors available for consultation by the diocesan bishop when he thinks it best to remove a pastor."
Personal correspondence to Reverend Norman H. Christian, US mail

02-25-1986
Archbishop John L. May
"Thank you for the very complete and helpful first report on ... Father Norman Christian at Foundation House."
Personal correspondence to Reverend William D. Perri, Director, Foundation House, US mail

10-12-1986
Reverend Norman H. Christian
"You have meant a great deal to me during 1986 ..."
Personal correspondence to Archbishop John L. May, US mail

01-29-1987
Reverend Norman H. Christian
"I am writing to you to indicate my desire for a change of assignment."
Personal correspondence to Archbishop John L. May, US mail

10-1995

Archdiocese Consultation Center

"Case File Summary ... Alleged Perpetrator: Father Norman Christian ... Initial report made by alleged victim 10-1995."

Archdiocesan Advisory Committee report, re: Father Norman H. Christian

12-1995

St. Louis Consultation Center

Fr. Norm Christian/discussion about future

12-05-1995

Reverend Norman H. Christian

"Dear Friends, my sisters and brothers in the Lord."

Personal correspondence to Saint William's Church parishioners, US mail

01-24-1996

Father Joe Naumann

"Beginning immediately, Father Norm Christian should receive his total compensation from the 'Clergy in Transition' Fund."

Memo to Mr. Gerard Hoeing, copy to Monsignor John Maguire and Mr. Fred Hummel

02-15-1996

Norman H. Christian

"For value received, the undersigned, Norman H. Christian, hereby promises to pay to the order of [victim]."

Promissory note prepared by archdiocese

05-1996

Former parishioners Mr. and Mrs. [names withheld] of Nativity Parish, 1996.

"I have never wrote [sic] to a bishop before, I hope I'm doing this right ..."

Personal correspondence to Archbishop Justin Rigali, US mail

05-24-1996
Archbishop Justin Rigali
"I have received your letter concerning efforts of one of the priests of the Archdiocese of Saint Louis."
Personal correspondence to former parishioners, Mr. and Mrs. [names withheld] of Nativity Parish, US mail

09-19-1996
Archdiocese Consultation Center
Advisory Committee Recommendations, re: Father Norman Christian; "Response to Allegation: Admission."
Memo to Archbishop Justin Rigali

09-25-1996
Archbishop Justin Rigali
"The Advisory Committee ... concluded the review and discussion of your case."
Personal correspondence to Reverend Norman H. Christian, US mail

10-17-1996
Reverend Norman H. Christian
"The Advisory Committee has given their recommendation to Archbishop Rigali."
Personal correspondence to Monsignor John Gaydos, VG, US mail

11-14-1996
Reverend Norman H. Christian
"I express my gratitude for our meeting in your office on October 24, 1996."
Personal correspondence to Monsignor John Gaydos, VG

12-12-1996
Monsignor John R. Gaydos
"I spoke with Dr. Paul Midden on Monday, December 9."
Memo, re: Father Norman Christian to file

01-06-1997
N. H. Christian
"This week I will travel to Oklahoma City, OK, to attend a national convention for Sexually Compulsive people."
Personal correspondence to Monsignor John Gaydos, VG, US mail

08-14-1998
Bishop M. Sheridan
"Today I received a phone call from a [redacted] year old man named [redacted] very upset as he recounted being sexually molested by a priest in 1974."
Memo, re: "Accusation by [redacted] sent to file

03-06-2002
Genevieve
"[redacted] called on behalf of her husband [redacted]. He had a problem with a priest and was told to call you."
Memo, re: [redacted] sent to Bishop Dolan

03-11-2004
Archdiocese of Saint Louis
"Statement of the Archdiocese of Saint Louis Regarding Father Norman Christian."
Copy sent to file.

03-26-2004
Norman H. Christian
"I am a 68 year old cleric of the Archdiocese ... retirement status living at Regina Cleri."
Personal correspondence to Archbishop Raymond Burke, US mail

04-05-2004
Norman Christian
"I am asking your response to several requests."
Personal correspondence to Monsignor Richard Stika, VG, US mail

04-12-2004
Monsignor Richard Stika, VG
"I have reviewed your letter regarding the reimbursement for activities."
Personal correspondence to Reverend Norman H. Christian, US mail

04-15-2004
Monsignor Richard Stika
"I spoke to the archbishop ... and we agreed to assist Father Christian with his legal fees."
Memo to Father Henry Breier

04-16-2004
J. Martin Hadican
"Re: John Doe TF vs. Father Norman H. Christian, et al."
Personal correspondence to Monsignor Richard F. Stika, VG, US mail

06-10-2004
Monsignor Richard Stika
"Norman Christian called this afternoon to inform us that he is going with Father "X" to his condo in Florida."
Memo to: File

10-06-2004
G. Vogel
"Fr. Norman Christian at St. Mary's Hospital."
Memo

10-07-2004
Genevieve Curtis
"Rev. Norman Christian Prognosis not good."
Memo

2004
Mariano Favazza
"Missouri Circuit Court Trial Docket Notice, John Doe TF plaintiff vs. Christian, Norman H; case assigned to Div. 01 on 09-07-04; Rollover for case not reached 11-01-04."
Notice given archdiocese following Father Christian's death

Undated
Circuit Court of Saint Louis City, State of Missouri
"John Doe KK, Plaintiff vs. Roman Catholic Archdiocese of Saint Louis ... Archbishop Raymond Burke ... Defendants, Case NO 052-01647 Division 17; Plaintiff's response to Defendant Archdiocese's motion for summary judgment."
Document given to archdiocese

Father Norman Christian's parish or chaplaincy appointments in Saint Louis Archdiocese

Saint Peter Parish in Kirkwood, Missouri (May 9, 1961)
Ascension Parish in Normandy, Missouri (March 16, 1967)
Sacred Heart Parish in Festus, Missouri (June 12, 1969)
Saint George Parish in Affton, Missouri (June 10, 1971)
Nativity Parish in Saint Louis, Missouri (January 3, 1978)
Saint Adalbert Parish in Saint Louis, Missouri (June 23, 1982)
Saint William Parish in Woodson Terrace, Missouri (June 18, 1987)

May 1995, sick leave. (In reality, he was removed from active ministry due to his pattern of sexual abuse of minors.)

For more information on accused priests mentioned in this book, as well as other clergy molesters, visit the Data of Publicly Accused Priests in the United States at www.BishopAccountability.org.

Also, see www.bishop-accountability.org/AbuseTracker regarding:

Father Gary Wolken (convicted)
Father James Funke (convicted)
Father John Hess (convicted)
Father Bryan Kuchar (convicted)